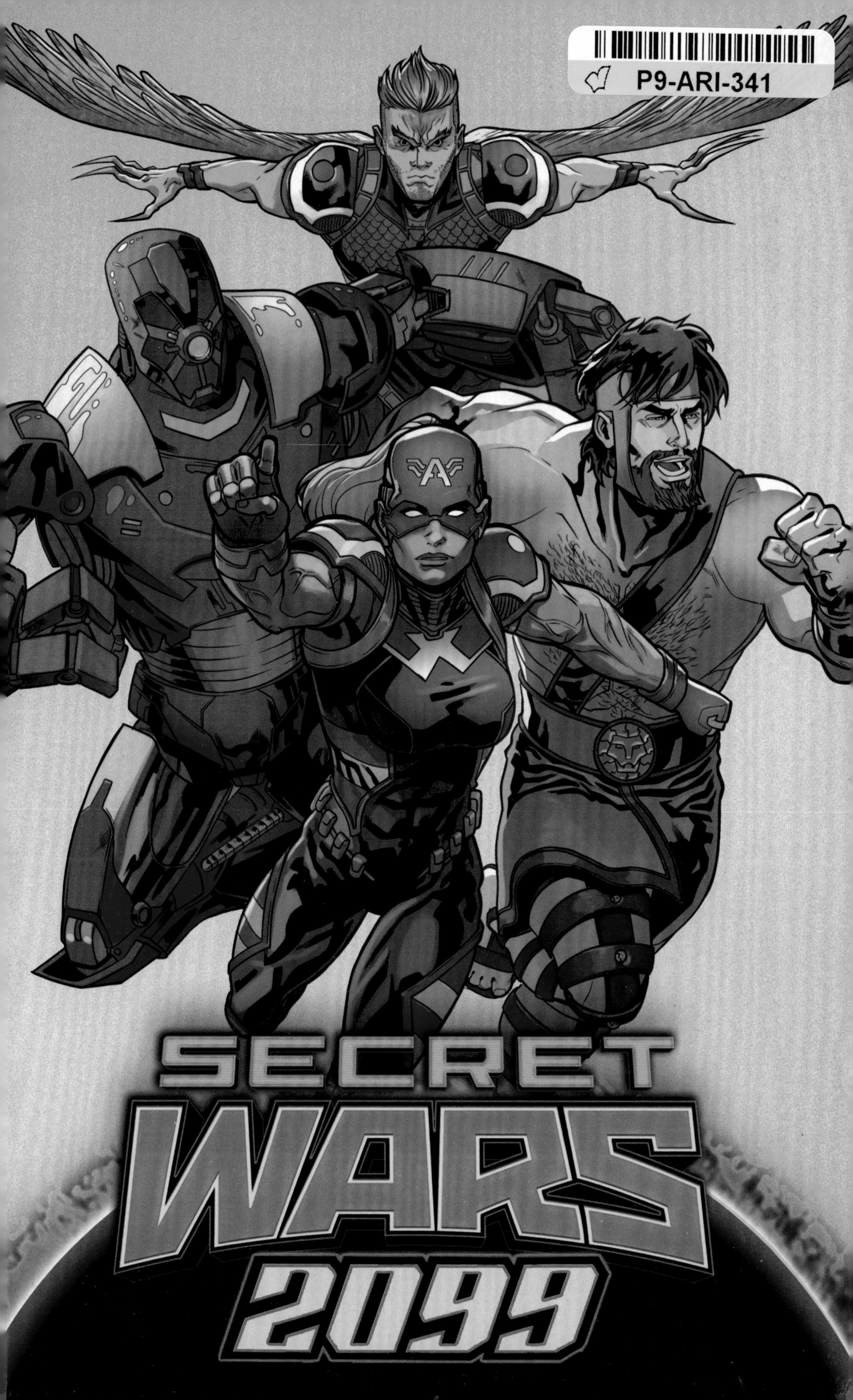
SECRET
WARS
2099

COLLECTION EDITOR JENNIFER GRÜNWALD
ASSISTANT EDITOR SARAH BRUNSTAD
ASSOCIATE MANAGING EDITOR ALEX STARBUCK
EDITOR, SPECIAL PROJECTS MARK D. BEAZLEY
SENIOR EDITOR, SPECIAL PROJECTS JEFF YOUNGQUIST
SVP PRINT, SALES & MARKETING DAVID GABRIEL
BOOK DESIGNER ADAM DEL RE

EDITOR IN CHIEF AXEL ALONSO
CHIEF CREATIVE OFFICER JOE QUESADA
PUBLISHER DAN BUCKLEY
EXECUTIVE PRODUCER ALAN FINE

SECRET WARS 2099. Contains material originally published in magazine form as SECRET WARS 2099 #1-5. First printing 2015. ISBN# 978-0-7851-9883-3. Published by MARVEL WORLDWIDE, INC., a subsidiary of MARVEL ENTERTAINMENT, LLC. OFFICE OF PUBLICATION: 135 West 50th Street, New York, NY 10020. Copyright © 2015 MARVEL No similarity between any of the names, characters, persons, and/or institutions in this magazine with those of any living or dead person or institution is intended, and any such similarity which may exist is purely coincidental. Printed in Canada. ALAN FINE, President, Marvel Entertainment; DAN BUCKLEY, President, TV, Publishing and Brand Management; JOE QUESADA, Chief Creative Officer; TOM BREVOORT, SVP of Publishing; DAVID BOGART, SVP of Operations & Procurement, Publishing; C.B. CEBULSKI, VP of International Development & Brand Management; DAVID GABRIEL, SVP Print, Sales & Marketing; JIM O'KEEFE, VP of Operations & Logistics; DAN CARR, Executive Director of Publishing Technology; SUSAN CRESPI, Editorial Operations Manager; ALEX MORALES, Publishing Operations Manager; STAN LEE, Chairman Emeritus. For information regarding advertising in Marvel Comics or on Marvel.com, please contact Jonathan Rheingold, VP of Custom Solutions & Ad Sales, at jrheingold@marvel.com. For Marvel subscription inquiries, please call 800-217-9158. Manufactured between 9/25/2015 and 11/2/2015 by SOLISCO PRINTERS, SCOTT, QC, CANADA.

10987654321

PETER DAVID
WRITER

WILL SLINEY
ARTIST

ANTONIO FABELA
WITH ANDRES MOSSA (#1)
COLORISTS

VC's JOE CARAMAGNA
LETTERER

DAVE RAPOZA
COVER ART

DEVIN LEWIS
EDITOR

NICK LOWE
SENIOR EDITOR

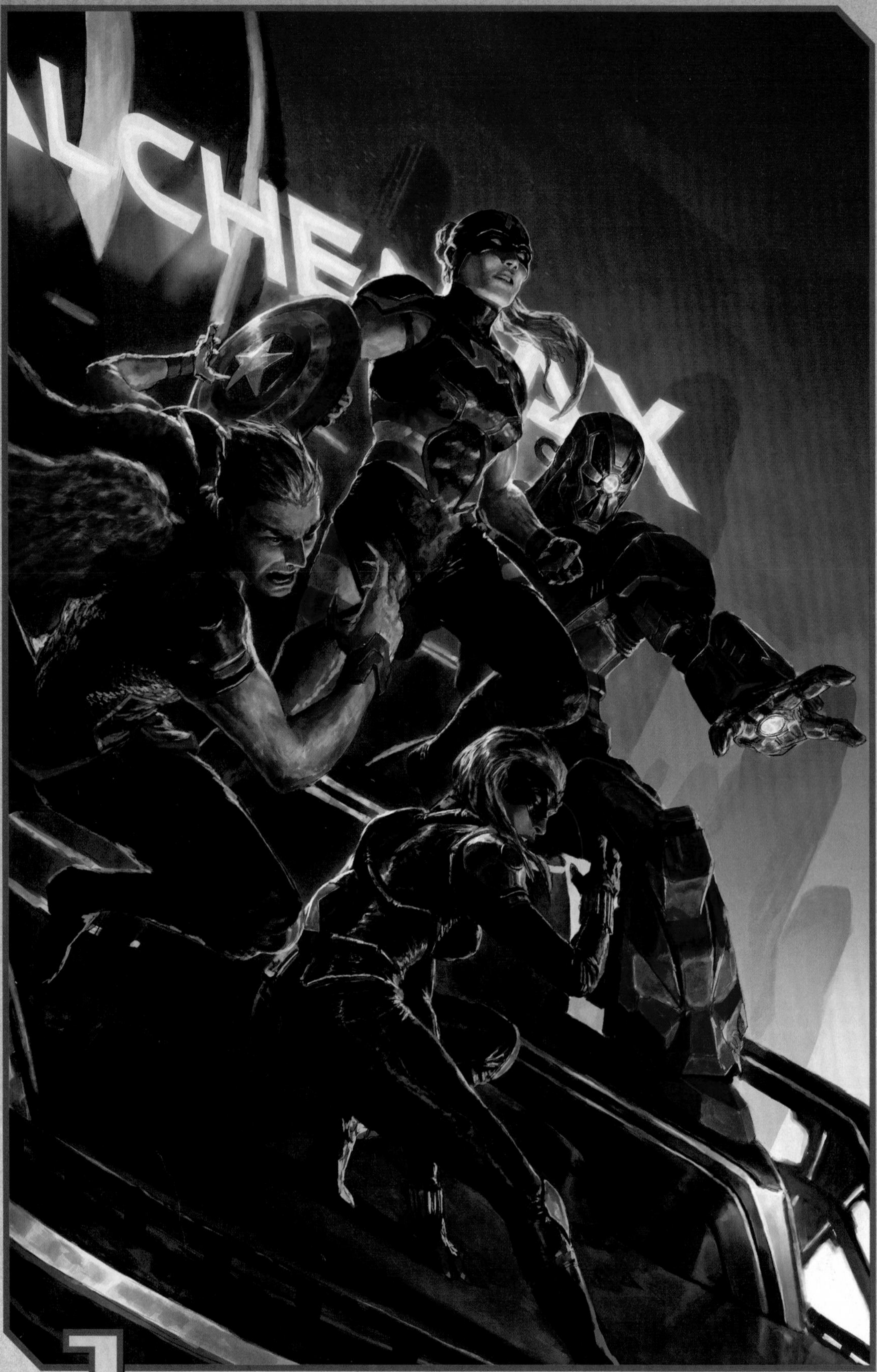

1

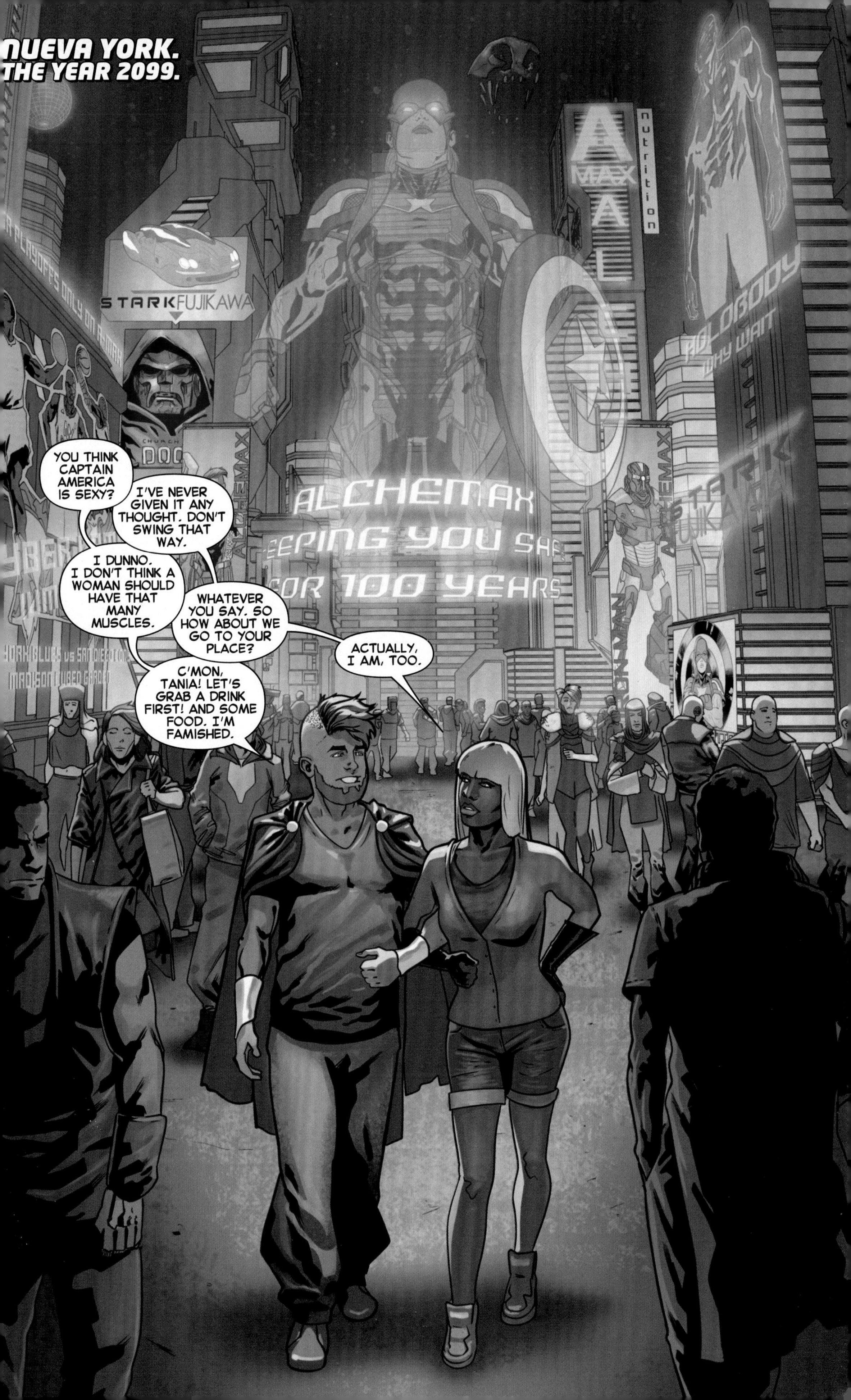
NUEVA YORK.
THE YEAR 2099.
YOU THINK CAPTAIN AMERICA IS SEXY?
I'VE NEVER GIVEN IT ANY THOUGHT. DON'T SWING THAT WAY.
I DUNNO. I DON'T THINK A WOMAN SHOULD HAVE THAT MANY MUSCLES.
WHATEVER YOU SAY. SO HOW ABOUT WE GO TO YOUR PLACE?
C'MON, TANIA! LET'S GRAB A DRINK FIRST! AND SOME FOOD. I'M FAMISHED.
ACTUALLY, I AM, TOO.
STARKFUJIKAWA
nutrition
HOLOBODY
WHY WAIT
ALCHEMAX

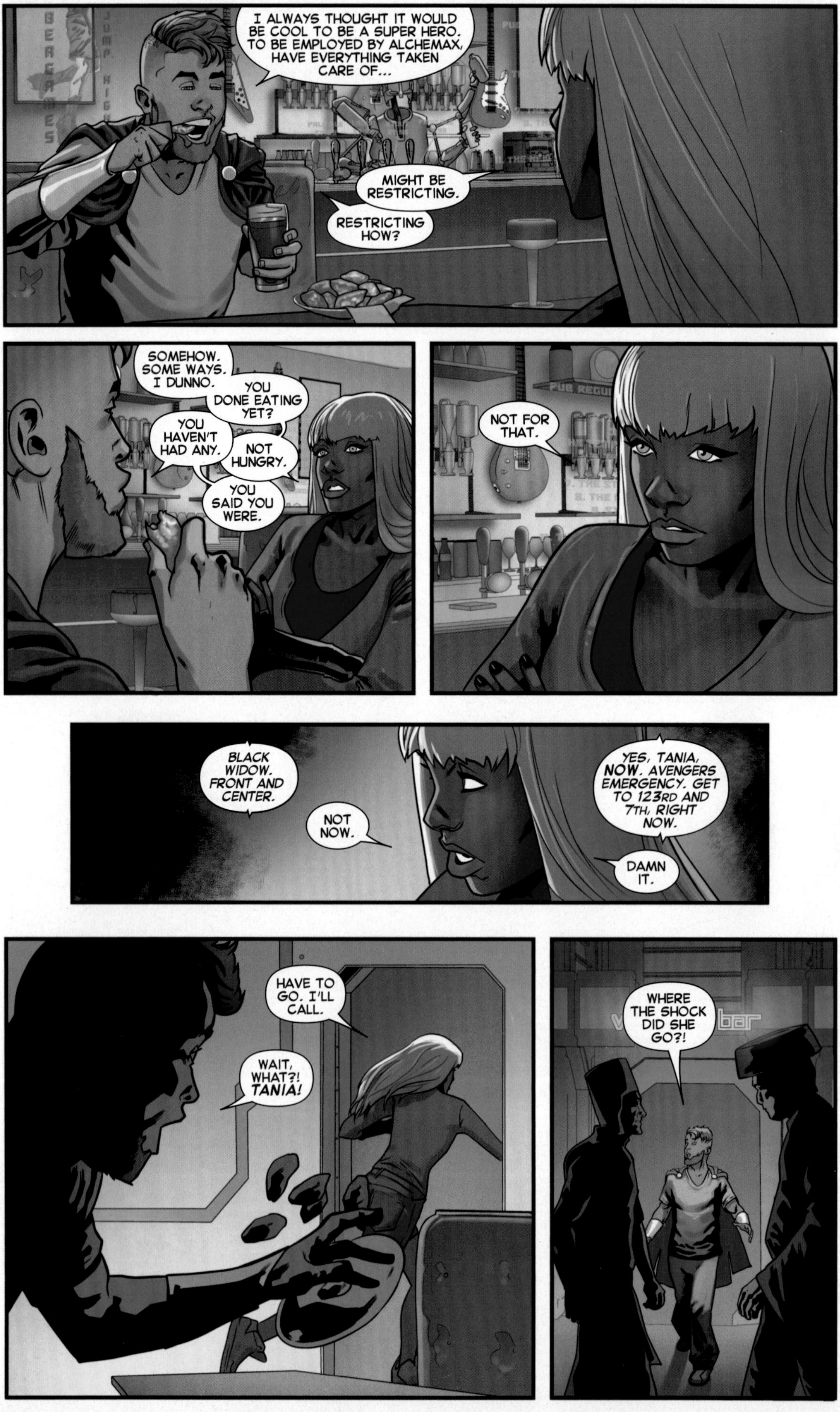
I ALWAYS THOUGHT IT WOULD BE COOL TO BE A SUPER HERO. TO BE EMPLOYED BY ALCHEMAX, HAVE EVERYTHING TAKEN CARE OF...
MIGHT BE RESTRICTING.
RESTRICTING HOW?
SOMEHOW. SOME WAYS. I DUNNO.
YOU DONE EATING YET?
YOU HAVEN'T HAD ANY.
NOT HUNGRY.
YOU SAID YOU WERE.
NOT FOR THAT.
BLACK WIDOW. FRONT AND CENTER.
NOT NOW.
YES, TANIA, NOW. AVENGERS EMERGENCY. GET TO 123RD AND 7TH, RIGHT NOW.
DAMN IT.
HAVE TO GO. I'LL CALL.
WAIT, WHAT?! TANIA!
WHERE THE SHOCK DID SHE GO?!

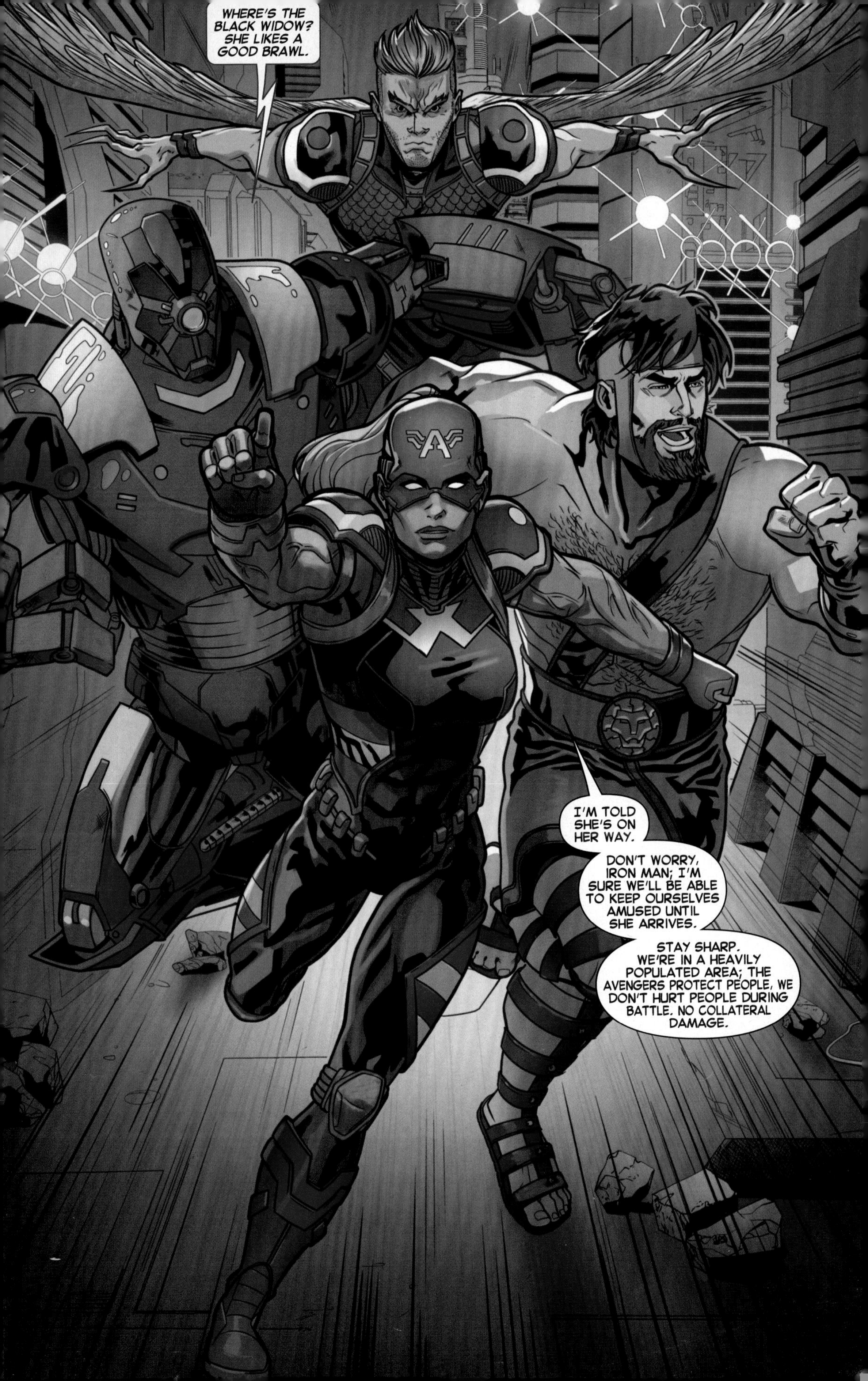
WHERE'S THE BLACK WIDOW? SHE LIKES A GOOD BRAWL.
I'M TOLD SHE'S ON HER WAY.
DON'T WORRY, IRON MAN; I'M SURE WE'LL BE ABLE TO KEEP OURSELVES AMUSED UNTIL SHE ARRIVES.
STAY SHARP. WE'RE IN A HEAVILY POPULATED AREA; THE AVENGERS PROTECT PEOPLE, WE DON'T HURT PEOPLE DURING BATTLE. NO COLLATERAL DAMAGE.

NEW YORK IS NO MORE! IN ITS PLACE STANDS NUEVA YORK, A TOWERING METROPOLIS FILLED WITH NEW INCARNATIONS OF THE HEROES OF THE PAST! TAKING ON THE MANTLES OF SUCH HEROES AS CAPTAIN AMERICA, IRON MAN, AND HAWKEYE, THESE NEW AVENGERS FIGHT FOR TRUTH, JUSTICE, AND MEGACORPORATIONS LIKE ALCHEMAX. THIS IS

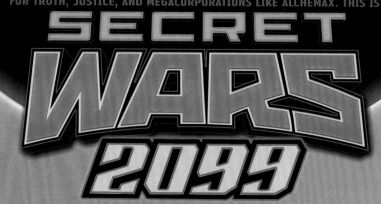

SECRET WARS 2099

THE MULTIVERSE WAS DESTROYED!

THE HEROES OF EARTH-616 AND EARTH-1610 WERE POWERLESS TO SAVE IT!

NOW ALL THAT REMAINS...IS BATTLEWORLD!

A MASSIVE PATCHWORK PLANET COMPOSED OF THE FRAGMENTS OF WORLDS THAT NO LONGER EXIST, MAINTAINED BY THE IRON WILL OF ITS GOD AND MASTER, VICTOR VON DOOM!

EACH REGION IS A DOMAIN UNTO ITSELF!

ONE OF THOSE REGIONS IS A NEW YORK OF THE NEAR FUTURE – ONE WHERE MEGACORPORATIONS CONTROL NOT ONLY THE CITIZENS, BUT THE AVENGERS, AS WELL!

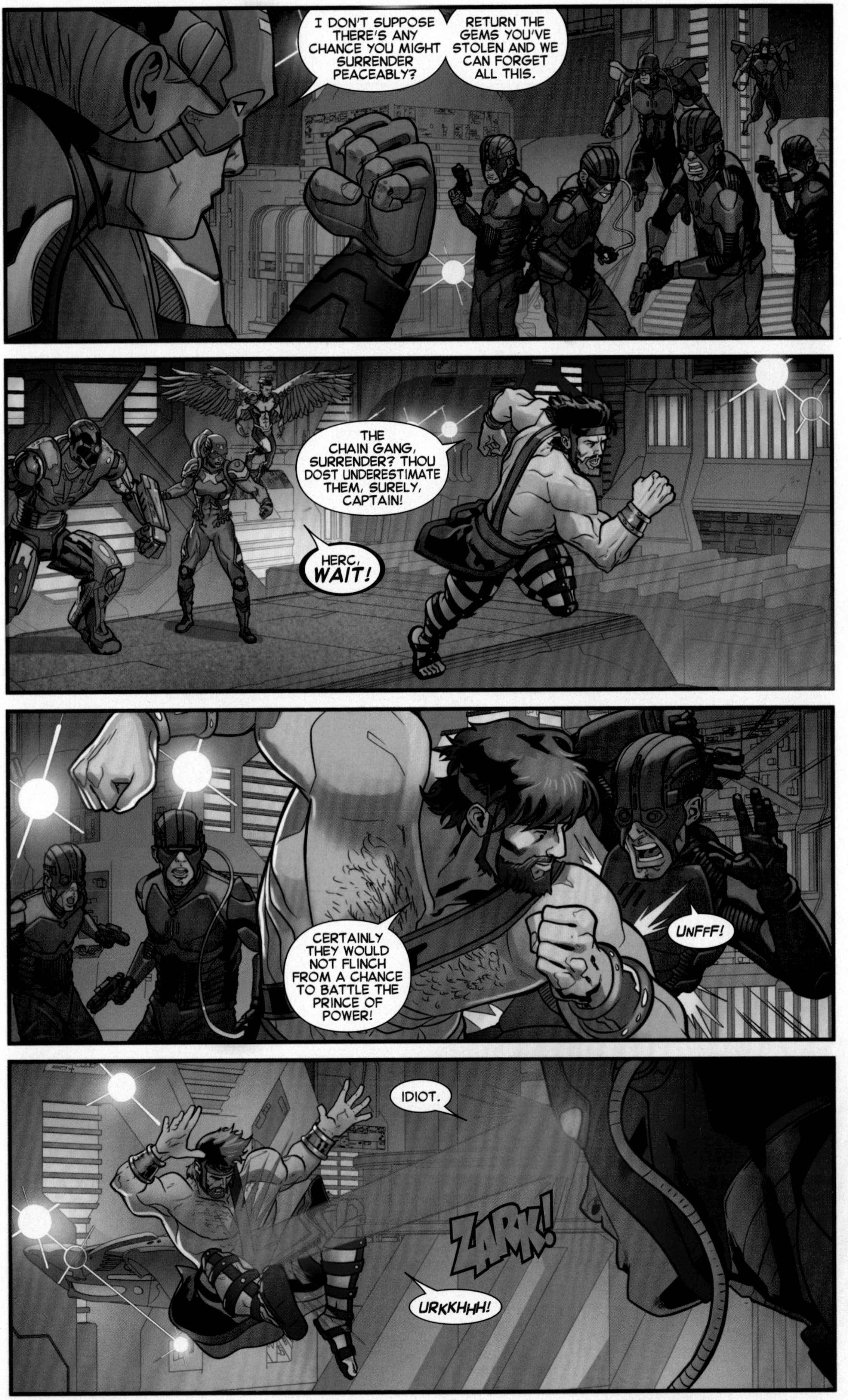
I DON'T SUPPOSE THERE'S ANY CHANCE YOU MIGHT SURRENDER PEACEABLY?
RETURN THE GEMS YOU'VE STOLEN AND WE CAN FORGET ALL THIS.
THE CHAIN GANG, SURRENDER? THOU DOST UNDERESTIMATE THEM, SURELY, CAPTAIN!
HERC, WAIT!
CERTAINLY THEY WOULD NOT FLINCH FROM A CHANCE TO BATTLE THE PRINCE OF POWER!
UNFFF!
IDIOT.
ZARK!
URKKHHH!

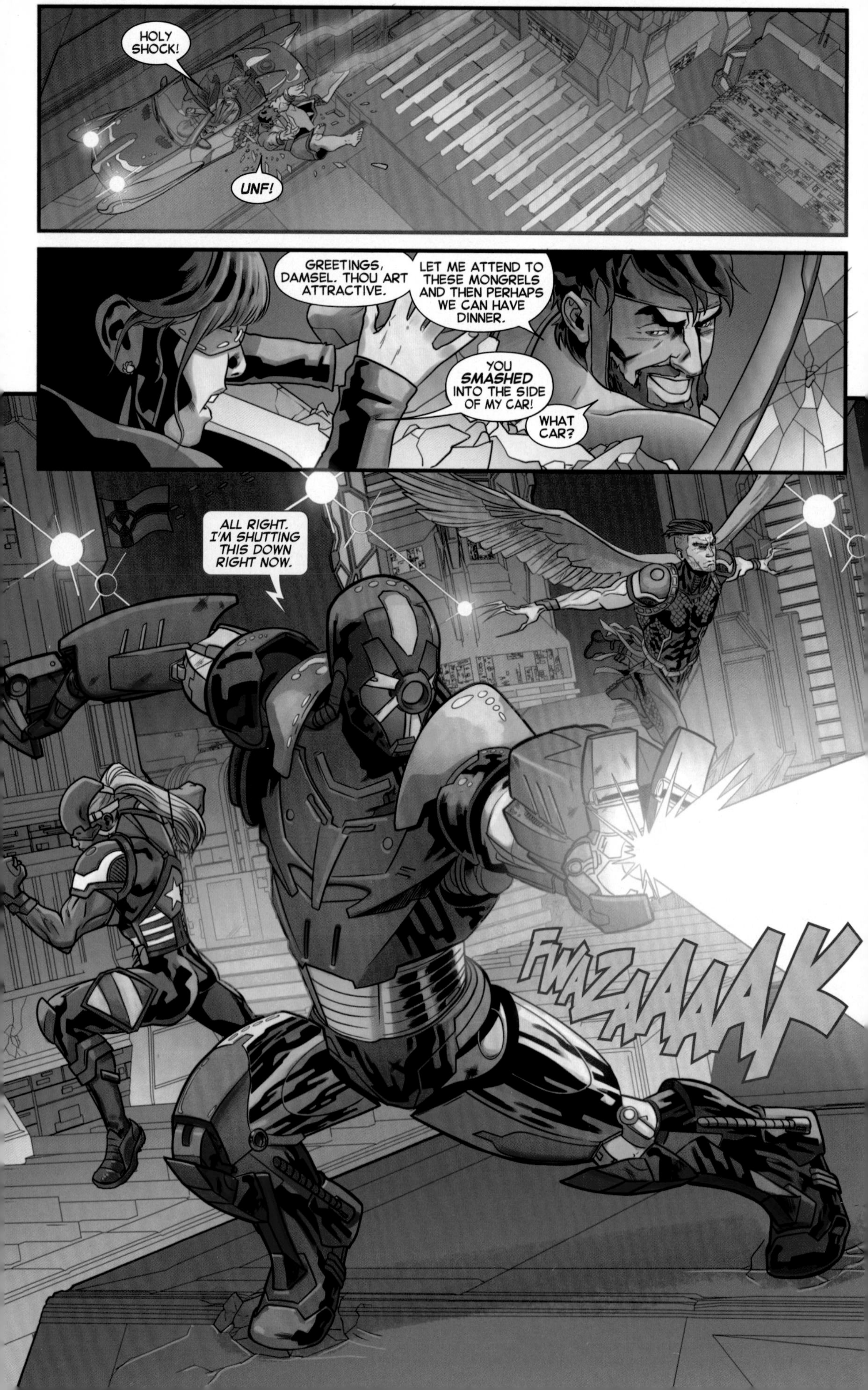
HOLY SHOCK!
UNF!
GREETINGS, DAMSEL. THOU ART ATTRACTIVE.
LET ME ATTEND TO THESE MONGRELS AND THEN PERHAPS WE CAN HAVE DINNER.
YOU SMASHED INTO THE SIDE OF MY CAR!
WHAT CAR?
ALL RIGHT. I'M SHUTTING THIS DOWN RIGHT NOW.
FWAZAAAAAK

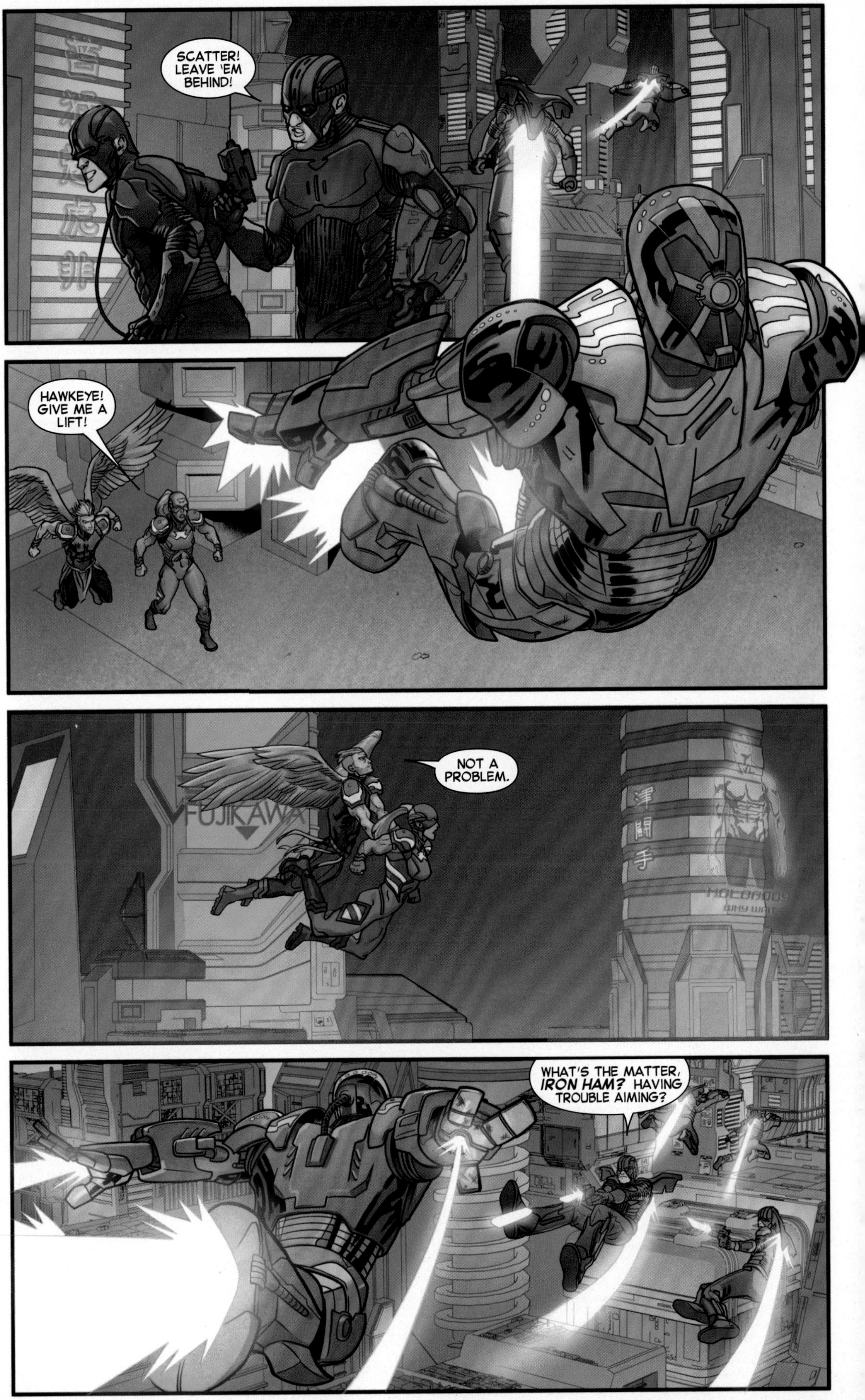
SCATTER! LEAVE 'EM BEHIND!
HAWKEYE! GIVE ME A LIFT!
FUJIKAWA
NOT A PROBLEM.
WHAT'S THE MATTER, *IRON HAM?* HAVING TROUBLE AIMING?

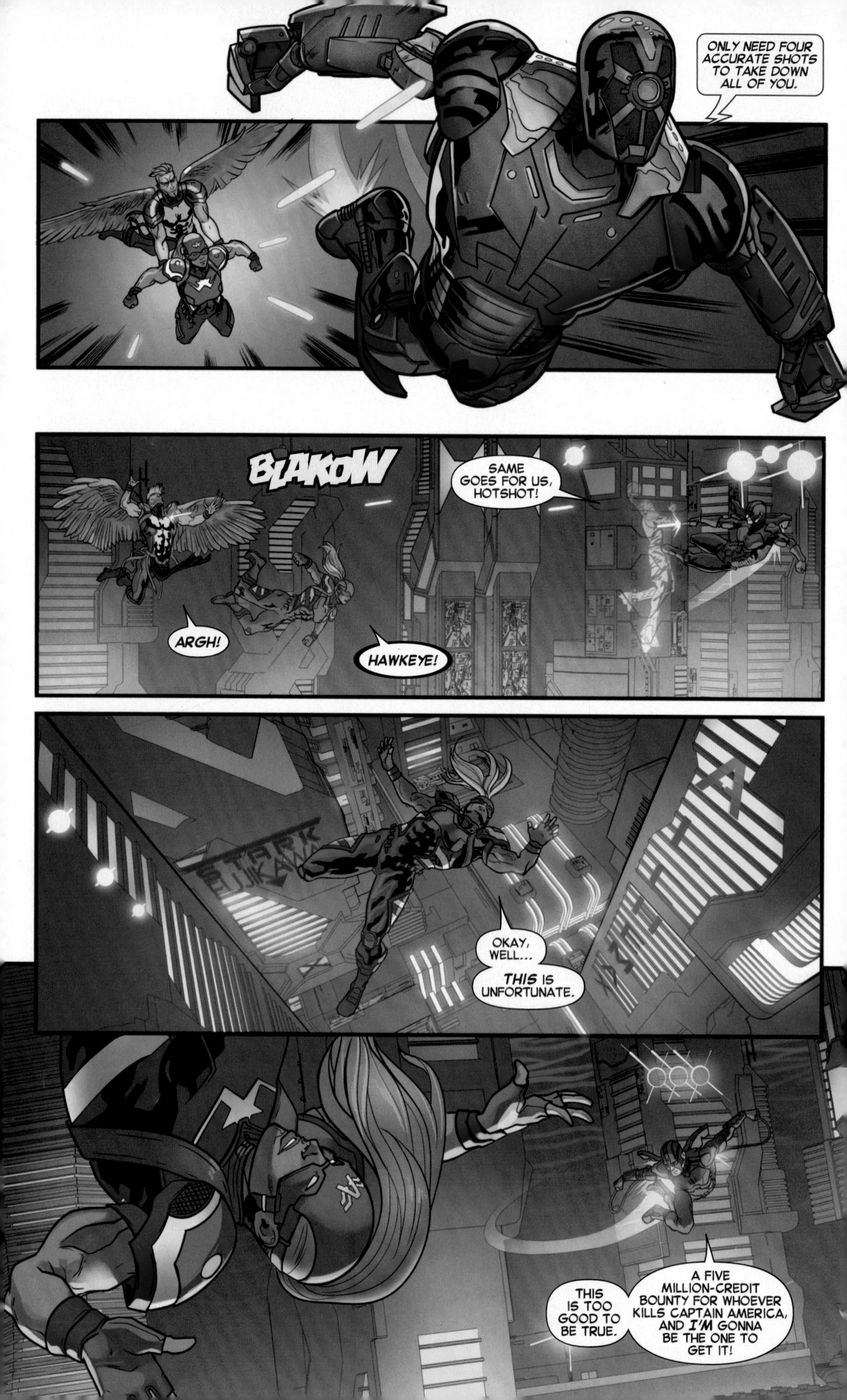
ONLY NEED FOUR ACCURATE SHOTS TO TAKE DOWN ALL OF YOU.
BLAKOW
SAME GOES FOR US, HOTSHOT!
ARGH!
HAWKEYE!
STARK FUJIKAWA
OKAY, WELL...
THIS IS UNFORTUNATE.
A FIVE MILLION-CREDIT BOUNTY FOR WHOEVER KILLS CAPTAIN AMERICA, AND I'M GONNA BE THE ONE TO GET IT!
THIS IS TOO GOOD TO BE TRUE.

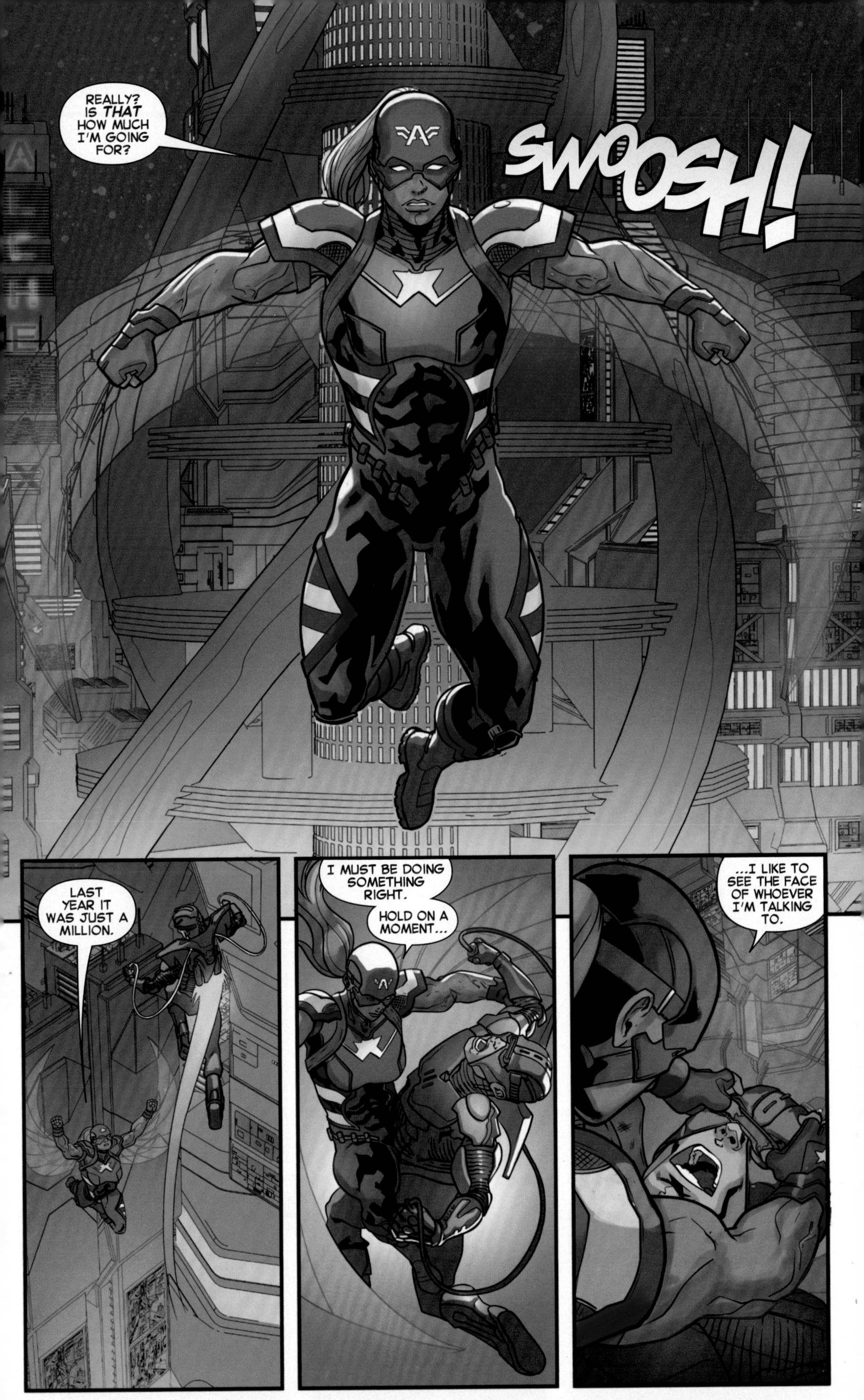
REALLY? IS THAT HOW MUCH I'M GOING FOR?
SWOOSH!
LAST YEAR IT WAS JUST A MILLION.
I MUST BE DOING SOMETHING RIGHT.
HOLD ON A MOMENT...
...I LIKE TO SEE THE FACE OF WHOEVER I'M TALKING TO.

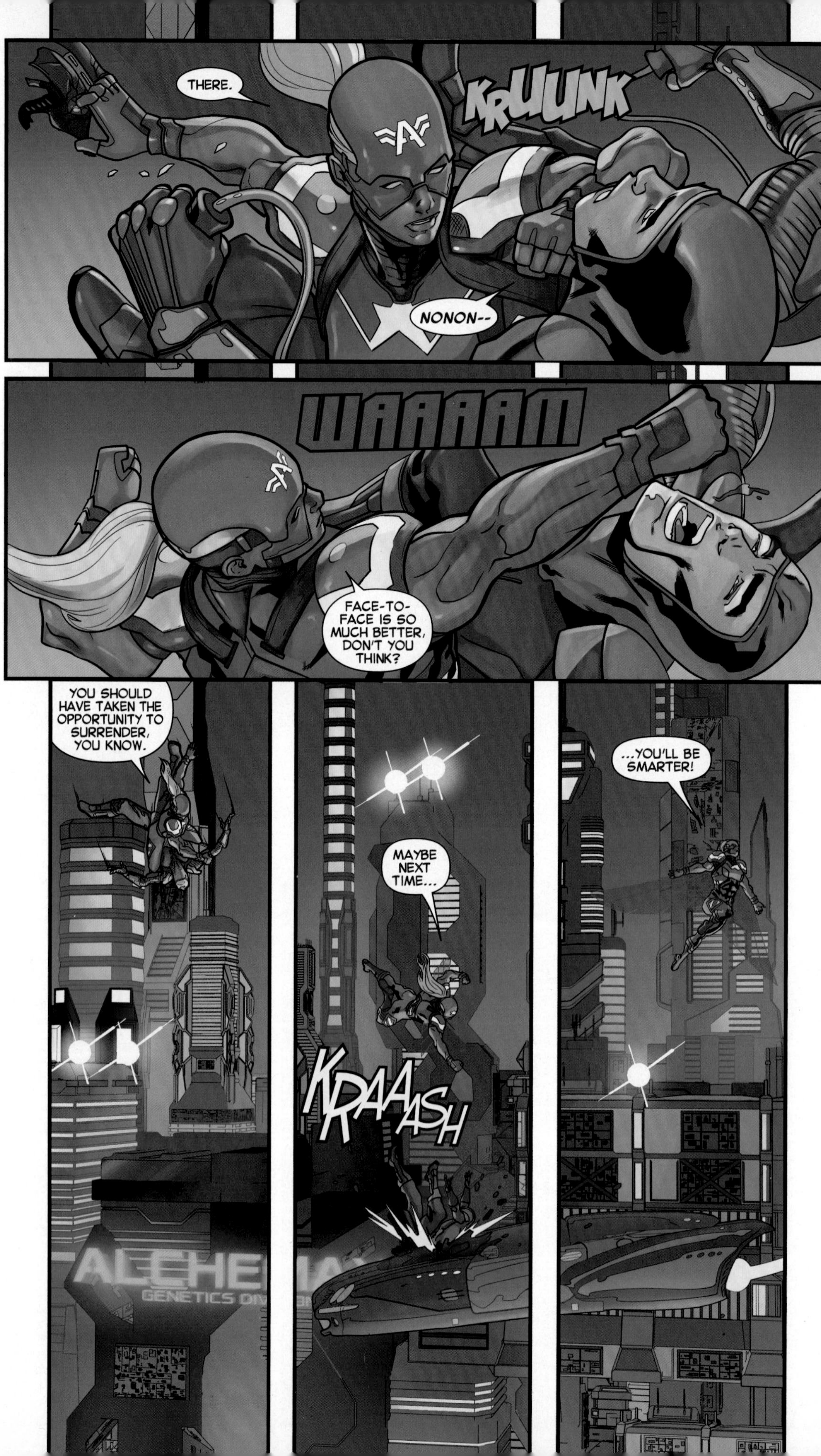
THERE.
KRUUUNK
NONON--
WAAAAAM
FACE-TO-FACE IS SO MUCH BETTER, DON'T YOU THINK?
YOU SHOULD HAVE TAKEN THE OPPORTUNITY TO SURRENDER, YOU KNOW.
MAYBE NEXT TIME...
KRAAASH
...YOU'LL BE SMARTER!

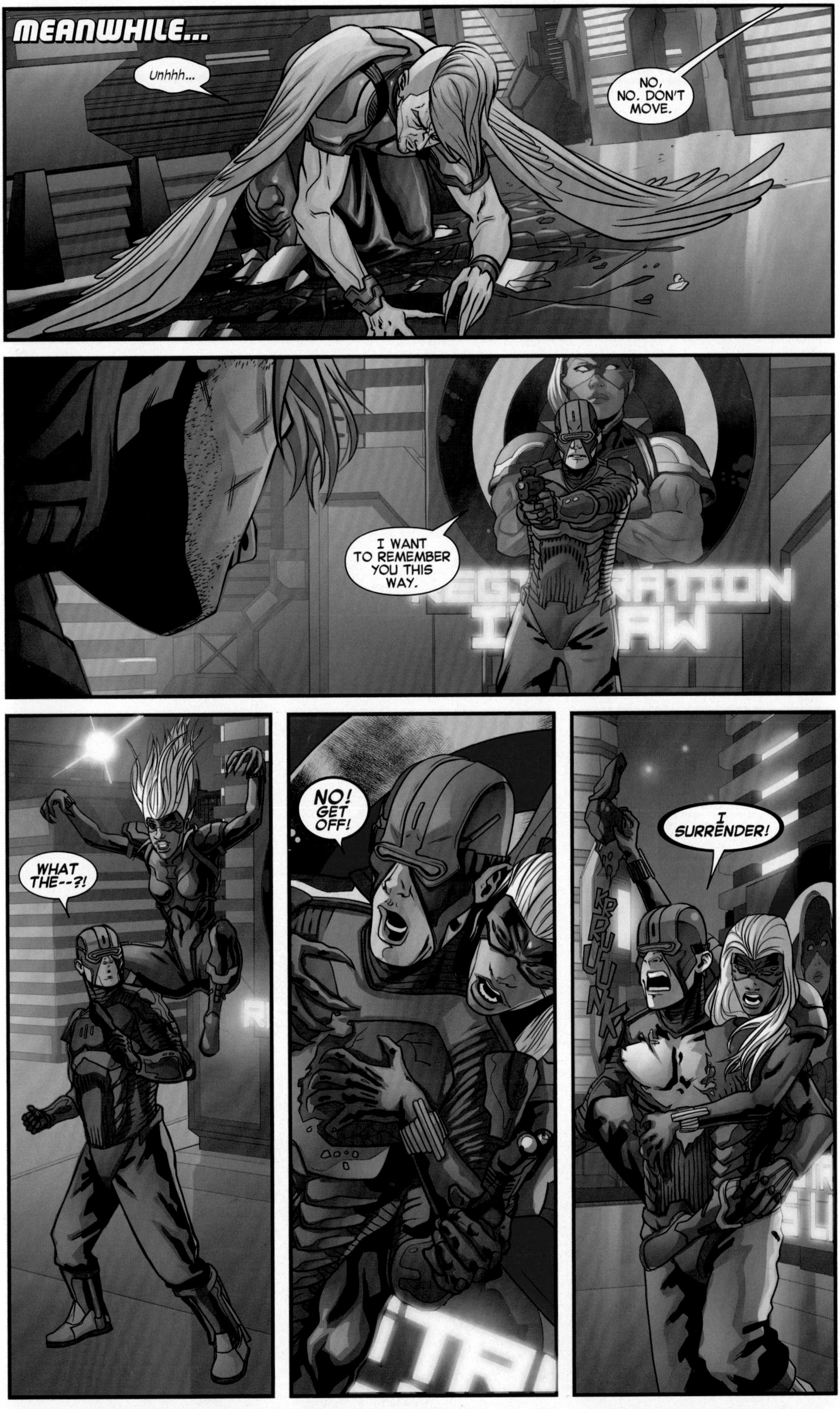
MEANWHILE...
Unhhh...
NO, NO. DON'T MOVE.
I WANT TO REMEMBER YOU THIS WAY.
WHAT THE--?!
NO! GET OFF!
I SURRENDER!
KRRUUNK

SNAKT

I DON'T RECALL GIVING YOU THE OPTION TO SURRENDER.

TANIA, STOP! THAT'S AN ORDER!

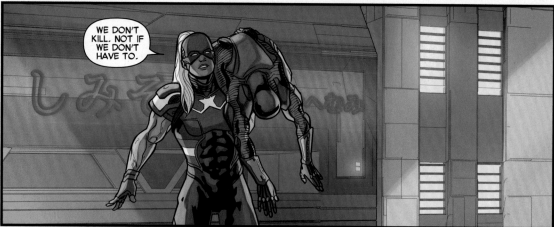

WE DON'T KILL. NOT IF WE DON'T HAVE TO.

AND IF I HAVE TO?

SHEATHE YOUR STINGER, WIDOW. I'M NOT KIDDING.

SHEATHE IT, OR I SWEAR...

...THE NEXT ONE WE HUNT WILL BE YOU.

SHUNT!

FINE. HAPPY?

ECSTATIC.

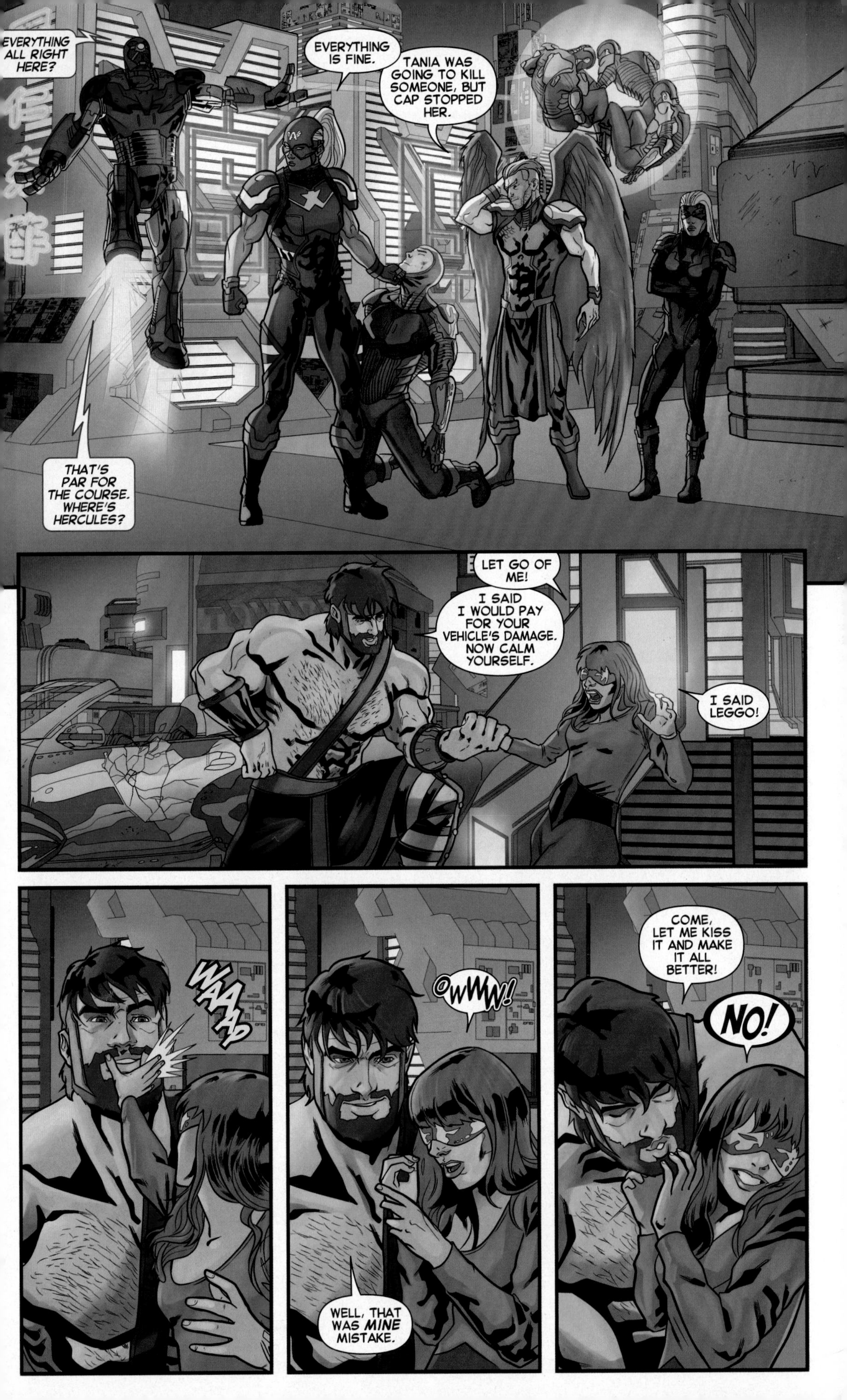
EVERYTHING ALL RIGHT HERE?
EVERYTHING IS FINE.
TANIA WAS GOING TO KILL SOMEONE, BUT CAP STOPPED HER.
THAT'S PAR FOR THE COURSE. WHERE'S HERCULES?
LET GO OF ME!
I SAID I WOULD PAY FOR YOUR VEHICLE'S DAMAGE. NOW CALM YOURSELF.
I SAID LEGGO!
WAAA!
OWWW!
WELL, THAT WAS MINE MISTAKE.
COME, LET ME KISS IT AND MAKE IT ALL BETTER!
NO!

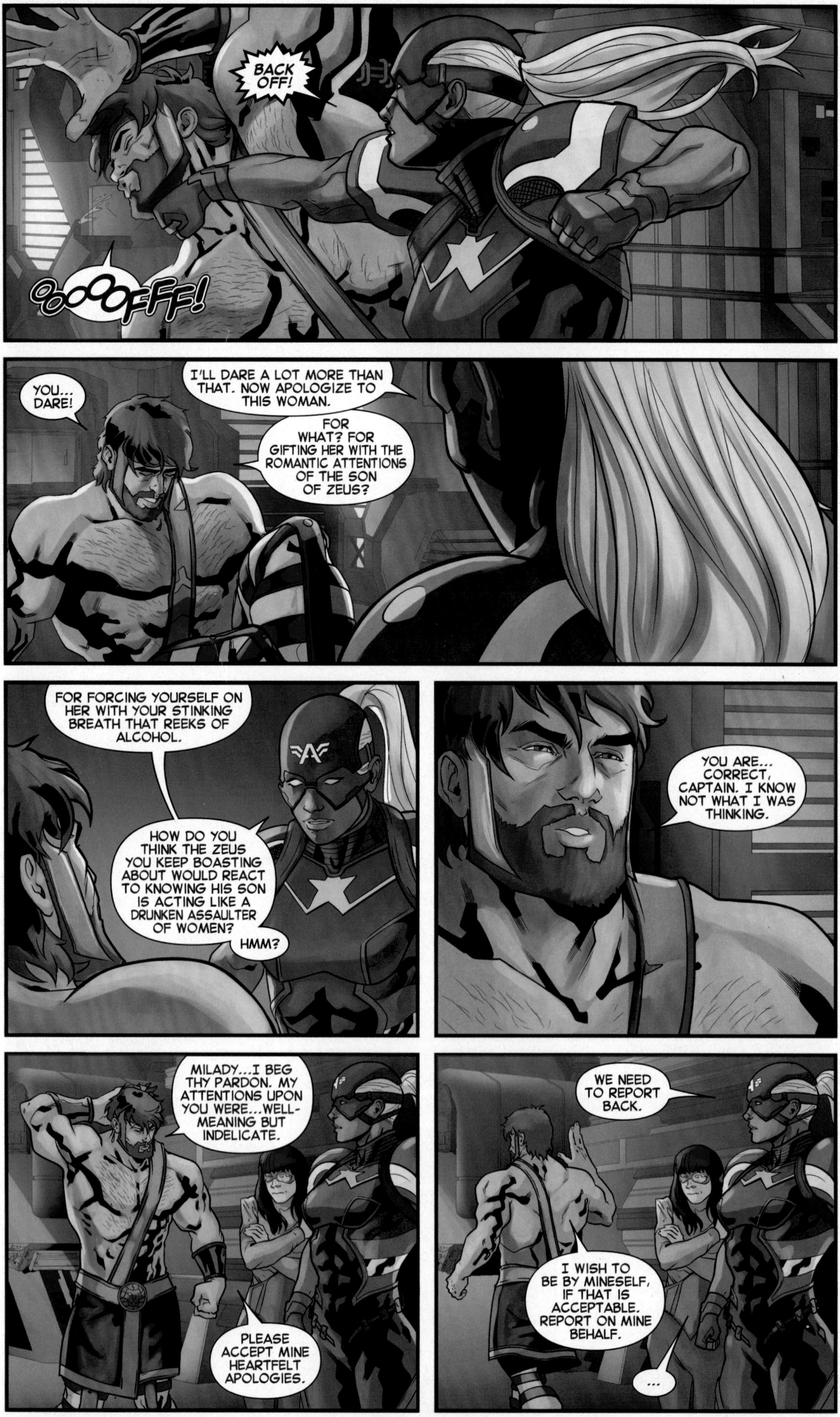
BACK OFF!
OOOOFFF!
YOU... DARE!
I'LL DARE A LOT MORE THAN THAT. NOW APOLOGIZE TO THIS WOMAN.
FOR WHAT? FOR GIFTING HER WITH THE ROMANTIC ATTENTIONS OF THE SON OF ZEUS?
FOR FORCING YOURSELF ON HER WITH YOUR STINKING BREATH THAT REEKS OF ALCOHOL.
HOW DO YOU THINK THE ZEUS YOU KEEP BOASTING ABOUT WOULD REACT TO KNOWING HIS SON IS ACTING LIKE A DRUNKEN ASSAULTER OF WOMEN?
HMM?
YOU ARE... CORRECT, CAPTAIN. I KNOW NOT WHAT I WAS THINKING.
MILADY...I BEG THY PARDON. MY ATTENTIONS UPON YOU WERE...WELL-MEANING BUT INDELICATE.
PLEASE ACCEPT MINE HEARTFELT APOLOGIES.
WE NEED TO REPORT BACK.
I WISH TO BE BY MINESELF, IF THAT IS ACCEPTABLE. REPORT ON MINE BEHALF.
...

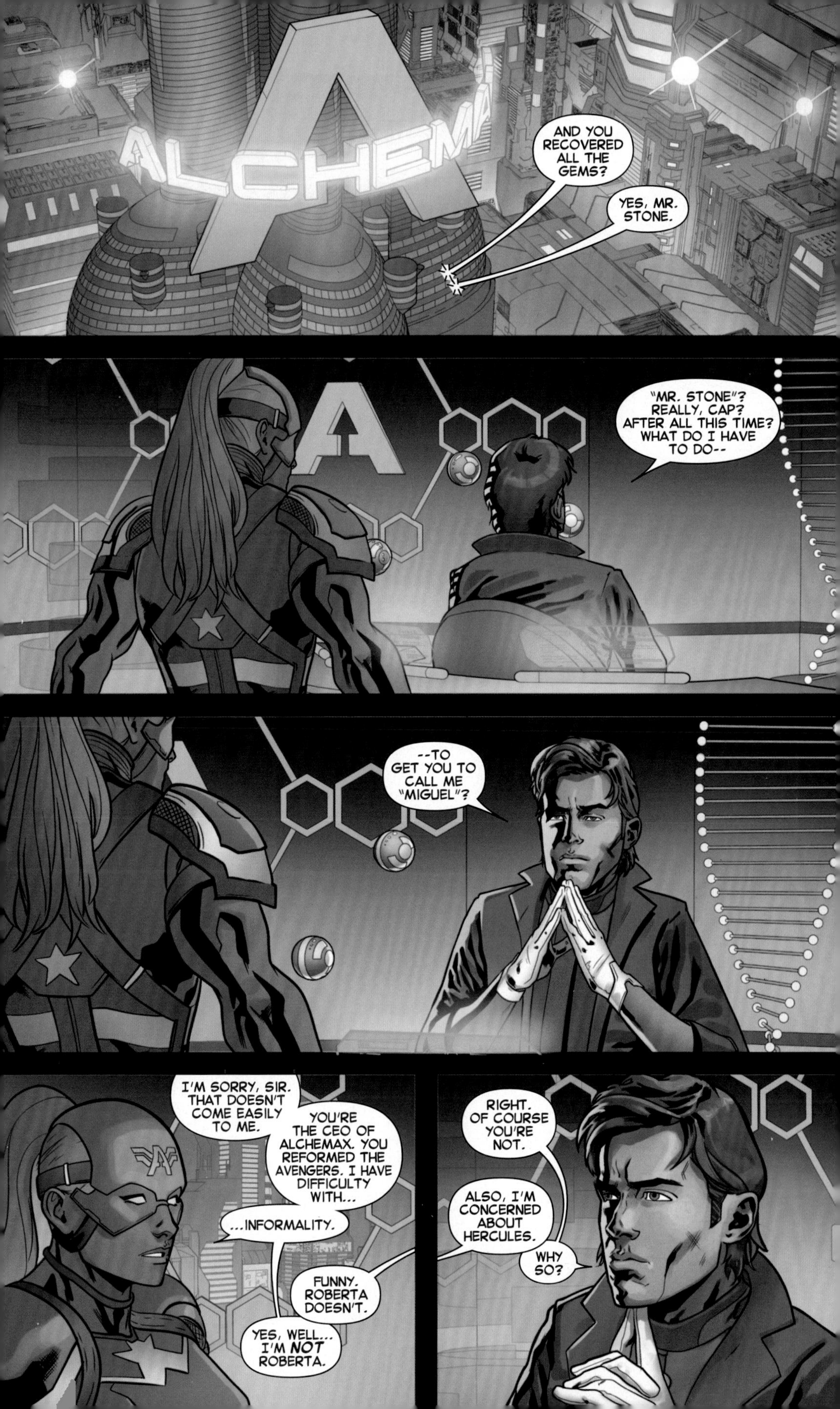
ALCHEMA
AND YOU RECOVERED ALL THE GEMS?
YES, MR. STONE.
"MR. STONE"? REALLY, CAP? AFTER ALL THIS TIME? WHAT DO I HAVE TO DO--
--TO GET YOU TO CALL ME "MIGUEL"?
I'M SORRY, SIR. THAT DOESN'T COME EASILY TO ME.
YOU'RE THE CEO OF ALCHEMAX. YOU REFORMED THE AVENGERS. I HAVE DIFFICULTY WITH...
...INFORMALITY.
FUNNY. ROBERTA DOESN'T.
YES, WELL... I'M *NOT* ROBERTA.
RIGHT. OF COURSE YOU'RE NOT.
ALSO, I'M CONCERNED ABOUT HERCULES.
WHY SO?

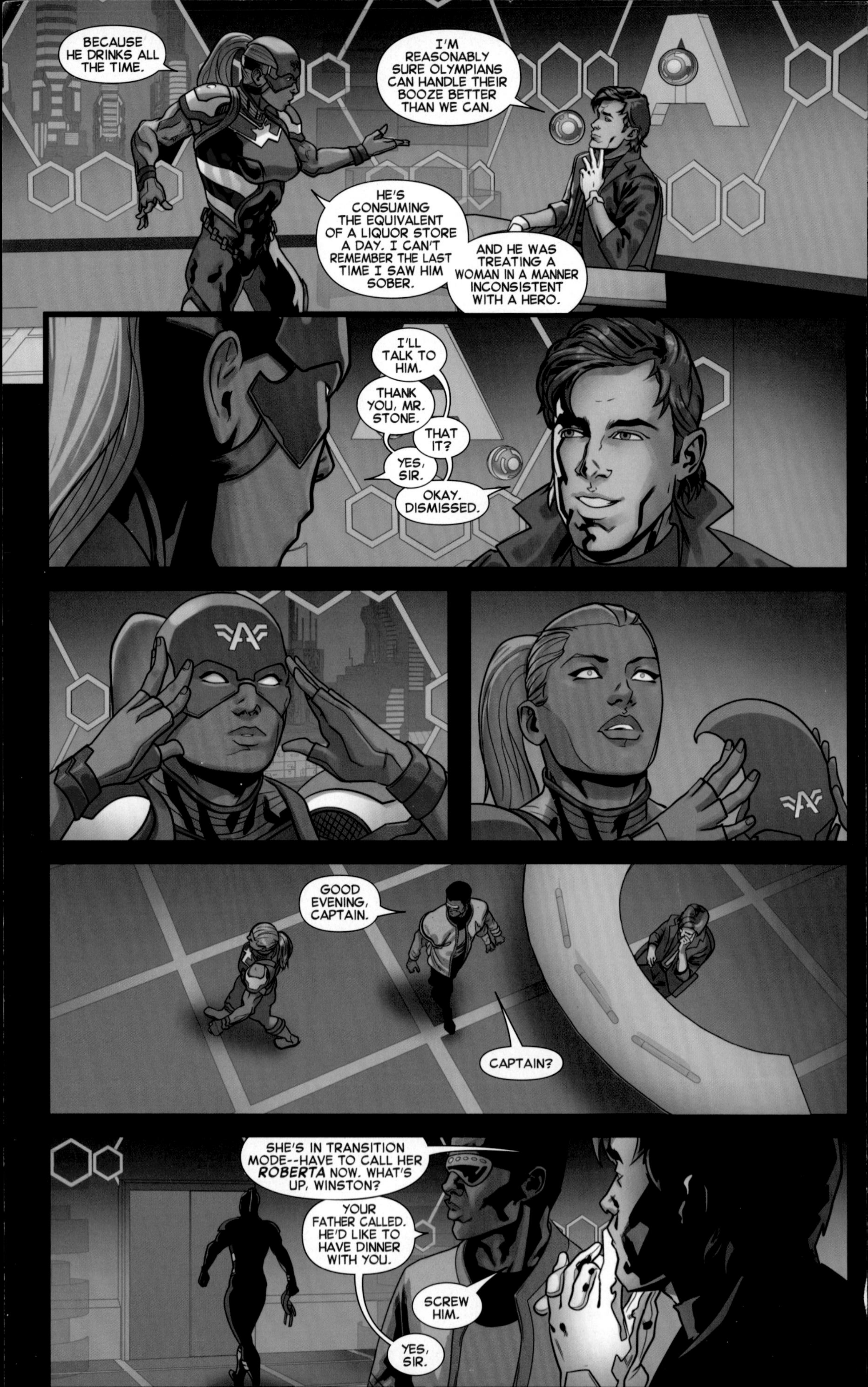

BECAUSE HE DRINKS ALL THE TIME.
I'M REASONABLY SURE OLYMPIANS CAN HANDLE THEIR BOOZE BETTER THAN WE CAN.
HE'S CONSUMING THE EQUIVALENT OF A LIQUOR STORE A DAY. I CAN'T REMEMBER THE LAST TIME I SAW HIM SOBER.
AND HE WAS TREATING A WOMAN IN A MANNER INCONSISTENT WITH A HERO.
I'LL TALK TO HIM.
THANK YOU, MR. STONE.
THAT IT?
YES, SIR.
OKAY. DISMISSED.
GOOD EVENING, CAPTAIN.
CAPTAIN?
SHE'S IN TRANSITION MODE--HAVE TO CALL HER *ROBERTA* NOW. WHAT'S UP, WINSTON?
YOUR FATHER CALLED. HE'D LIKE TO HAVE DINNER WITH YOU.
SCREW HIM.
YES, SIR.

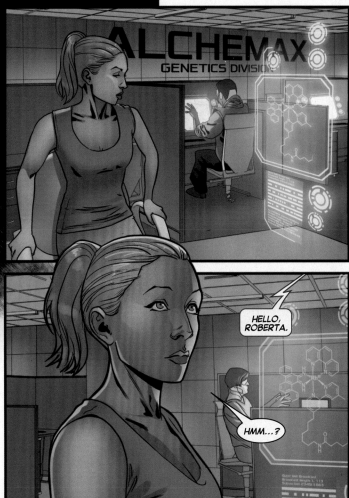

ALCHEMAX
GENETICS DIVISION

HELLO, ROBERTA.

HMM...?

OH! HELLO, IRON MAN. UHM... ...CAN I HELP YOU WITH SOMETHING?

NO. I'M FINE.

I WAS JUST GOING TO GO DOWNSTAIRS AND CHECK IN WITH THE VISION.

WELL, DON'T LET ME STOP YOU.

Incredible.

INCOMING TRANSMISSION

BEEP BEEP

INCOMING CALL. HUSBAND.

ANSWER.

INCOMING TRANSMISSION

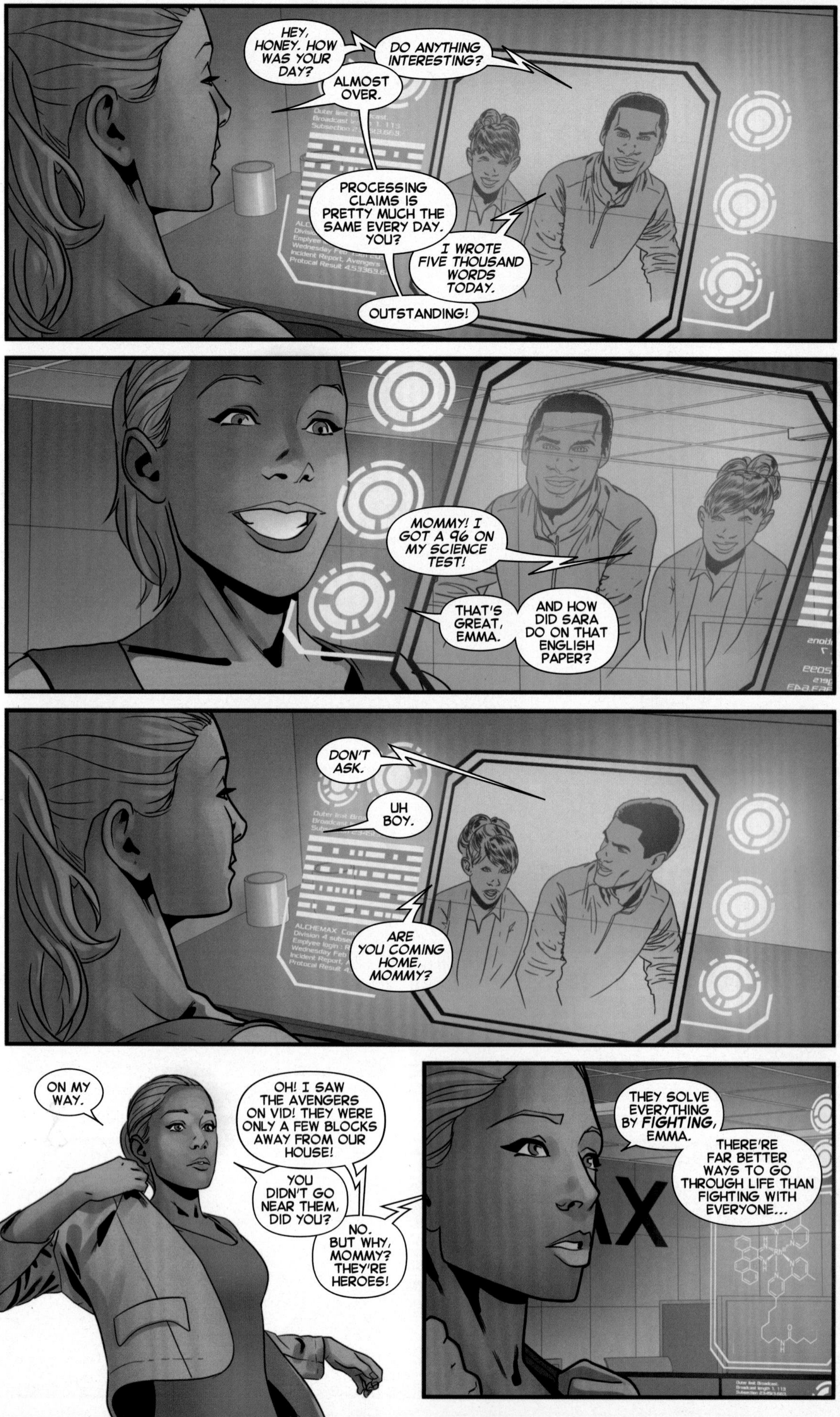
HEY, HONEY. HOW WAS YOUR DAY?
DO ANYTHING INTERESTING?
ALMOST OVER.
PROCESSING CLAIMS IS PRETTY MUCH THE SAME EVERY DAY. YOU?
I WROTE FIVE THOUSAND WORDS TODAY.
OUTSTANDING!
MOMMY! I GOT A 96 ON MY SCIENCE TEST!
THAT'S GREAT, EMMA.
AND HOW DID SARA DO ON THAT ENGLISH PAPER?
DON'T ASK.
UH BOY.
ARE YOU COMING HOME, MOMMY?
ON MY WAY.
OH! I SAW THE AVENGERS ON VID! THEY WERE ONLY A FEW BLOCKS AWAY FROM OUR HOUSE!
YOU DIDN'T GO NEAR THEM, DID YOU?
NO. BUT WHY, MOMMY? THEY'RE HEROES!
THEY SOLVE EVERYTHING BY FIGHTING, EMMA.
THERE'RE FAR BETTER WAYS TO GO THROUGH LIFE THAN FIGHTING WITH EVERYONE...

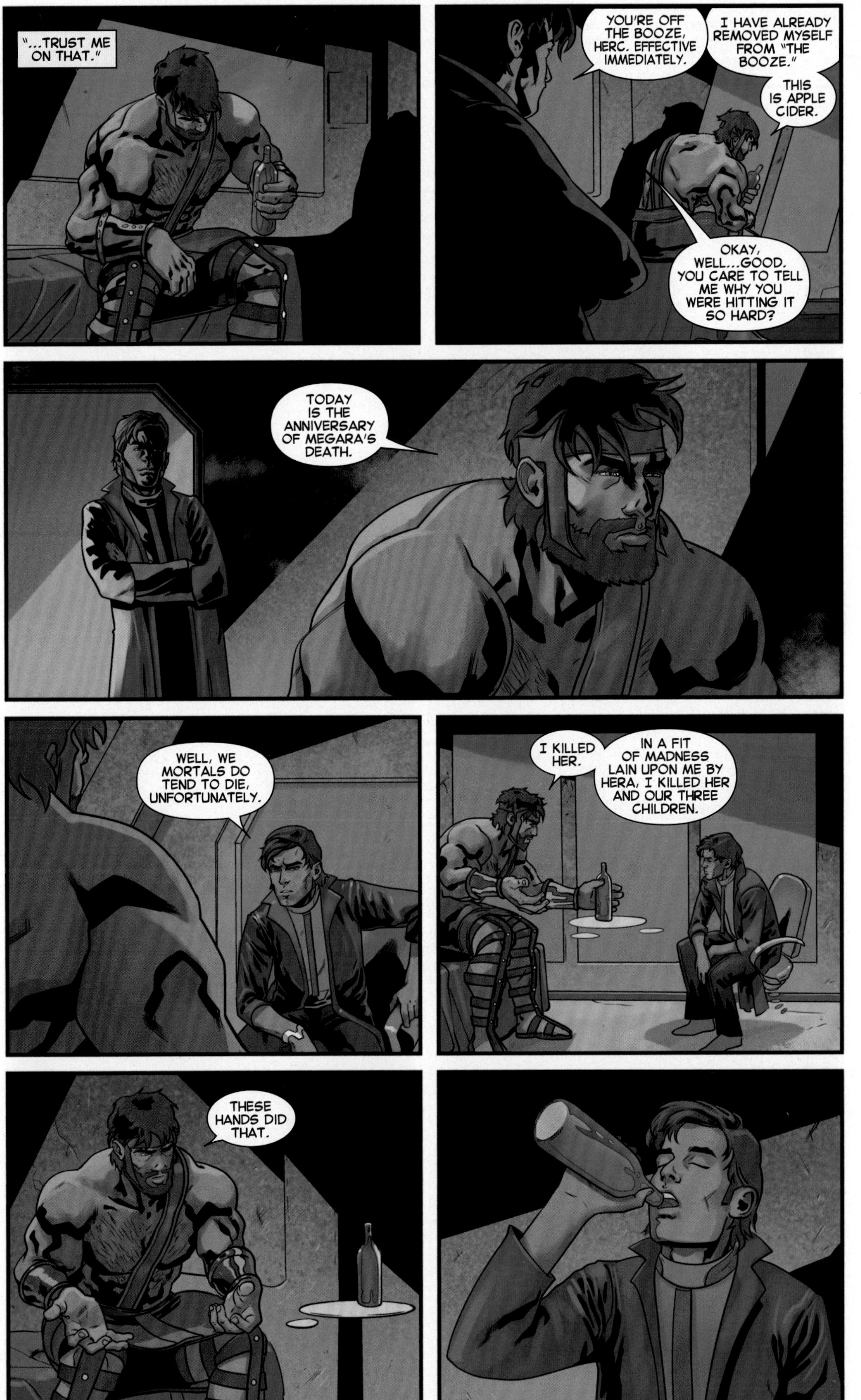
"...TRUST ME ON THAT."
YOU'RE OFF THE BOOZE, HERC. EFFECTIVE IMMEDIATELY.
I HAVE ALREADY REMOVED MYSELF FROM "THE BOOZE."
THIS IS APPLE CIDER.
OKAY, WELL...GOOD. YOU CARE TO TELL ME WHY YOU WERE HITTING IT SO HARD?
TODAY IS THE ANNIVERSARY OF MEGARA'S DEATH.
WELL, WE MORTALS DO TEND TO DIE, UNFORTUNATELY.
I KILLED HER.
IN A FIT OF MADNESS LAIN UPON ME BY HERA, I KILLED HER AND OUR THREE CHILDREN.
THESE HANDS DID THAT.

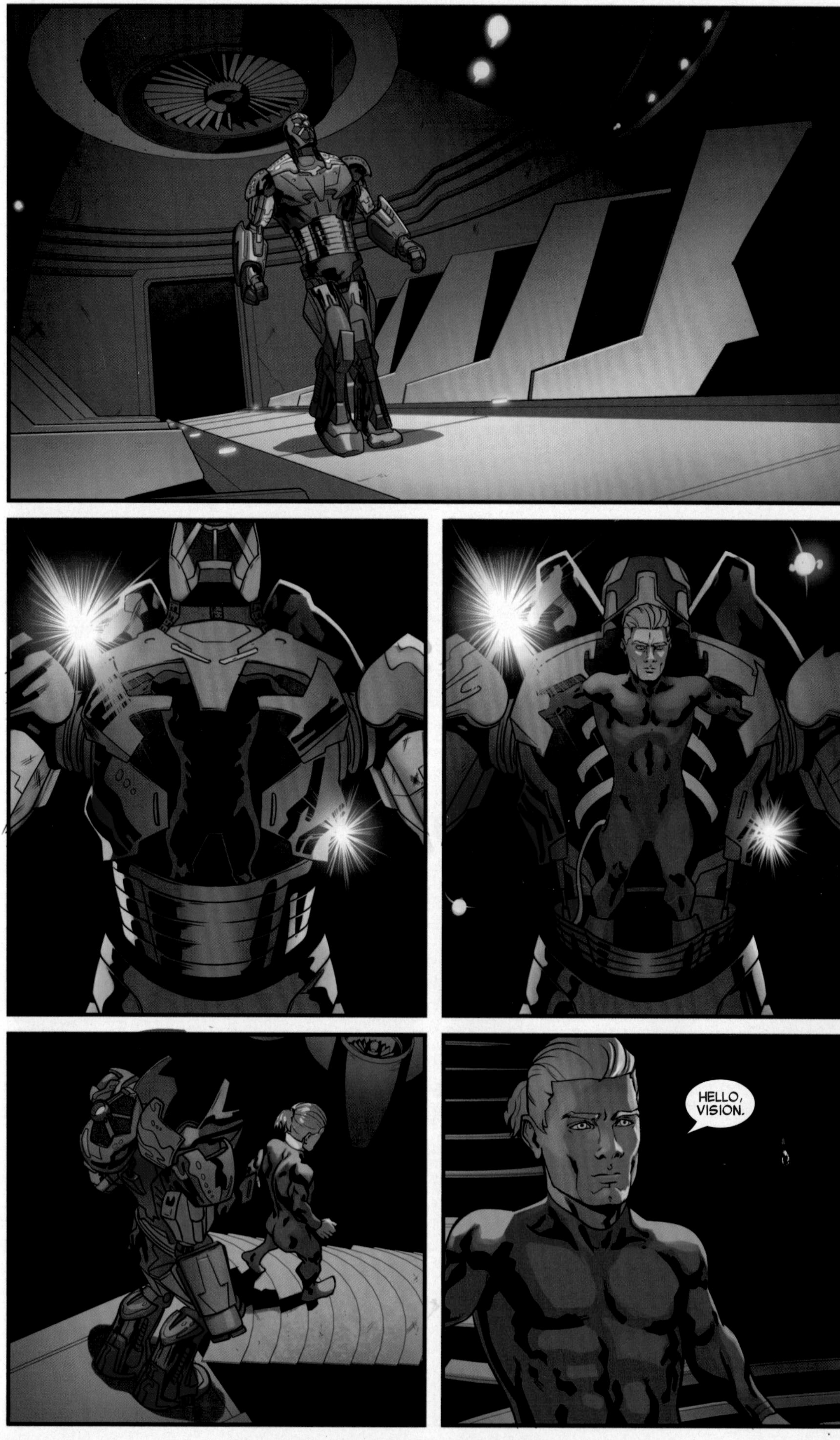
HELLO, VISION.

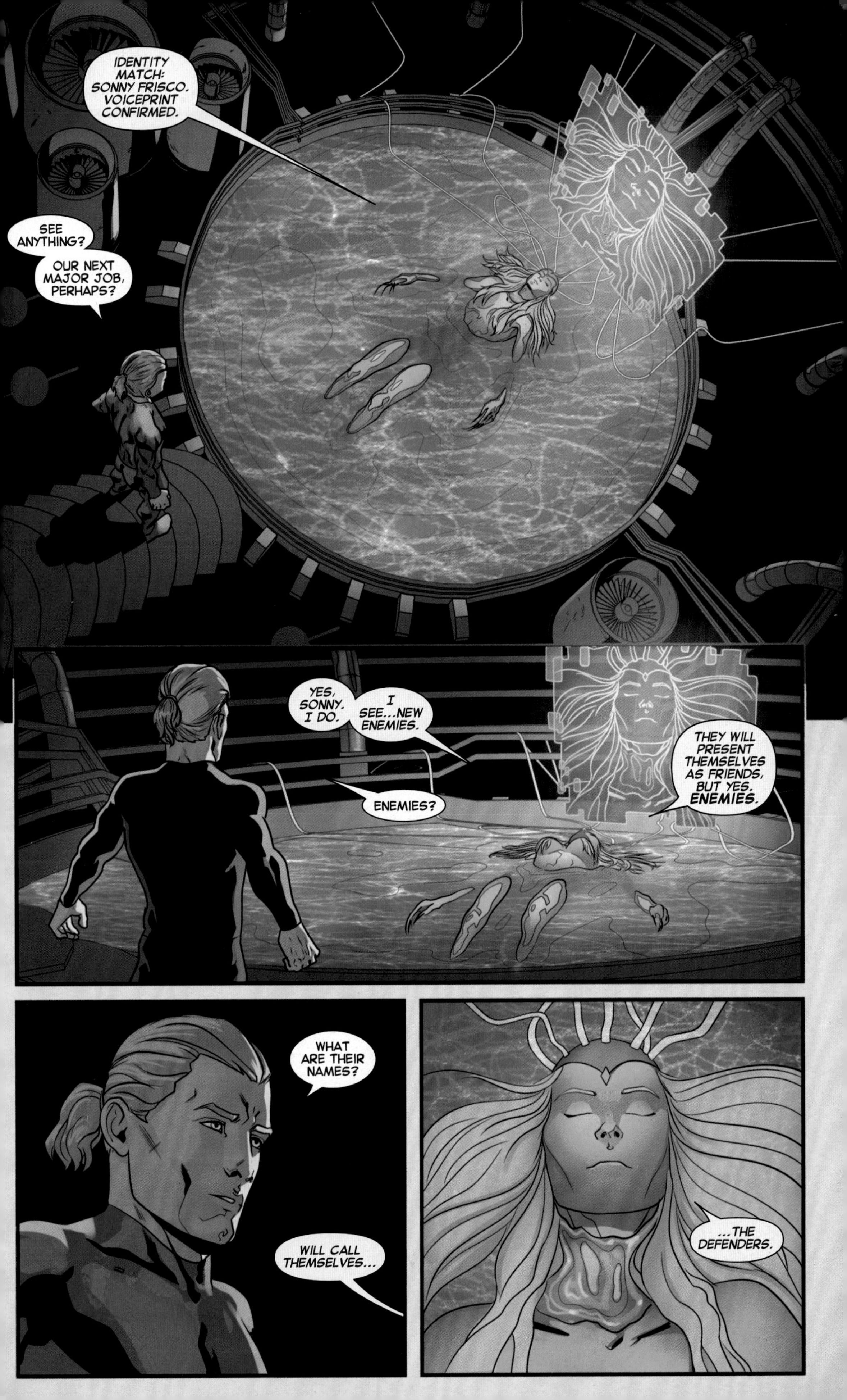
IDENTITY MATCH: SONNY FRISCO. VOICEPRINT CONFIRMED.
SEE ANYTHING?
OUR NEXT MAJOR JOB, PERHAPS?
YES, SONNY. I DO.
I SEE...NEW ENEMIES.
ENEMIES?
THEY WILL PRESENT THEMSELVES AS FRIENDS, BUT YES. ENEMIES.
WHAT ARE THEIR NAMES?
WILL CALL THEMSELVES...
...THE DEFENDERS.

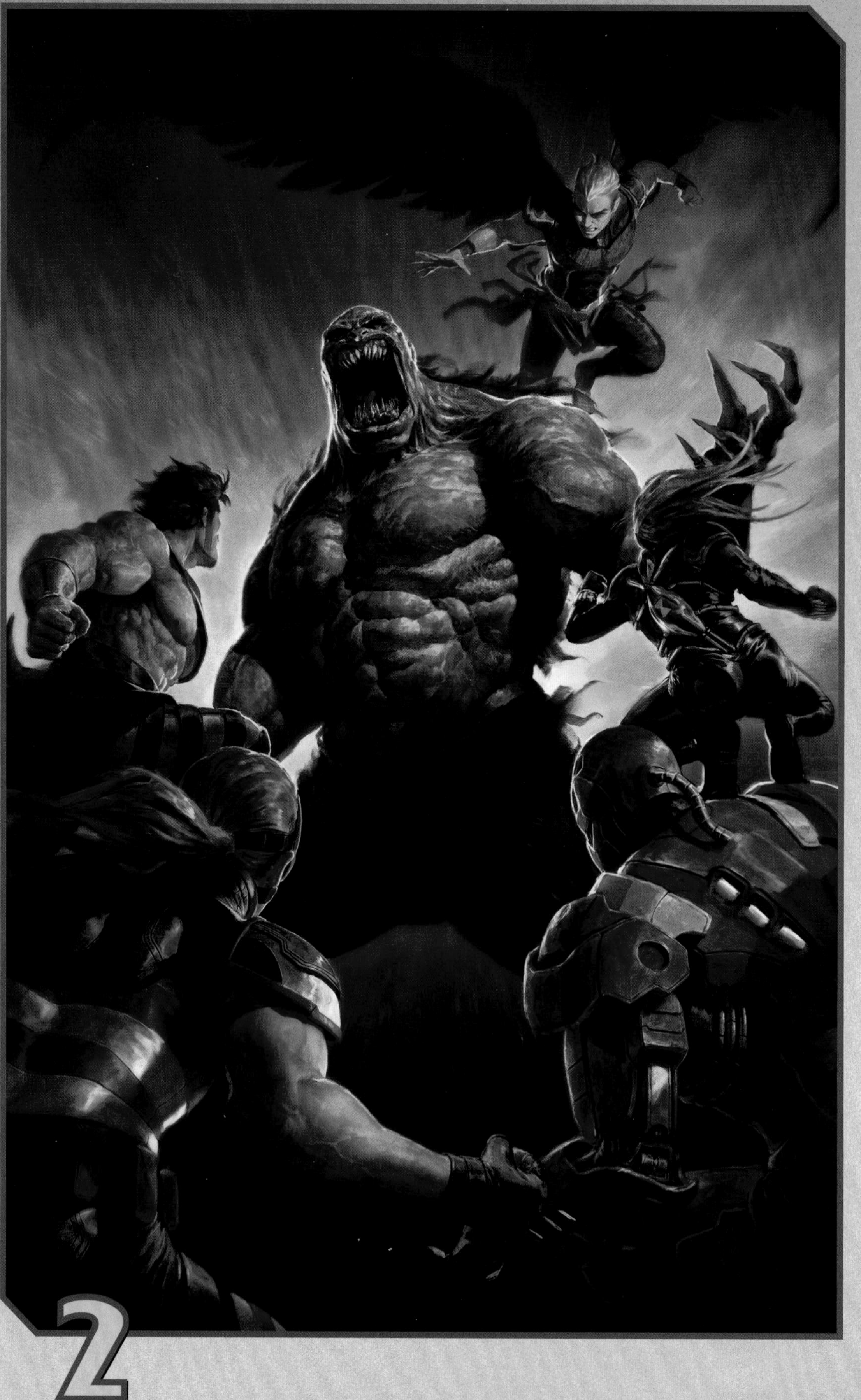

2

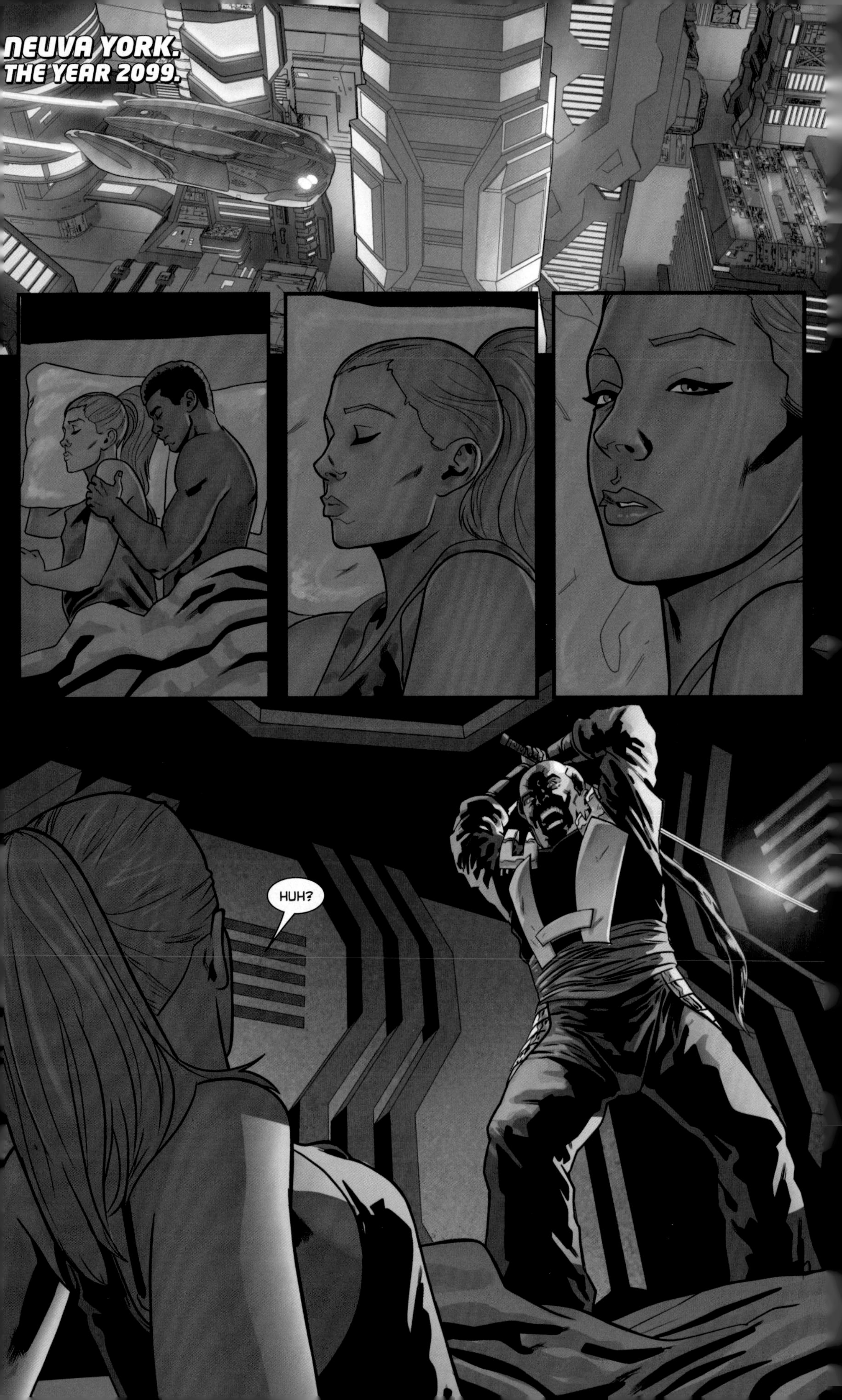
NEUVA YORK.
THE YEAR 2099.
HUH?

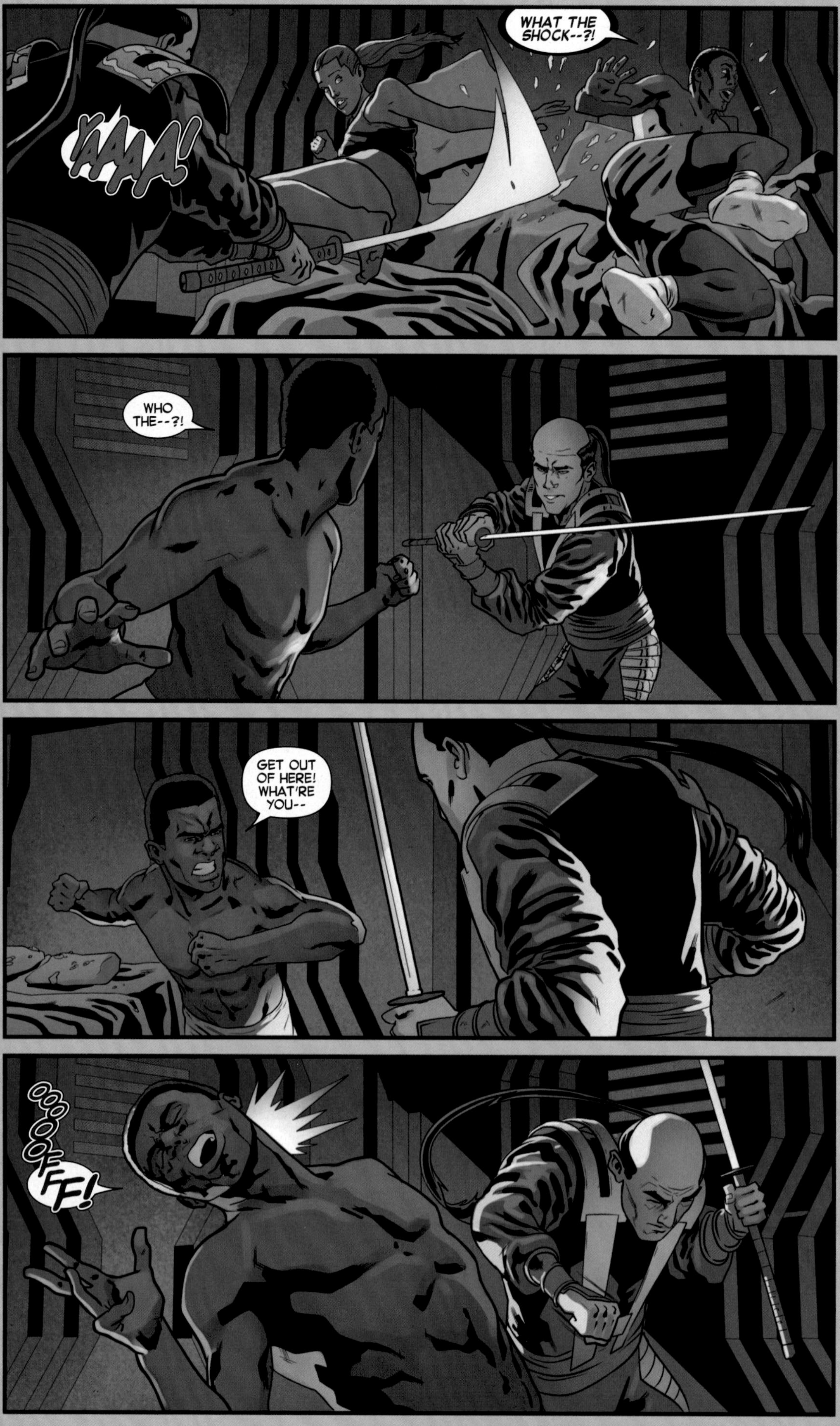
YAAAA!
WHAT THE SHOCK--?!
WHO THE--?!
GET OUT OF HERE! WHAT'RE YOU--
OOOOOFF!

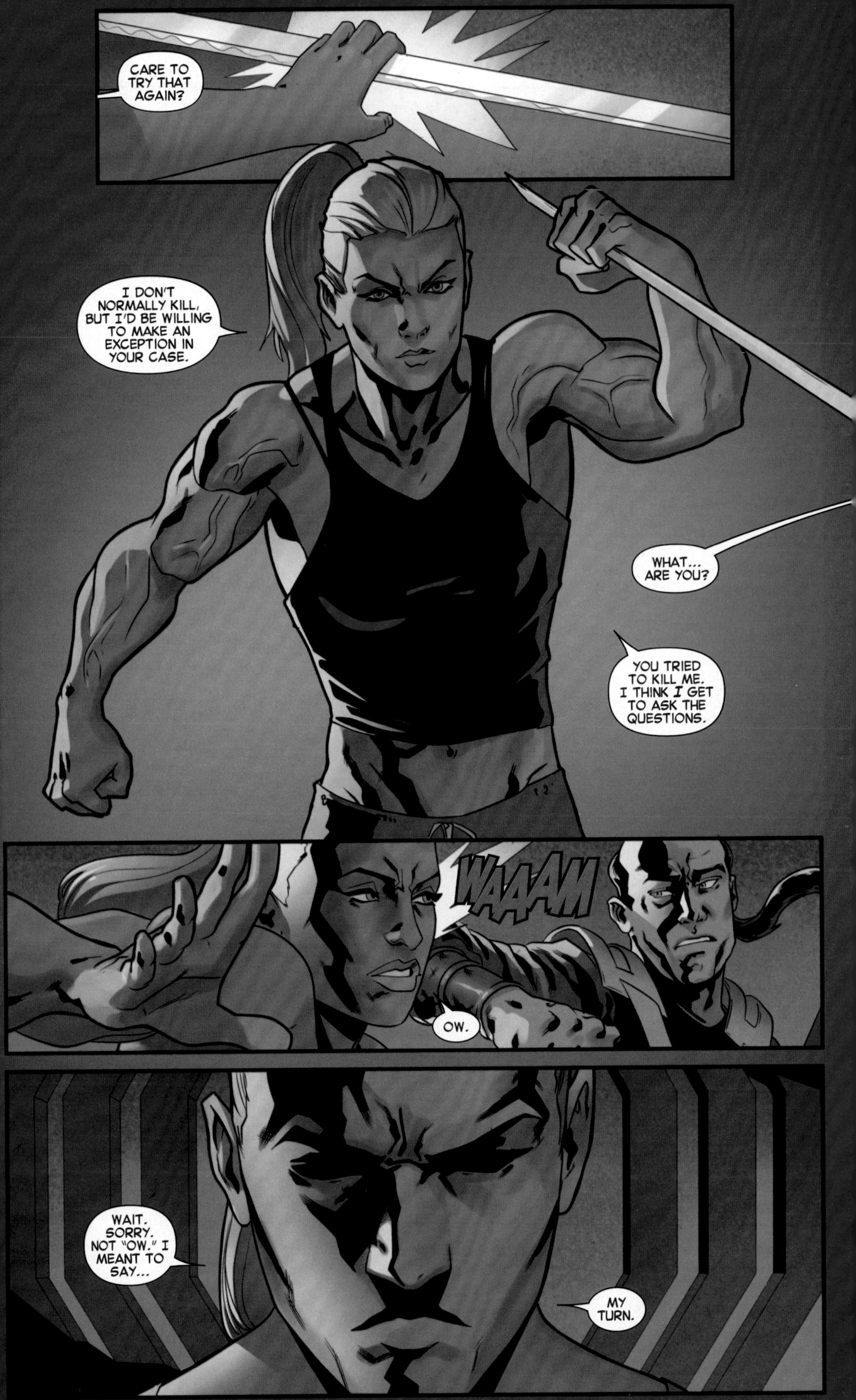
CARE TO TRY THAT AGAIN?
I DON'T NORMALLY KILL, BUT I'D BE WILLING TO MAKE AN EXCEPTION IN YOUR CASE.
WHAT... ARE YOU?
YOU TRIED TO KILL ME. I THINK I GET TO ASK THE QUESTIONS.
WAAAM
OW.
WAIT. SORRY. NOT "OW." I MEANT TO SAY...
MY TURN.

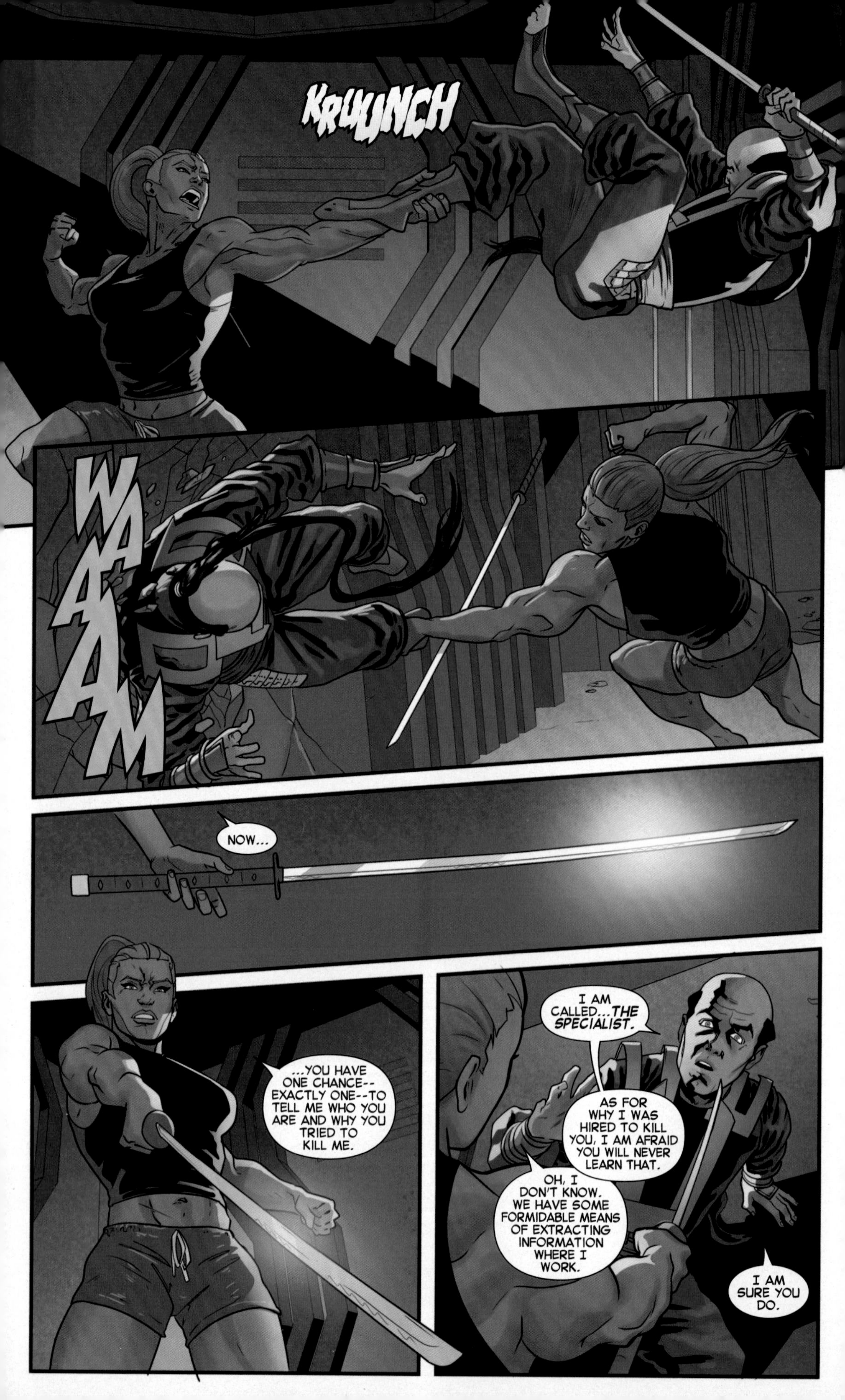
KRUUNCH
WAAAM
NOW...
...YOU HAVE ONE CHANCE--EXACTLY ONE--TO TELL ME WHO YOU ARE AND WHY YOU TRIED TO KILL ME.
I AM CALLED... THE SPECIALIST.
AS FOR WHY I WAS HIRED TO KILL YOU, I AM AFRAID YOU WILL NEVER LEARN THAT.
OH, I DON'T KNOW. WE HAVE SOME FORMIDABLE MEANS OF EXTRACTING INFORMATION WHERE I WORK.
I AM SURE YOU DO.

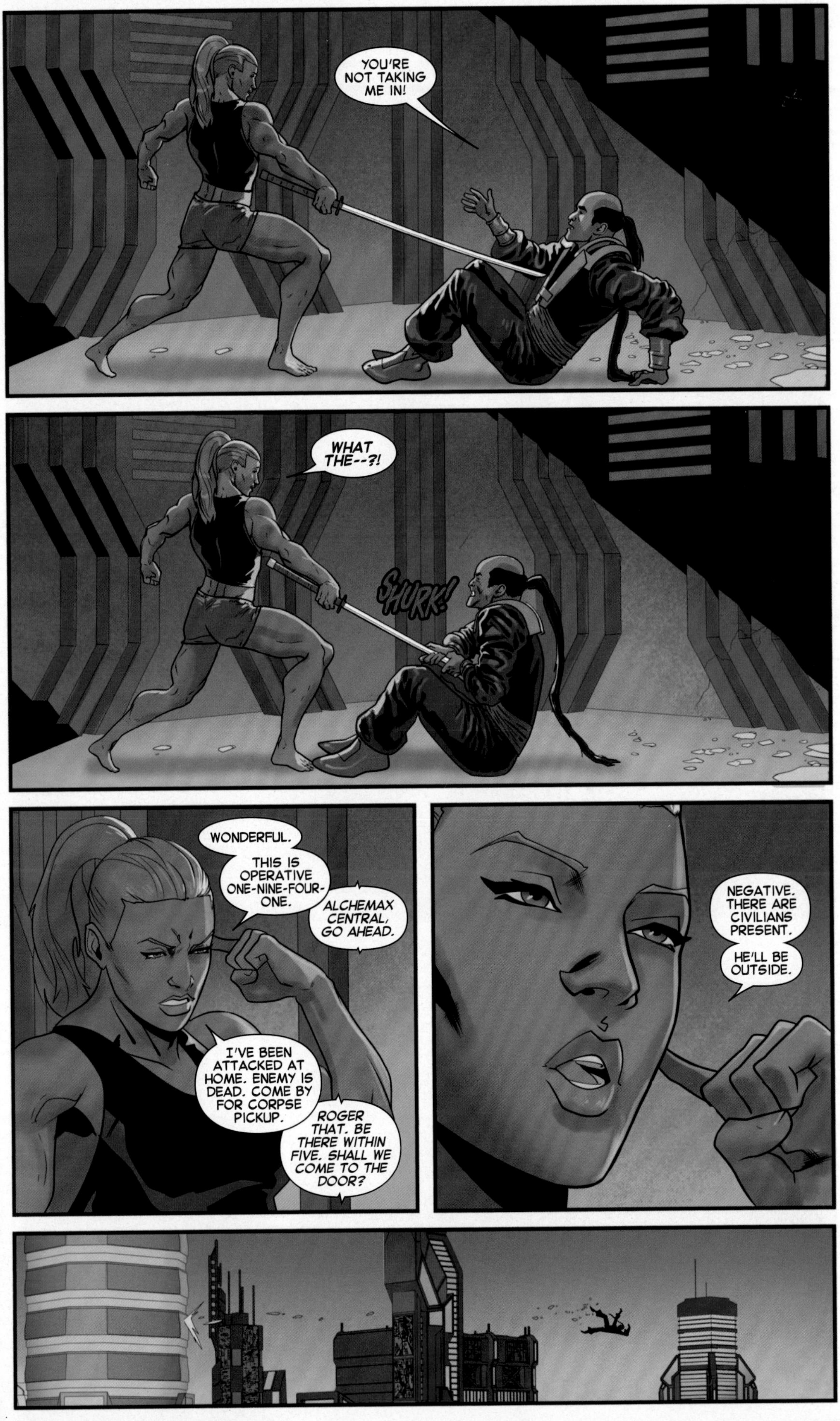

YOU'RE NOT TAKING ME IN!
WHAT THE--?!
SHURK!
WONDERFUL.
THIS IS OPERATIVE ONE-NINE-FOUR-ONE.
ALCHEMAX CENTRAL, GO AHEAD.
I'VE BEEN ATTACKED AT HOME. ENEMY IS DEAD. COME BY FOR CORPSE PICKUP.
ROGER THAT. BE THERE WITHIN FIVE. SHALL WE COME TO THE DOOR?
NEGATIVE. THERE ARE CIVILIANS PRESENT.
HE'LL BE OUTSIDE.

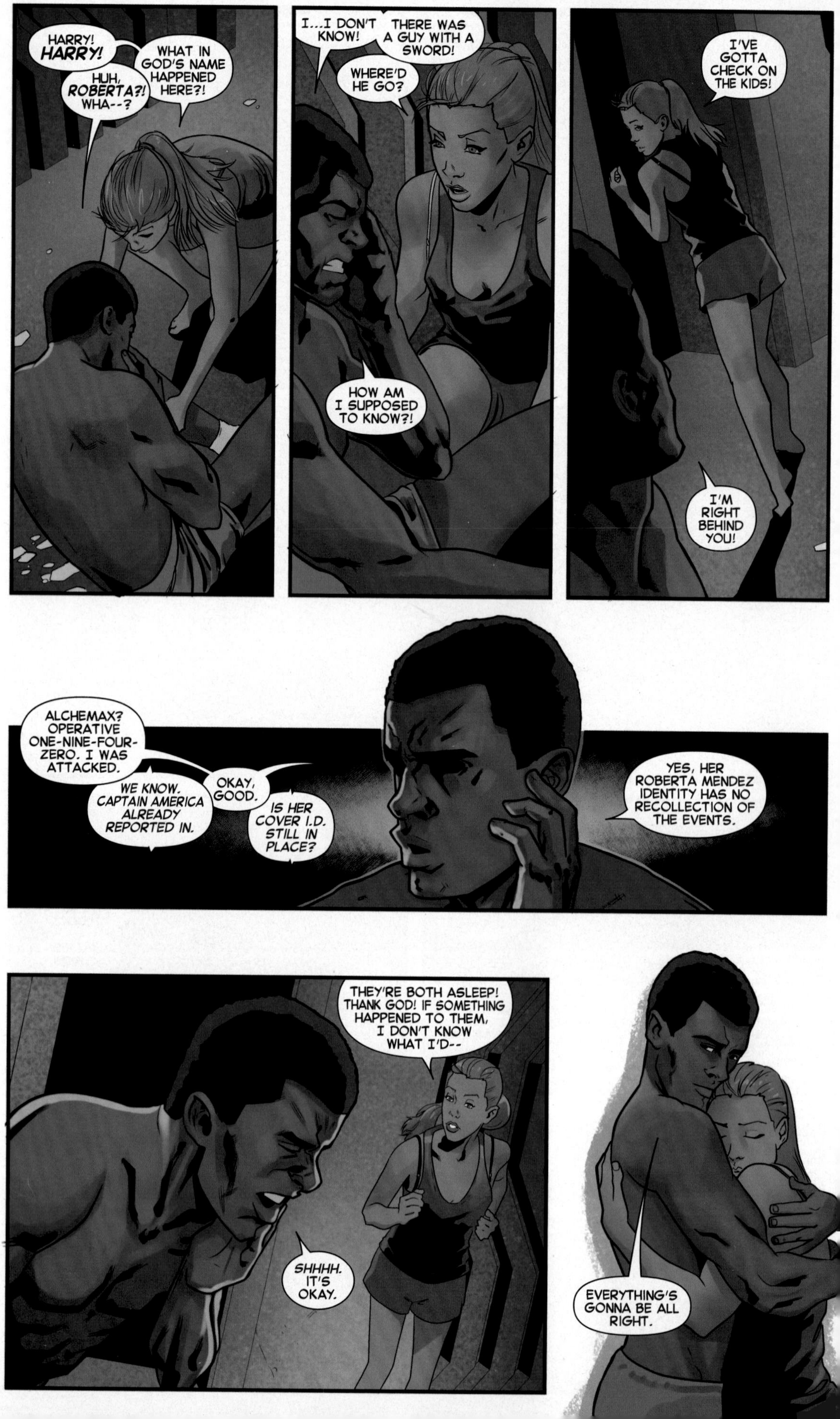
HARRY! HARRY!
HUH, ROBERTA?! WHA--?
WHAT IN GOD'S NAME HAPPENED HERE?!
I...I DON'T KNOW!
THERE WAS A GUY WITH A SWORD!
WHERE'D HE GO?
HOW AM I SUPPOSED TO KNOW?!
I'VE GOTTA CHECK ON THE KIDS!
I'M RIGHT BEHIND YOU!
ALCHEMAX? OPERATIVE ONE-NINE-FOUR-ZERO. I WAS ATTACKED.
WE KNOW. CAPTAIN AMERICA ALREADY REPORTED IN.
OKAY, GOOD.
IS HER COVER I.D. STILL IN PLACE?
YES, HER ROBERTA MENDEZ IDENTITY HAS NO RECOLLECTION OF THE EVENTS.
THEY'RE BOTH ASLEEP! THANK GOD! IF SOMETHING HAPPENED TO THEM, I DON'T KNOW WHAT I'D--
SHHHH. IT'S OKAY.
EVERYTHING'S GONNA BE ALL RIGHT.

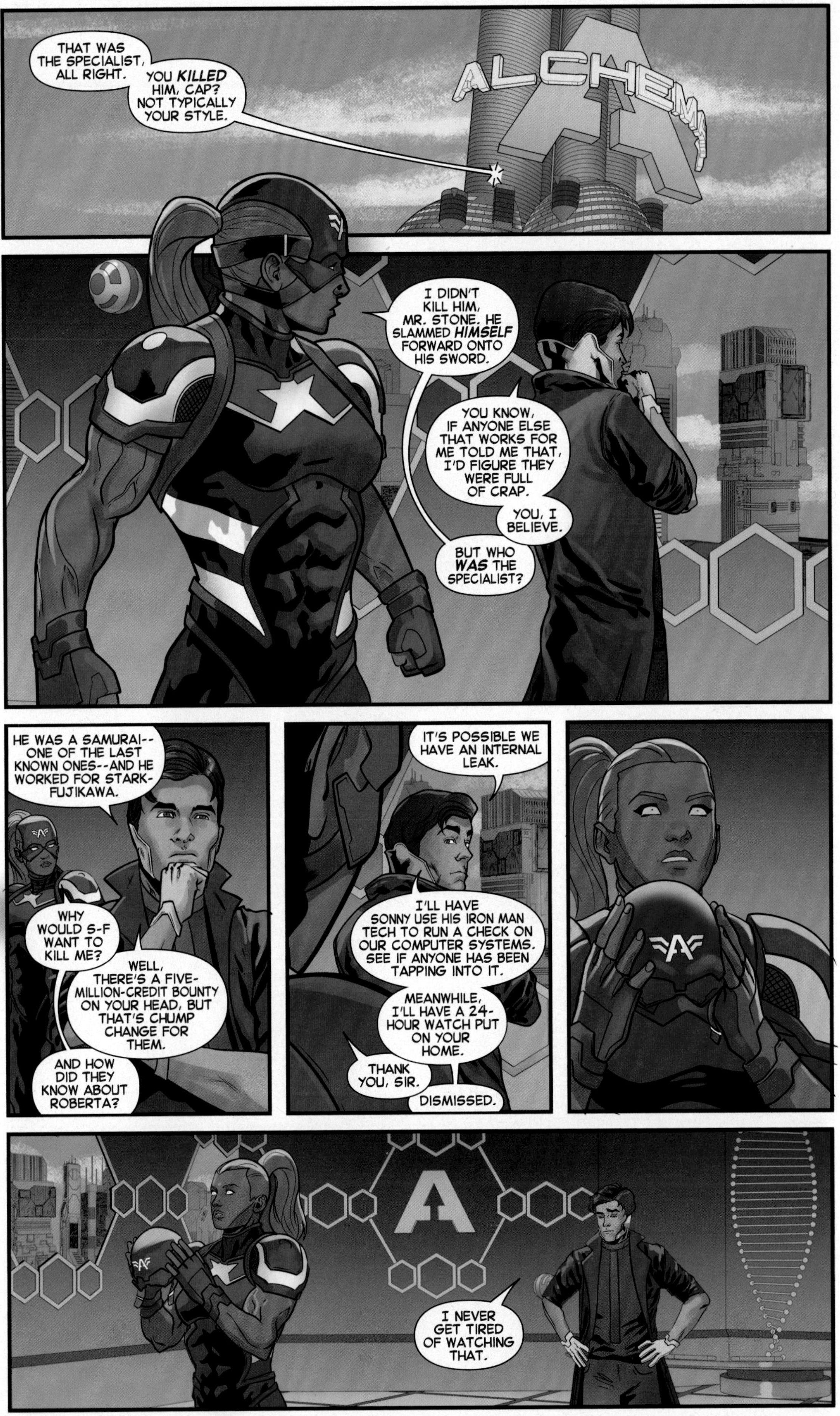
THAT WAS THE SPECIALIST, ALL RIGHT.
YOU KILLED HIM, CAP? NOT TYPICALLY YOUR STYLE.
ALCHEM
I DIDN'T KILL HIM, MR. STONE. HE SLAMMED HIMSELF FORWARD ONTO HIS SWORD.
YOU KNOW, IF ANYONE ELSE THAT WORKS FOR ME TOLD ME THAT, I'D FIGURE THEY WERE FULL OF CRAP.
YOU, I BELIEVE.
BUT WHO WAS THE SPECIALIST?
HE WAS A SAMURAI--ONE OF THE LAST KNOWN ONES--AND HE WORKED FOR STARK-FUJIKAWA.
WHY WOULD S-F WANT TO KILL ME?
WELL, THERE'S A FIVE-MILLION-CREDIT BOUNTY ON YOUR HEAD, BUT THAT'S CHUMP CHANGE FOR THEM.
AND HOW DID THEY KNOW ABOUT ROBERTA?
IT'S POSSIBLE WE HAVE AN INTERNAL LEAK.
I'LL HAVE SONNY USE HIS IRON MAN TECH TO RUN A CHECK ON OUR COMPUTER SYSTEMS. SEE IF ANYONE HAS BEEN TAPPING INTO IT.
MEANWHILE, I'LL HAVE A 24-HOUR WATCH PUT ON YOUR HOME.
THANK YOU, SIR.
DISMISSED.
I NEVER GET TIRED OF WATCHING THAT.

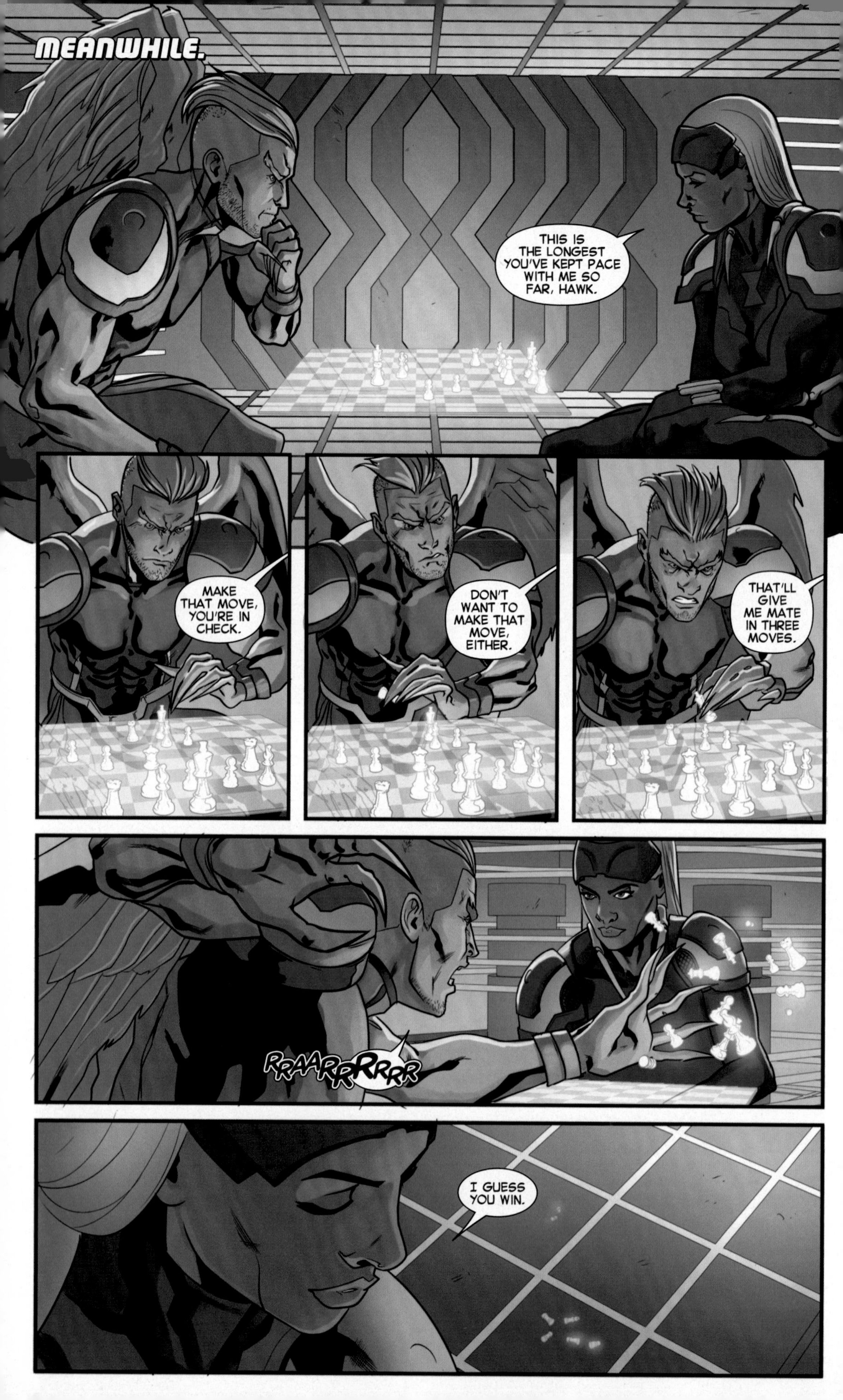
MEANWHILE.
THIS IS THE LONGEST YOU'VE KEPT PACE WITH ME SO FAR, HAWK.
MAKE THAT MOVE, YOU'RE IN CHECK.
DON'T WANT TO MAKE THAT MOVE, EITHER.
THAT'LL GIVE ME MATE IN THREE MOVES.
RRAARRRRRR
I GUESS YOU WIN.

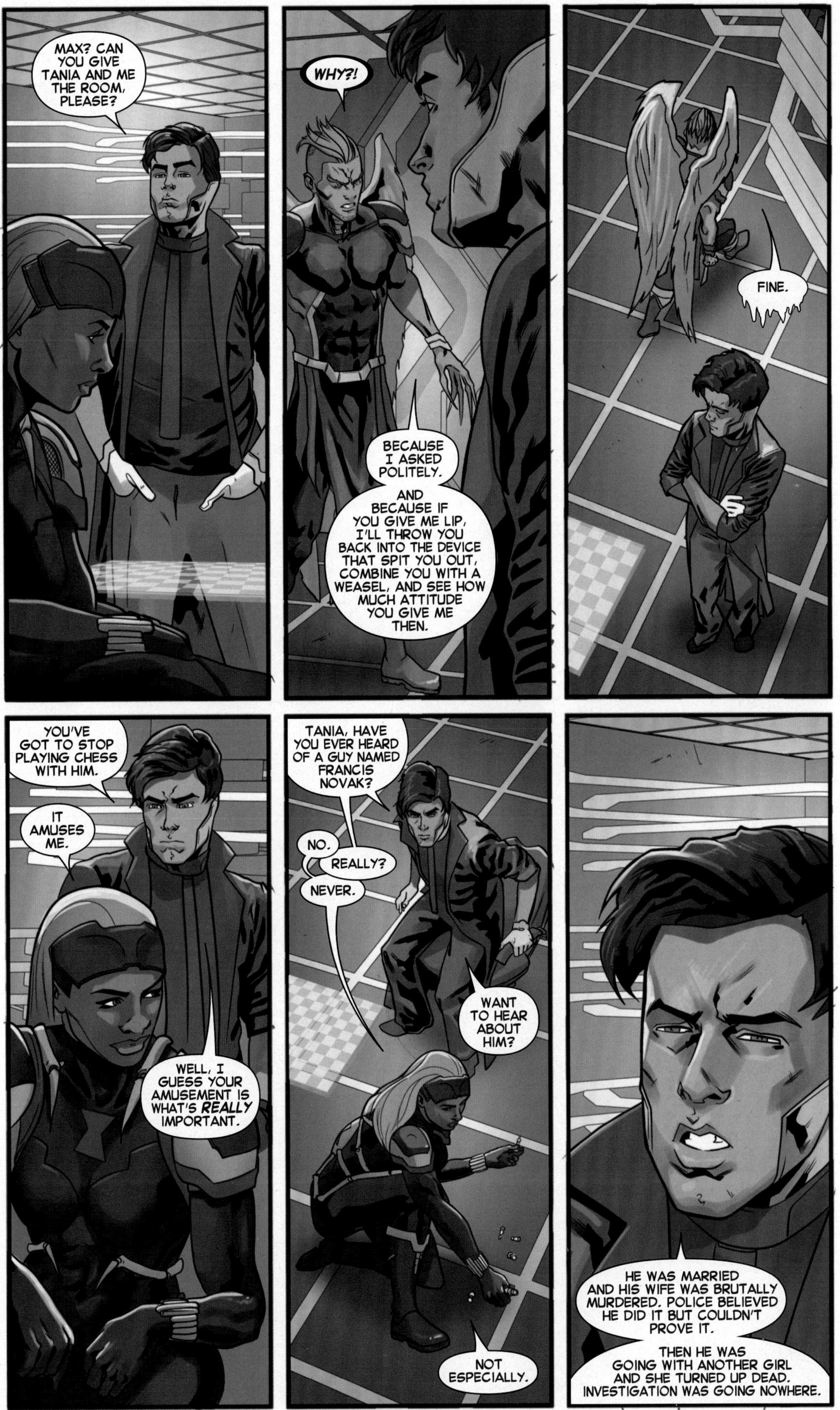
MAX? CAN YOU GIVE TANIA AND ME THE ROOM, PLEASE?
WHY?!
BECAUSE I ASKED POLITELY.
AND BECAUSE IF YOU GIVE ME LIP, I'LL THROW YOU BACK INTO THE DEVICE THAT SPIT YOU OUT, COMBINE YOU WITH A WEASEL, AND SEE HOW MUCH ATTITUDE YOU GIVE ME THEN.
FINE.
YOU'VE GOT TO STOP PLAYING CHESS WITH HIM.
IT AMUSES ME.
WELL, I GUESS YOUR AMUSEMENT IS WHAT'S REALLY IMPORTANT.
TANIA, HAVE YOU EVER HEARD OF A GUY NAMED FRANCIS NOVAK?
NO.
REALLY?
NEVER.
WANT TO HEAR ABOUT HIM?
NOT ESPECIALLY.
HE WAS MARRIED AND HIS WIFE WAS BRUTALLY MURDERED. POLICE BELIEVED HE DID IT BUT COULDN'T PROVE IT.
THEN HE WAS GOING WITH ANOTHER GIRL AND SHE TURNED UP DEAD. INVESTIGATION WAS GOING NOWHERE.

SOUNDS NASTY. WOMEN SHOULD WATCH OUT FOR HIM.

FUNNY YOU SHOULD SAY THAT.

OH? WHY?

HE WAS FOUND DEAD THIS MORNING.

DEAD AND HALF EATEN.

THAT SOUNDS NASTY.

IT WAS. SO TELL ME, TANIA...

IF I RUN A DNA SCAN ON HIS CORPSE, HOW MANY SECONDS DO YOU THINK IT WILL TAKE ME TO FIND TRACES OF YOUR SALIVA IN HIM?

I HAVE NO IDEA WHAT YOU'RE TALKING ABOUT, MIGUEL.

OF COURSE YOU DON'T.

I FIND THIS AGAIN, TANIA, AND WE'RE GOING TO HAVE ANOTHER CONVERSATION THAT WON'T END THIS PEACEFULLY.

SO EITHER STOP DOING IT OR GET BETTER AT HIDING YOUR KILLS. UNDERSTOOD?

YES, SIR. HEY, MIGUEL--?

YEAH?

HAVE ANY PLANS TONIGHT?

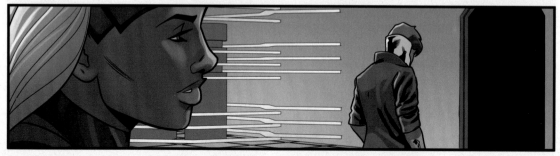

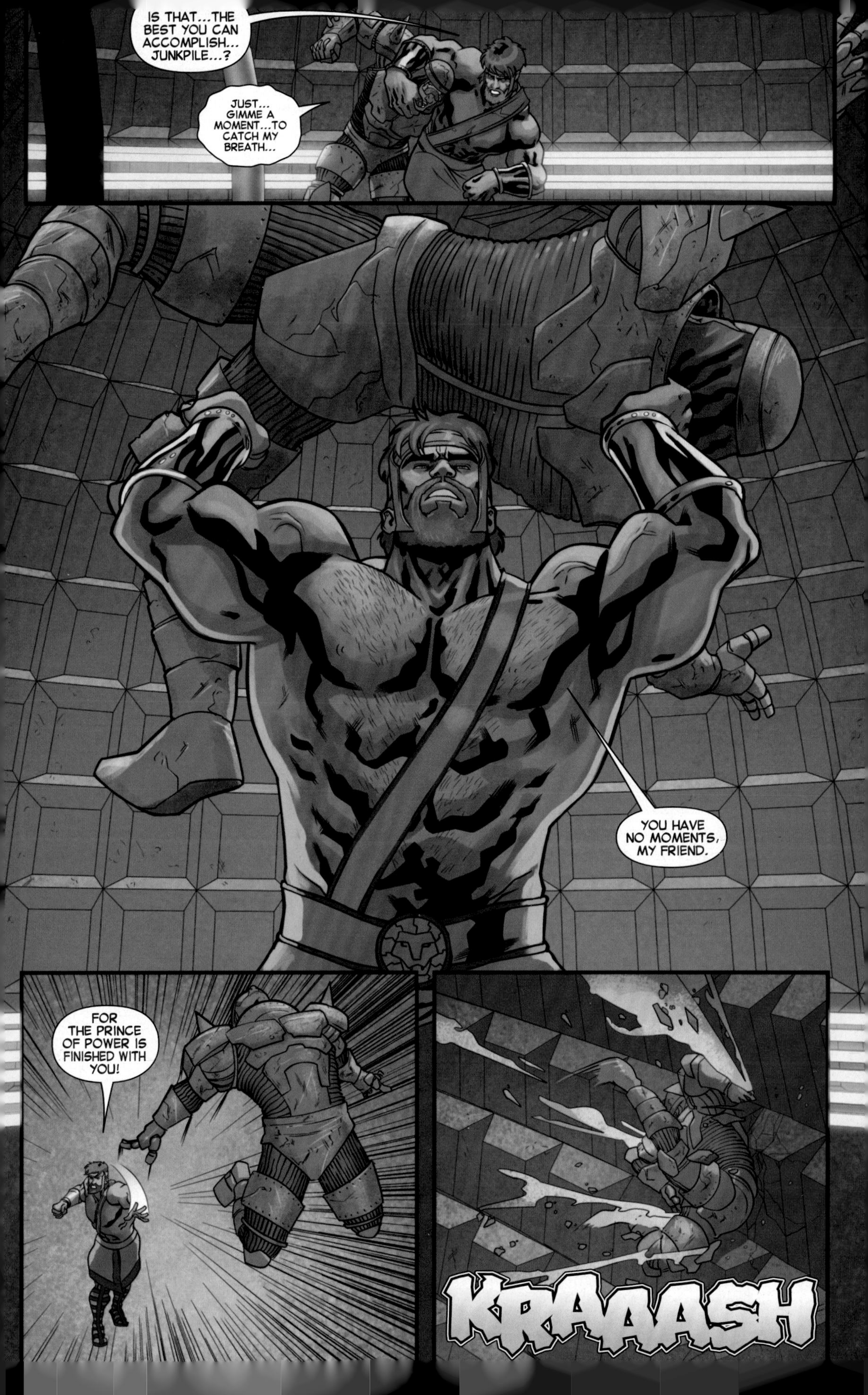

IS THAT...THE BEST YOU CAN ACCOMPLISH... JUNKPILE...?
JUST... GIMME A MOMENT...TO CATCH MY BREATH...
YOU HAVE NO MOMENTS, MY FRIEND.
FOR THE PRINCE OF POWER IS FINISHED WITH YOU!
KRAAASH

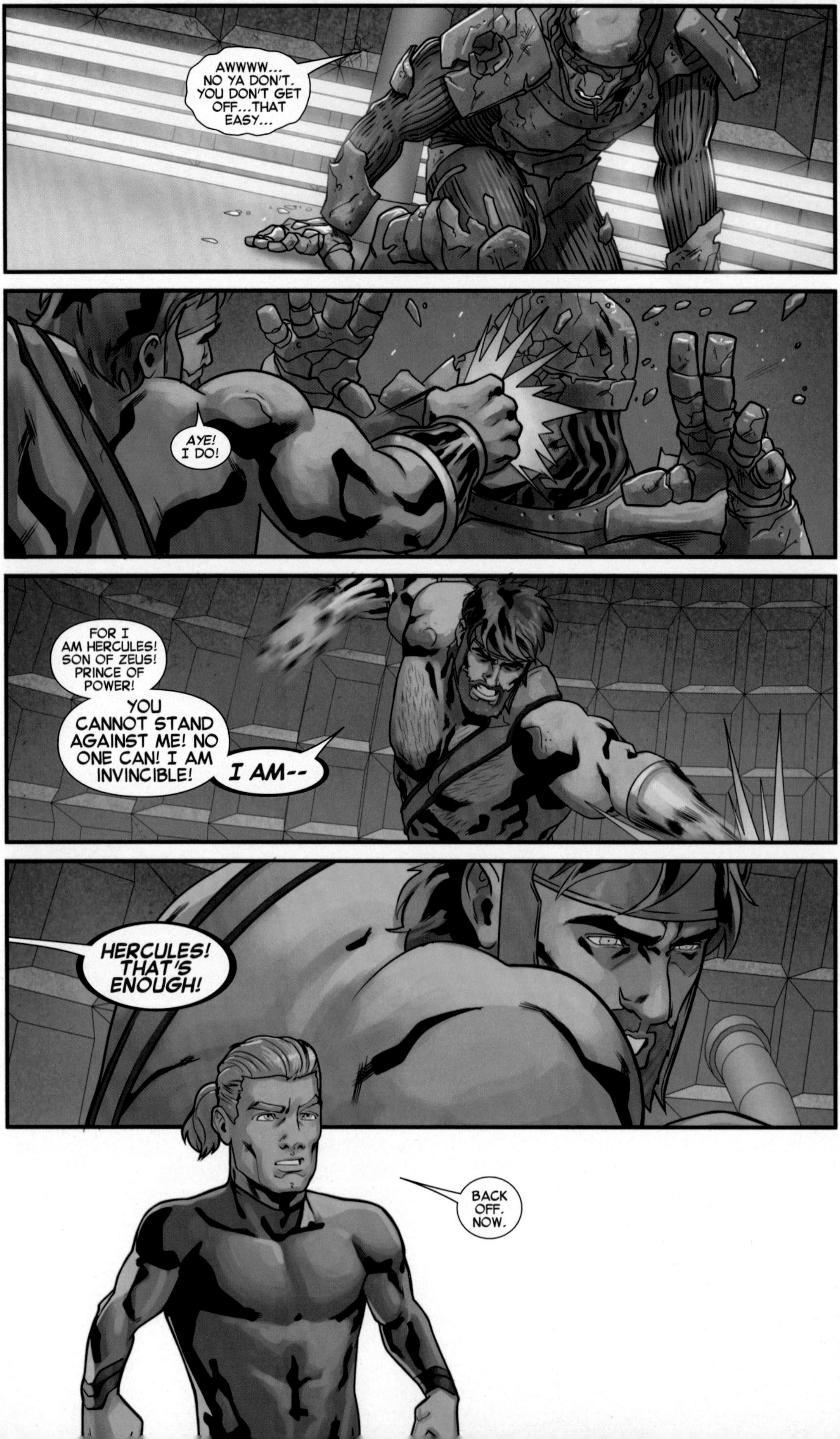

AWWWW... NO YA DON'T. YOU DON'T GET OFF...THAT EASY...
AYE! I DO!
FOR I AM HERCULES! SON OF ZEUS! PRINCE OF POWER!
YOU CANNOT STAND AGAINST ME! NO ONE CAN! I AM INVINCIBLE!
I AM--
HERCULES! THAT'S ENOUGH!
BACK OFF. NOW.

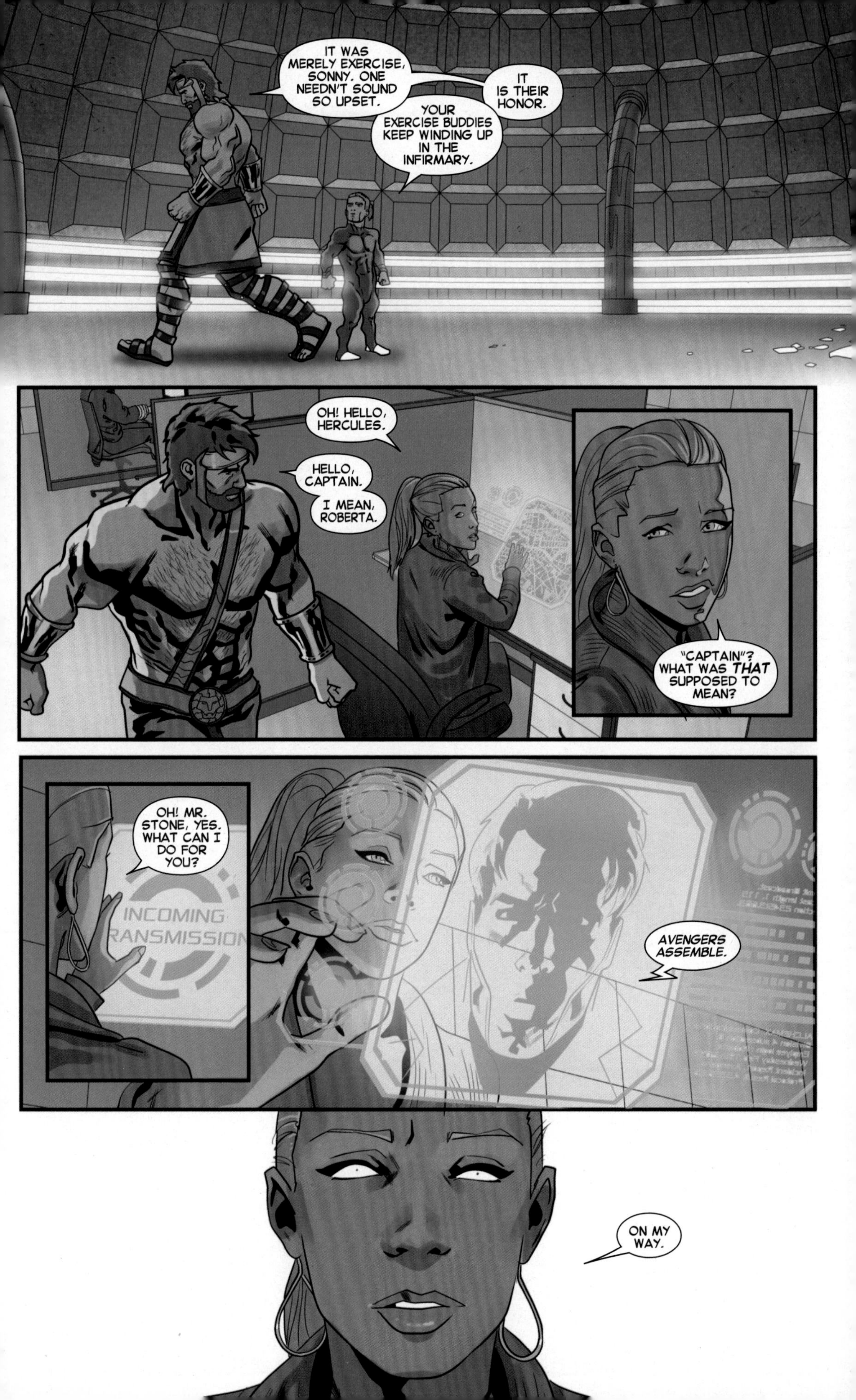
IT WAS MERELY EXERCISE, SONNY. ONE NEEDN'T SOUND SO UPSET.
IT IS THEIR HONOR.
YOUR EXERCISE BUDDIES KEEP WINDING UP IN THE INFIRMARY.
OH! HELLO, HERCULES.
HELLO, CAPTAIN.
I MEAN, ROBERTA.
"CAPTAIN"? WHAT WAS THAT SUPPOSED TO MEAN?
OH! MR. STONE, YES. WHAT CAN I DO FOR YOU?
INCOMING
RANSMISSION
AVENGERS ASSEMBLE.
ON MY WAY.

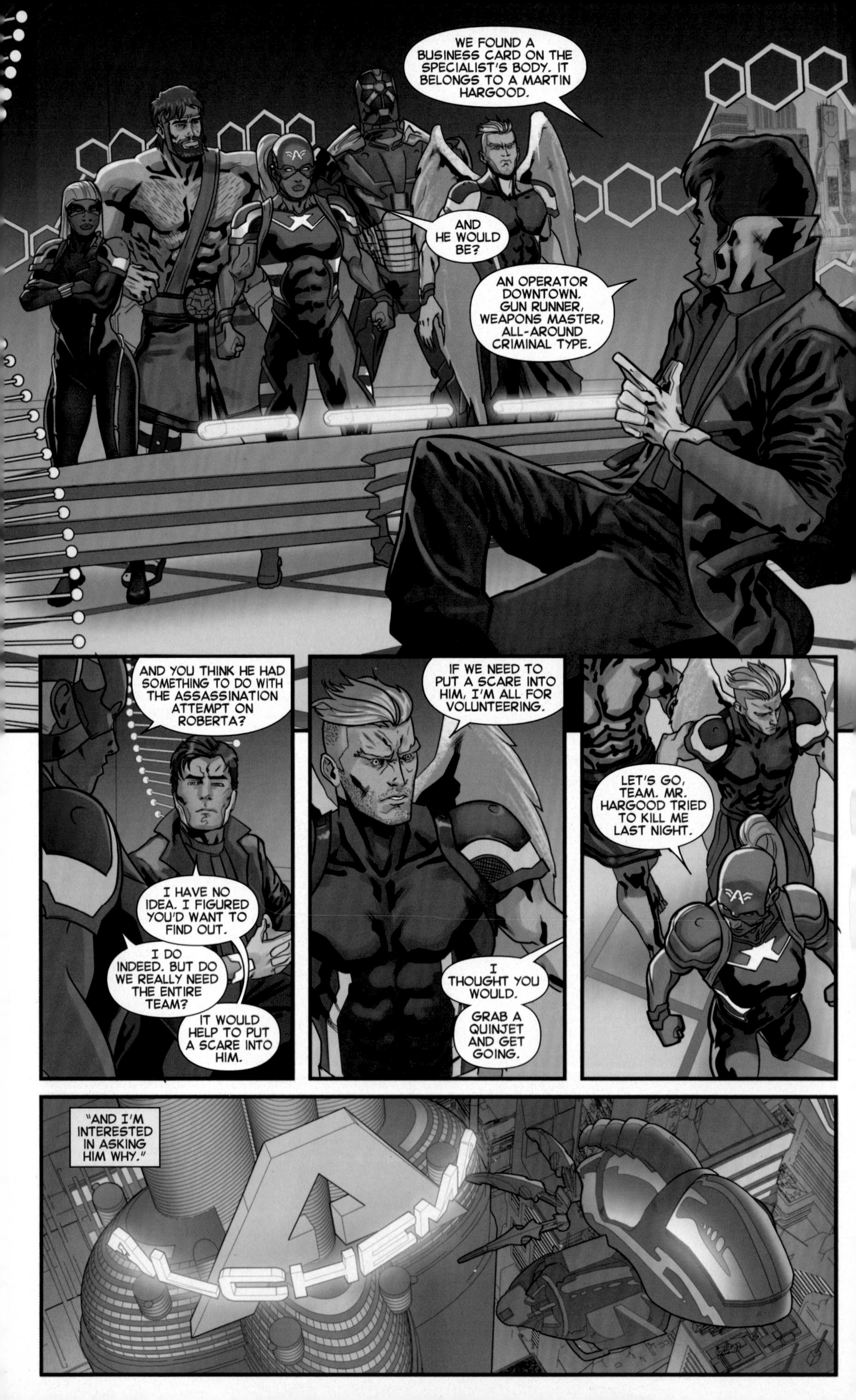
WE FOUND A BUSINESS CARD ON THE SPECIALIST'S BODY. IT BELONGS TO A MARTIN HARGOOD.
AND HE WOULD BE?
AN OPERATOR DOWNTOWN. GUN RUNNER, WEAPONS MASTER, ALL-AROUND CRIMINAL TYPE.
AND YOU THINK HE HAD SOMETHING TO DO WITH THE ASSASSINATION ATTEMPT ON ROBERTA?
I HAVE NO IDEA. I FIGURED YOU'D WANT TO FIND OUT.
I DO INDEED. BUT DO WE REALLY NEED THE ENTIRE TEAM?
IT WOULD HELP TO PUT A SCARE INTO HIM.
IF WE NEED TO PUT A SCARE INTO HIM, I'M ALL FOR VOLUNTEERING.
I THOUGHT YOU WOULD.
GRAB A QUINJET AND GET GOING.
LET'S GO, TEAM. MR. HARGOOD TRIED TO KILL ME LAST NIGHT.
"AND I'M INTERESTED IN ASKING HIM WHY."
ALCHEMAX

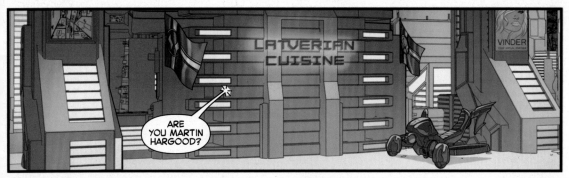

LATVERIAN CUISINE

VINDER

ARE YOU MARTIN HARGOOD?

I AM INDEED. AND YOU WOULD BE?

JOHN EISENHART. I NEED TO HAVE WORDS WITH YOU.

AS YOU SEE, I'M IN THE MIDDLE OF LUNCH. SO IF YOU WOULDN'T MIND--

KRAAAASH

I'M SORRY, I DON'T SEEM TO HAVE HAD YOUR ATTENTION. IS THIS BETTER?

WHAT DO YOU WANT, MR. EISENHART?

I HAVE AN ISSUE WITH YOUR AFTER-HOURS ACTIVITIES.

AND WHAT WOULD THOSE BE?

WE GOING TO PLAY THIS GAME?

FINE. LET'S PLAY.

PUT HIM DOWN.

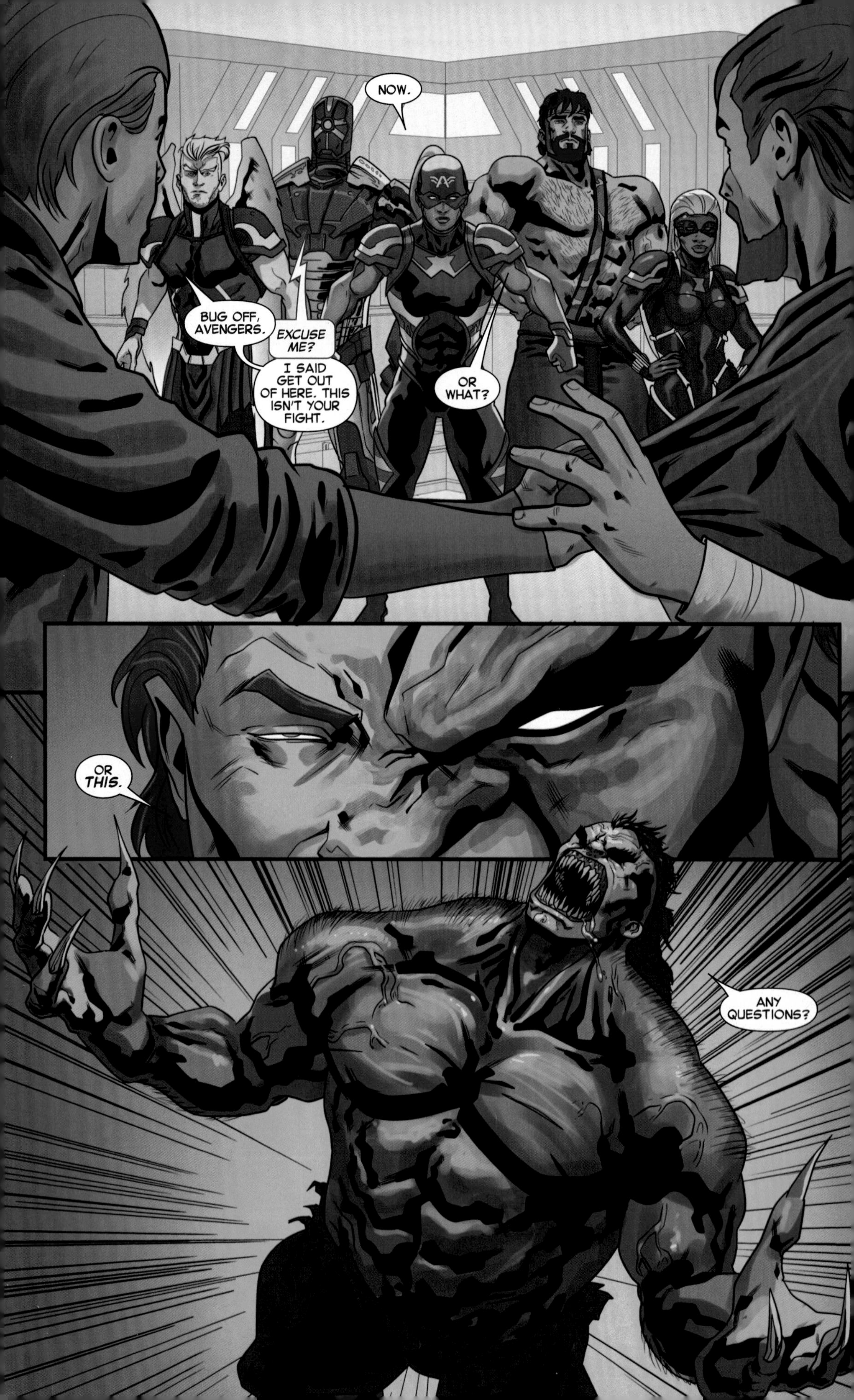
NOW.
BUG OFF, AVENGERS.
EXCUSE ME?
I SAID GET OUT OF HERE. THIS ISN'T YOUR FIGHT.
OR WHAT?
OR THIS.
ANY QUESTIONS?

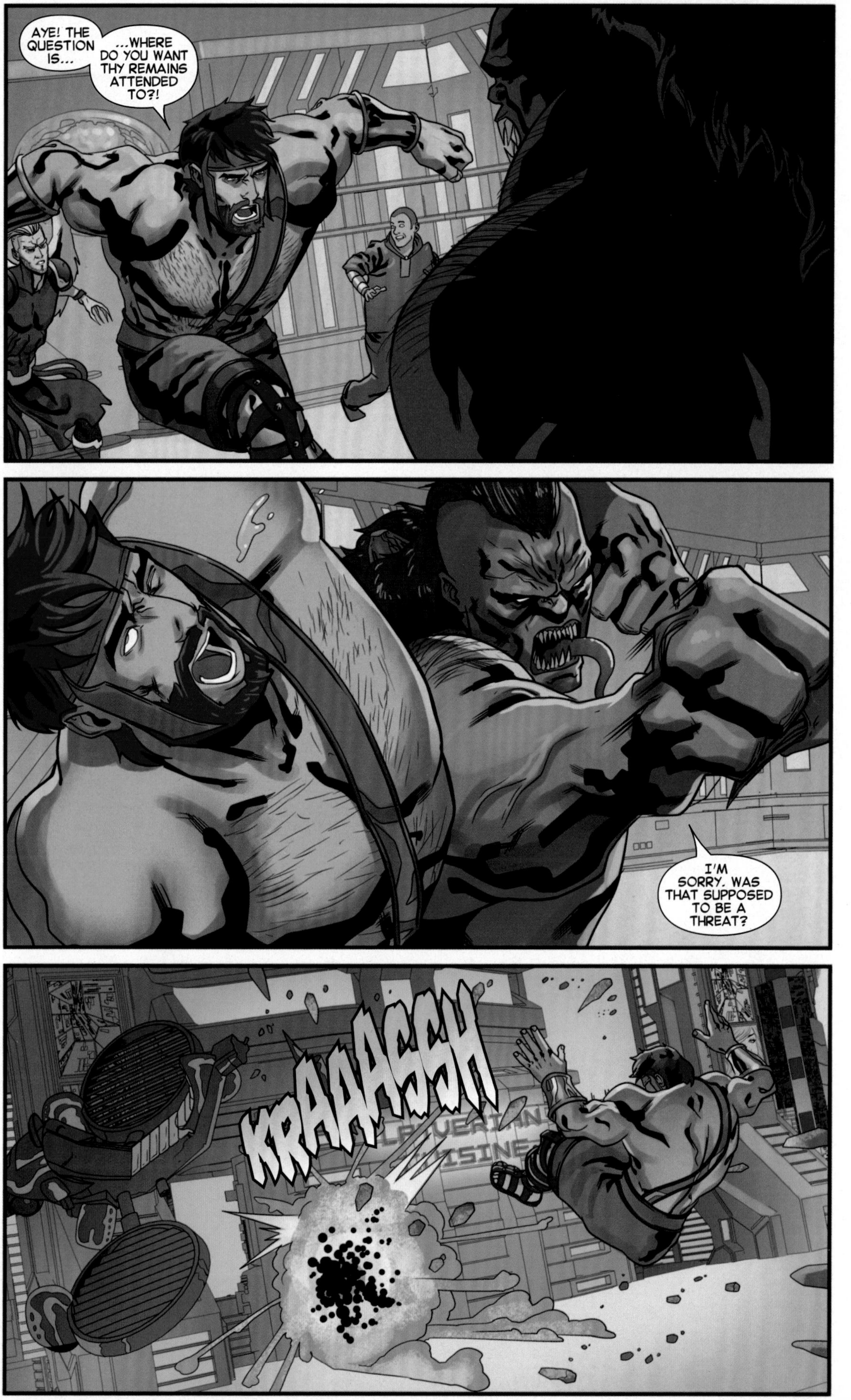
AYE! THE QUESTION IS...
...WHERE DO YOU WANT THY REMAINS ATTENDED TO?!
I'M SORRY. WAS THAT SUPPOSED TO BE A THREAT?
KRAAASCH

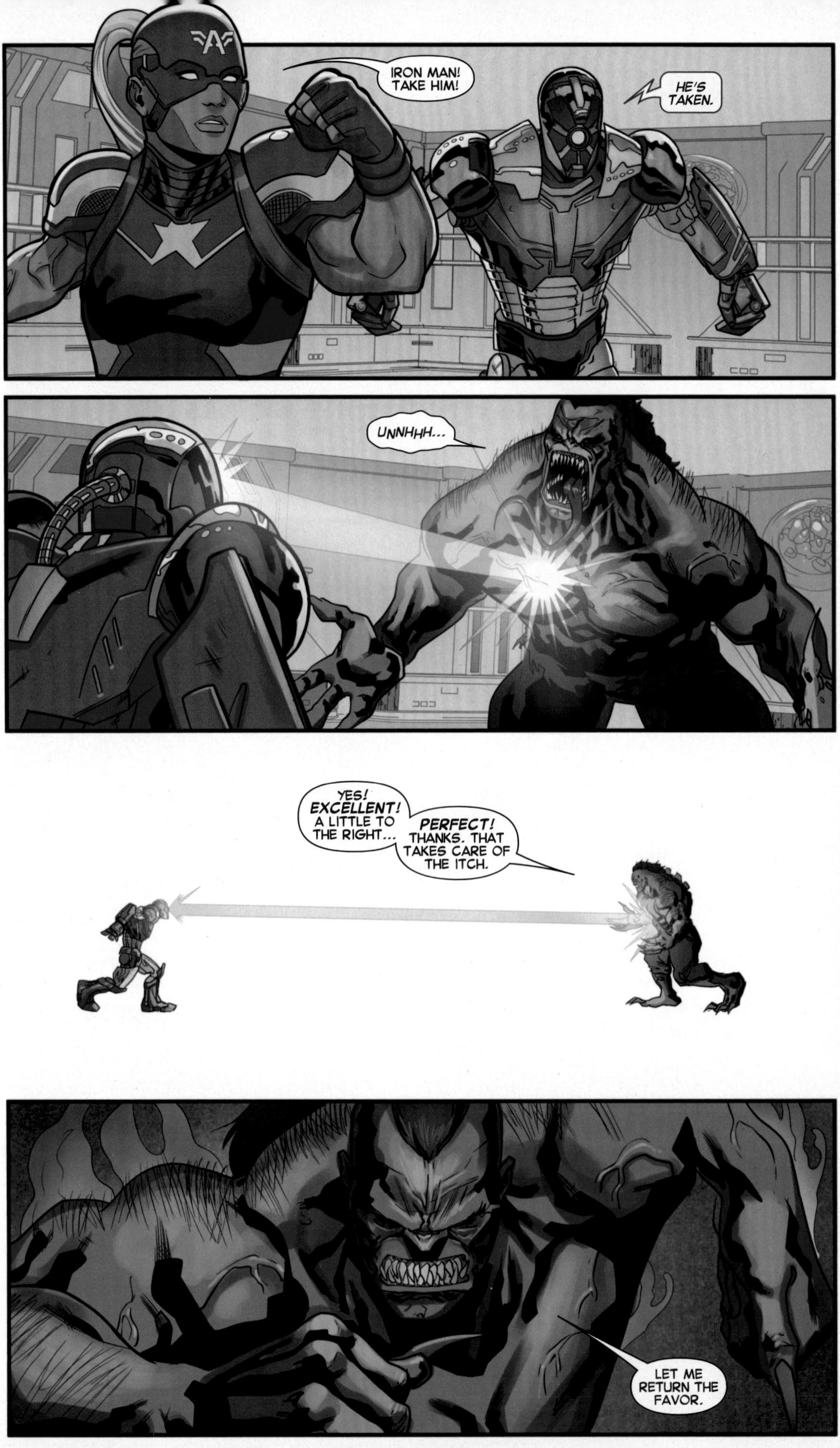
IRON MAN! TAKE HIM!
HE'S TAKEN.
UNNHHH...
YES! EXCELLENT! A LITTLE TO THE RIGHT...
PERFECT! THANKS. THAT TAKES CARE OF THE ITCH.
LET ME RETURN THE FAVOR.

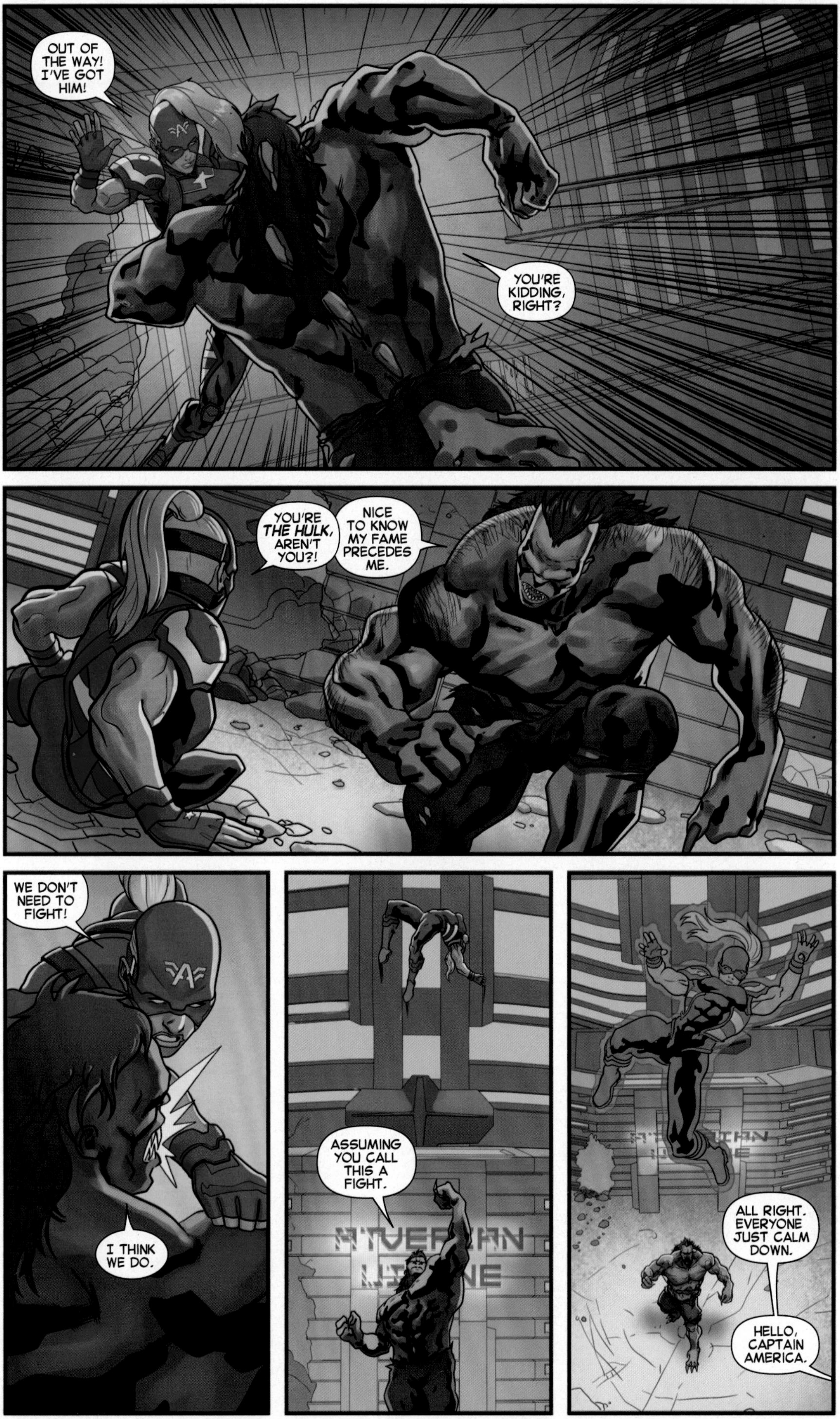
OUT OF THE WAY! I'VE GOT HIM!
YOU'RE KIDDING, RIGHT?
YOU'RE *THE HULK*, AREN'T YOU?!
NICE TO KNOW MY FAME PRECEDES ME.
WE DON'T NEED TO FIGHT!
I THINK WE DO.
ASSUMING YOU CALL THIS A FIGHT.
ALL RIGHT. EVERYONE JUST CALM DOWN.
HELLO, CAPTAIN AMERICA.

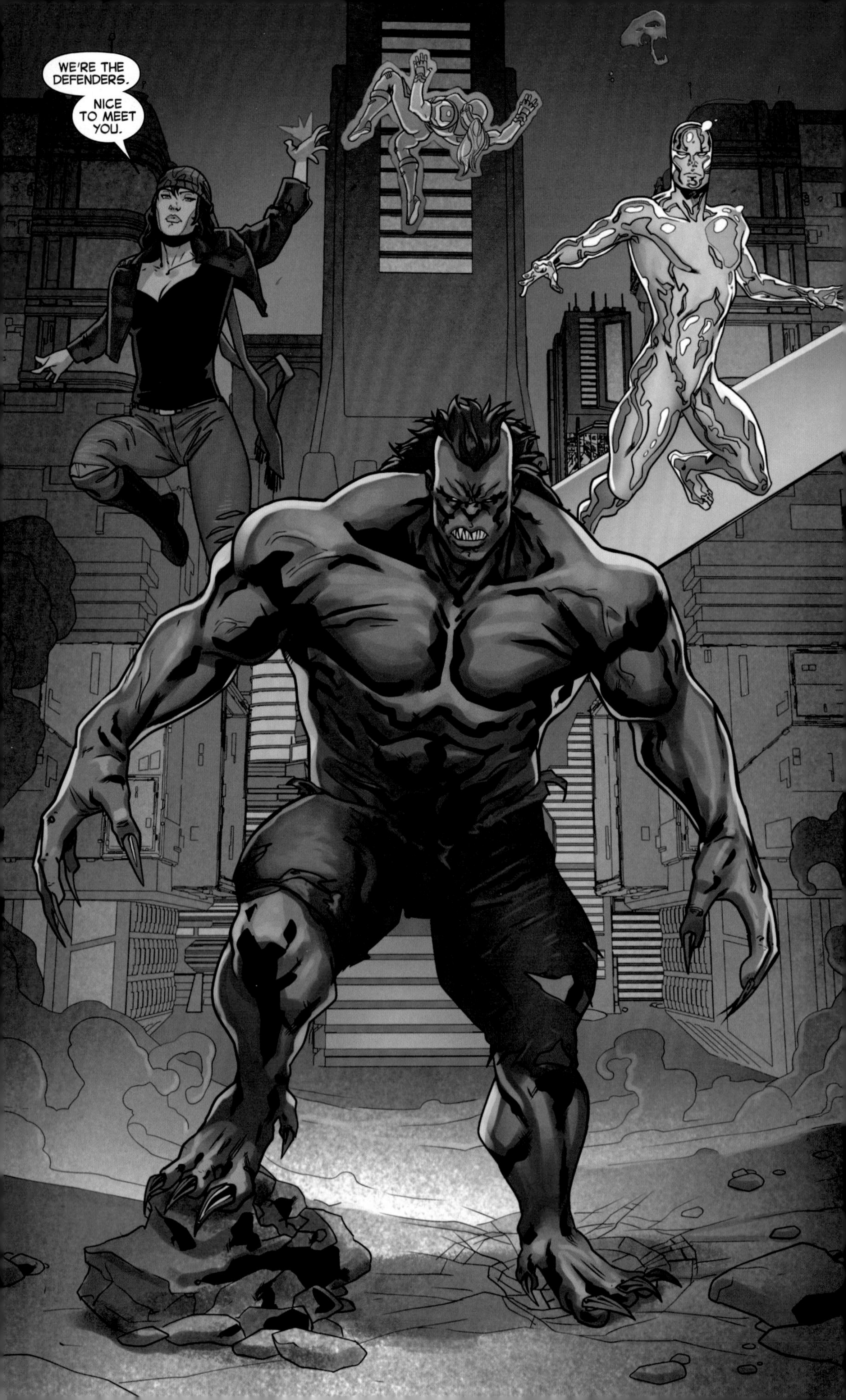

WE'RE THE DEFENDERS.
NICE TO MEET YOU.

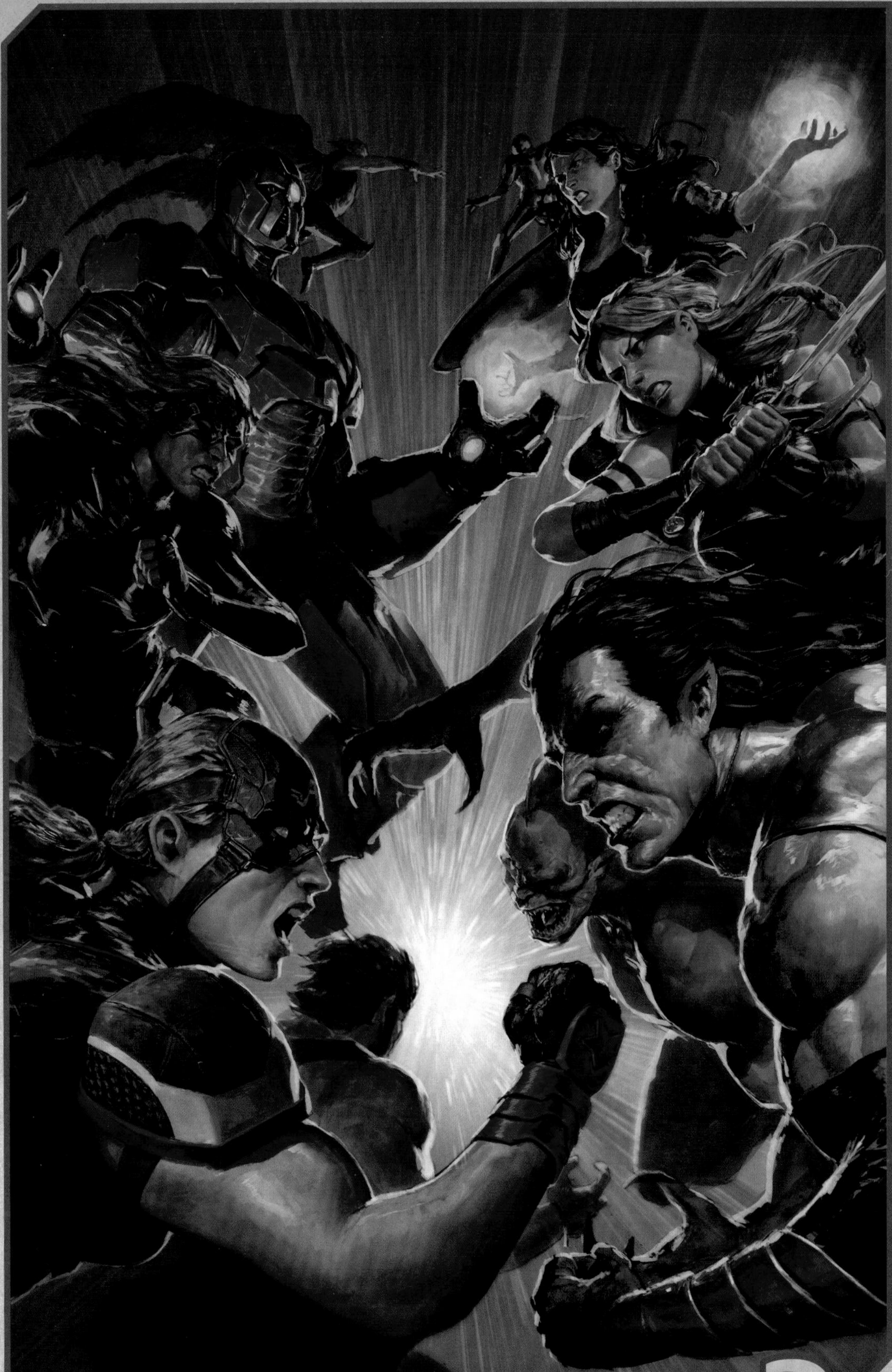

3

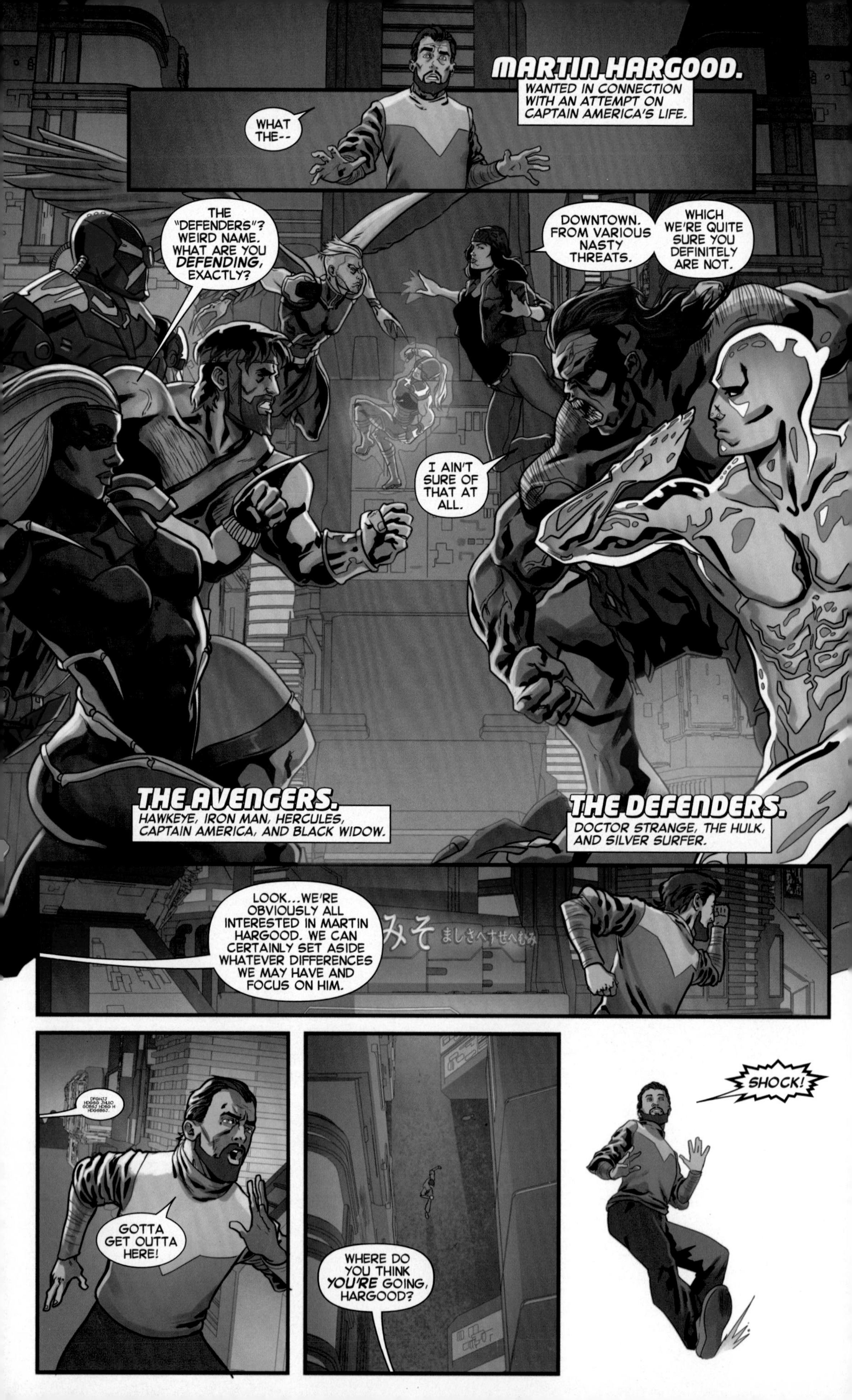
MARTIN HARGOOD.
WANTED IN CONNECTION WITH AN ATTEMPT ON CAPTAIN AMERICA'S LIFE.
WHAT THE--
THE "DEFENDERS"? WEIRD NAME. WHAT ARE YOU DEFENDING, EXACTLY?
DOWNTOWN. FROM VARIOUS NASTY THREATS.
WHICH WE'RE QUITE SURE YOU DEFINITELY ARE NOT.
I AIN'T SURE OF THAT AT ALL.
THE AVENGERS.
HAWKEYE, IRON MAN, HERCULES, CAPTAIN AMERICA, AND BLACK WIDOW.
THE DEFENDERS.
DOCTOR STRANGE, THE HULK, AND SILVER SURFER.
LOOK...WE'RE OBVIOUSLY ALL INTERESTED IN MARTIN HARGOOD. WE CAN CERTAINLY SET ASIDE WHATEVER DIFFERENCES WE MAY HAVE AND FOCUS ON HIM.
みそ
GOTTA GET OUTTA HERE!
WHERE DO YOU THINK YOU'RE GOING, HARGOOD?
SHOCK!

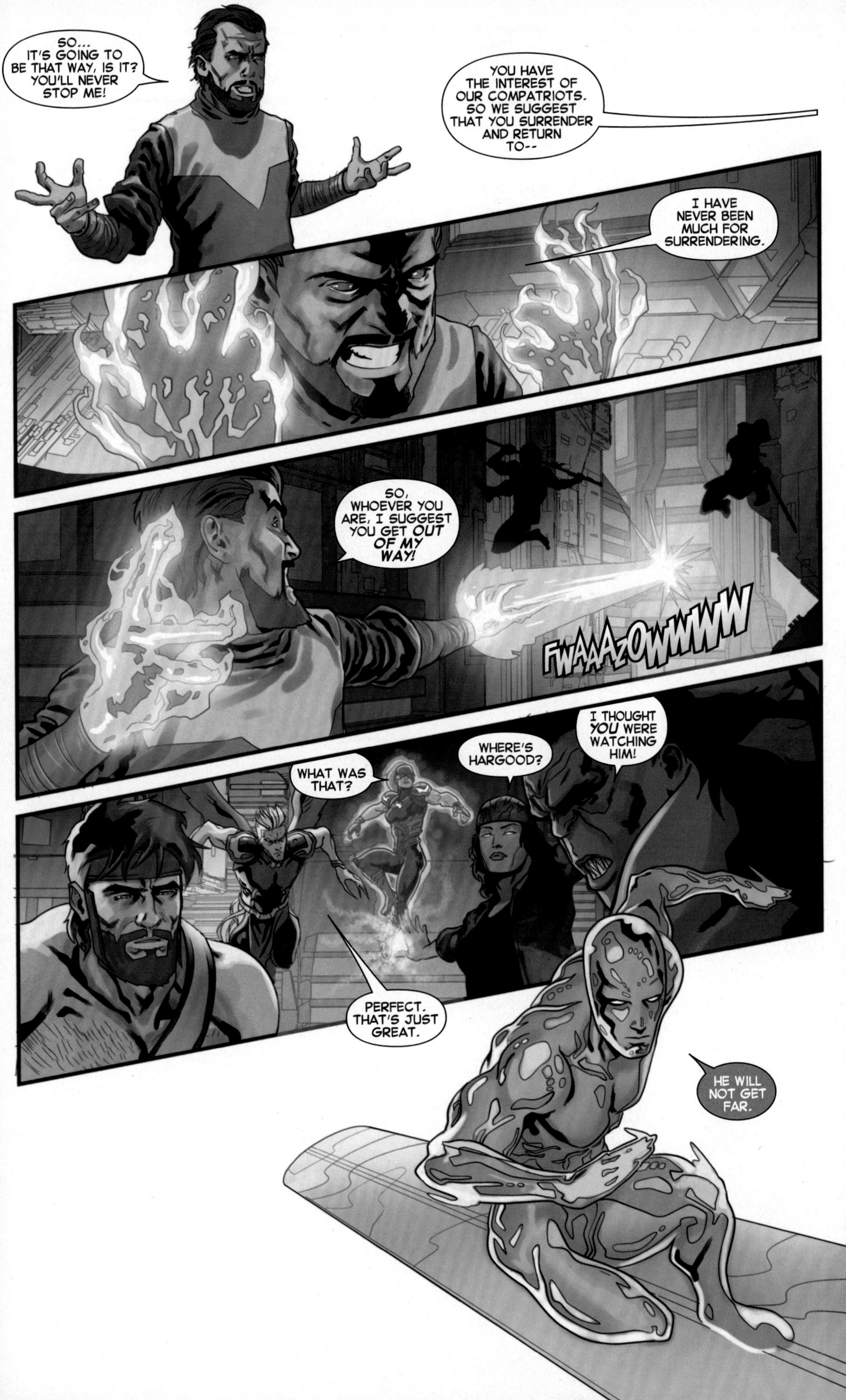

SO... IT'S GOING TO BE THAT WAY, IS IT? YOU'LL NEVER STOP ME!
YOU HAVE THE INTEREST OF OUR COMPATRIOTS. SO WE SUGGEST THAT YOU SURRENDER AND RETURN TO--
I HAVE NEVER BEEN MUCH FOR SURRENDERING.
SO, WHOEVER YOU ARE, I SUGGEST YOU GET OUT OF MY WAY!
FWAAAZOWWWW
WHAT WAS THAT?
WHERE'S HARGOOD?
I THOUGHT YOU WERE WATCHING HIM!
PERFECT. THAT'S JUST GREAT.
HE WILL NOT GET FAR.

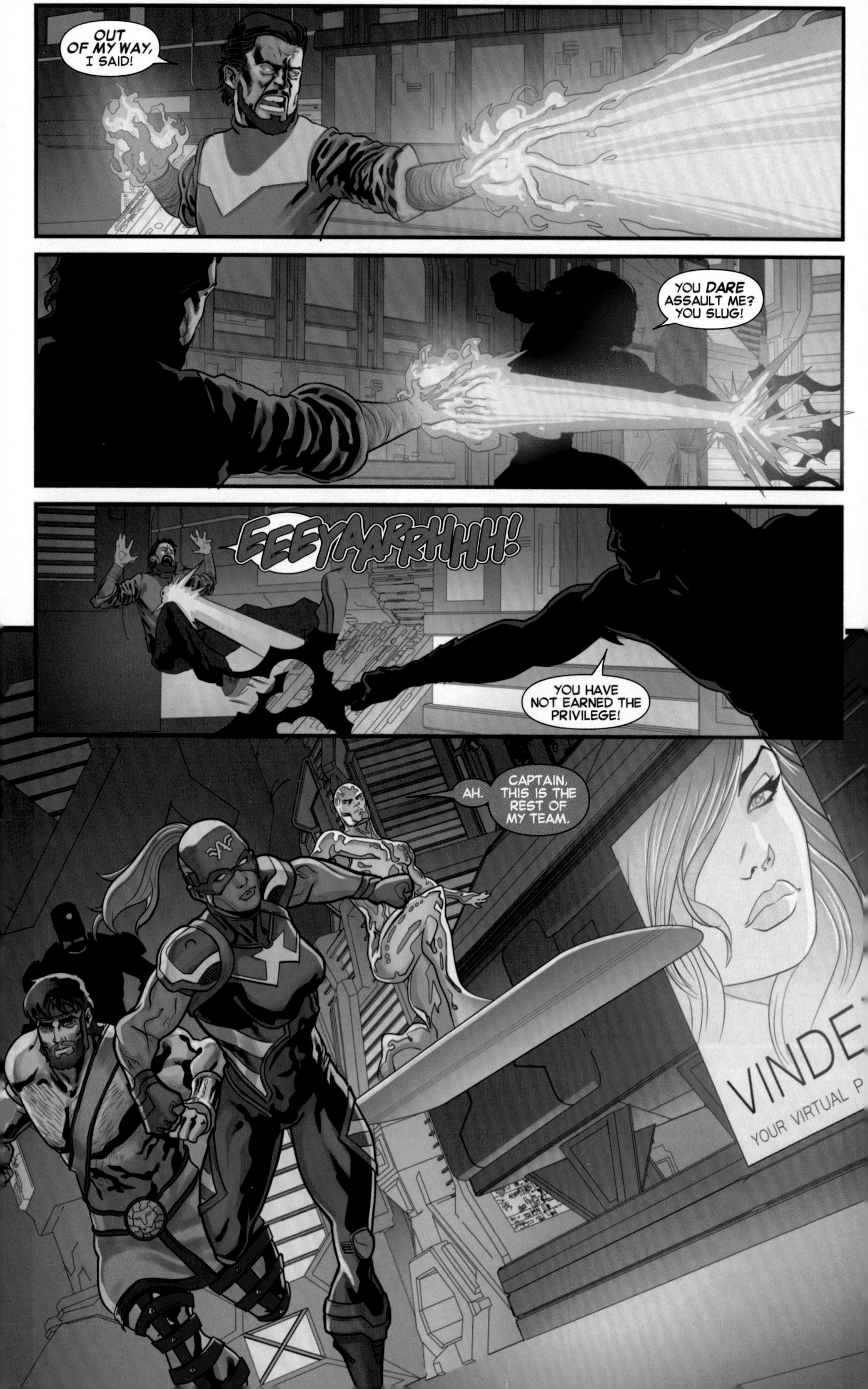
OUT OF MY WAY, I SAID!
YOU DARE ASSAULT ME? YOU SLUG!
EEEYAARRHHH!
YOU HAVE NOT EARNED THE PRIVILEGE!
AH.
CAPTAIN, THIS IS THE REST OF MY TEAM.
VINDE
YOUR VIRTUAL P

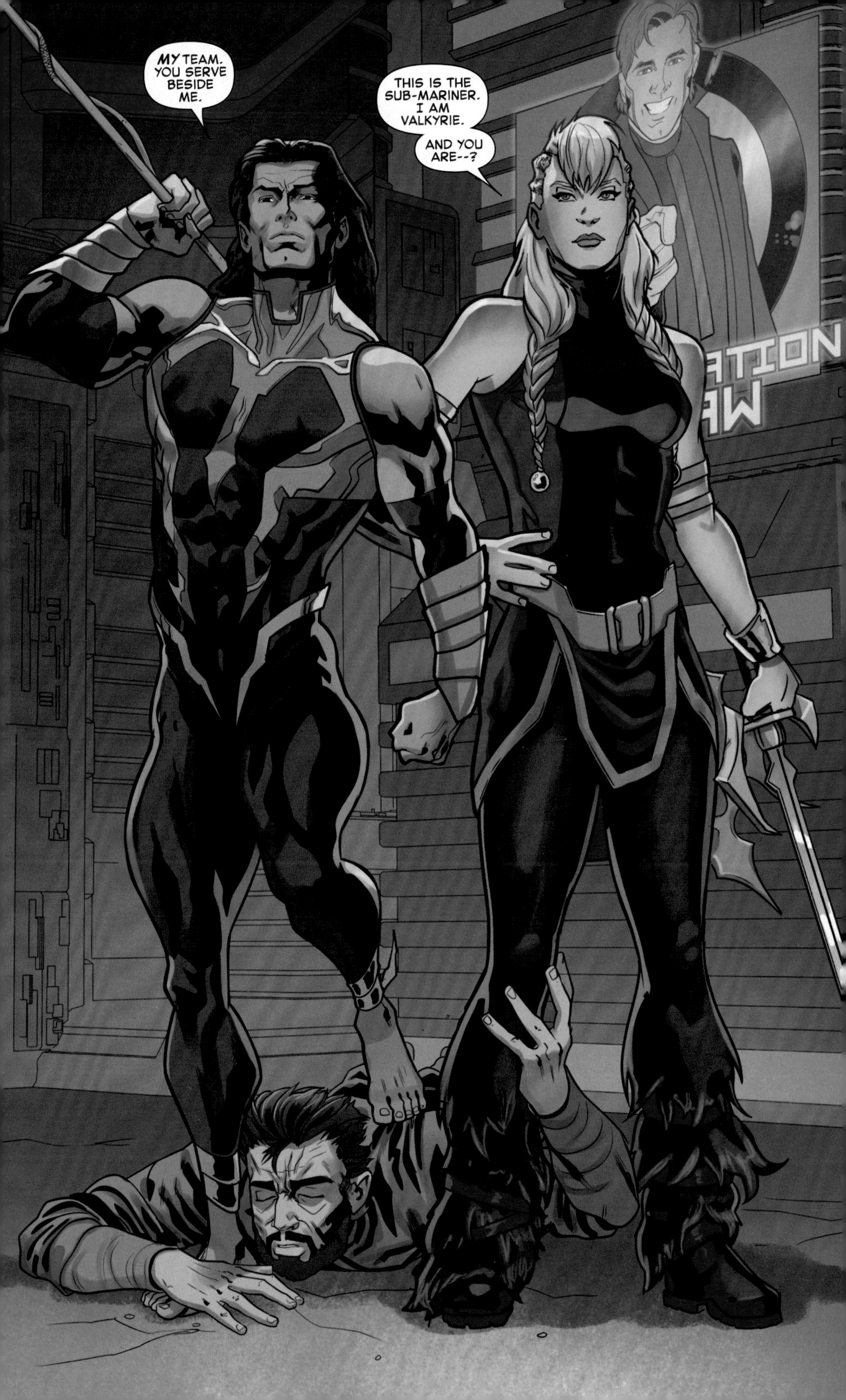
MY TEAM. YOU SERVE BESIDE ME.
THIS IS THE SUB-MARINER. I AM VALKYRIE.
AND YOU ARE--?

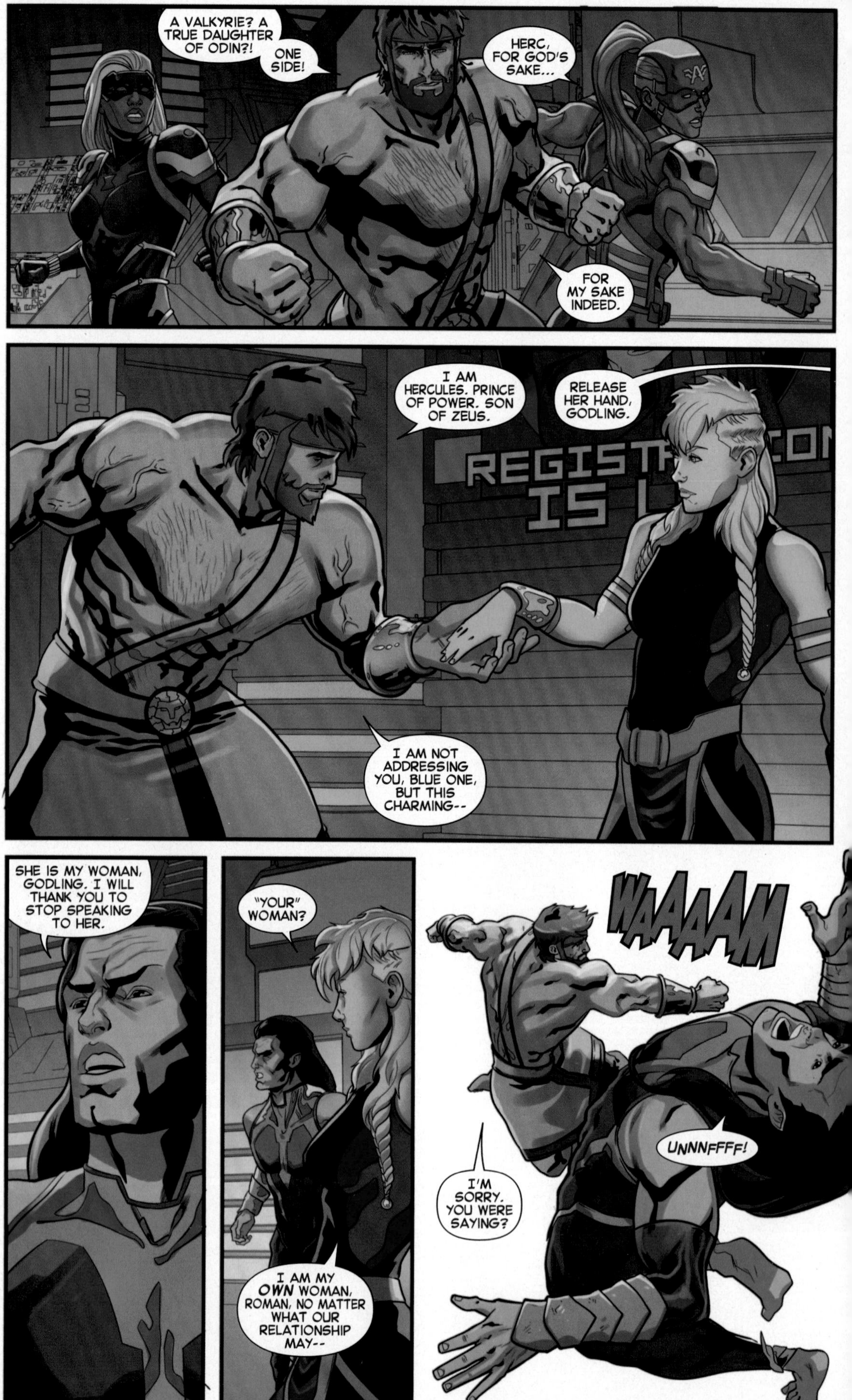
A VALKYRIE? A TRUE DAUGHTER OF ODIN?!
ONE SIDE!
HERC, FOR GOD'S SAKE...
FOR MY SAKE INDEED.
I AM HERCULES. PRINCE OF POWER. SON OF ZEUS.
RELEASE HER HAND, GODLING.
REGIST
IS
I AM NOT ADDRESSING YOU, BLUE ONE, BUT THIS CHARMING--
SHE IS MY WOMAN, GODLING. I WILL THANK YOU TO STOP SPEAKING TO HER.
"YOUR" WOMAN?
I AM MY OWN WOMAN, ROMAN, NO MATTER WHAT OUR RELATIONSHIP MAY--
WAAAAM
UNNNFFFF!
I'M SORRY. YOU WERE SAYING?

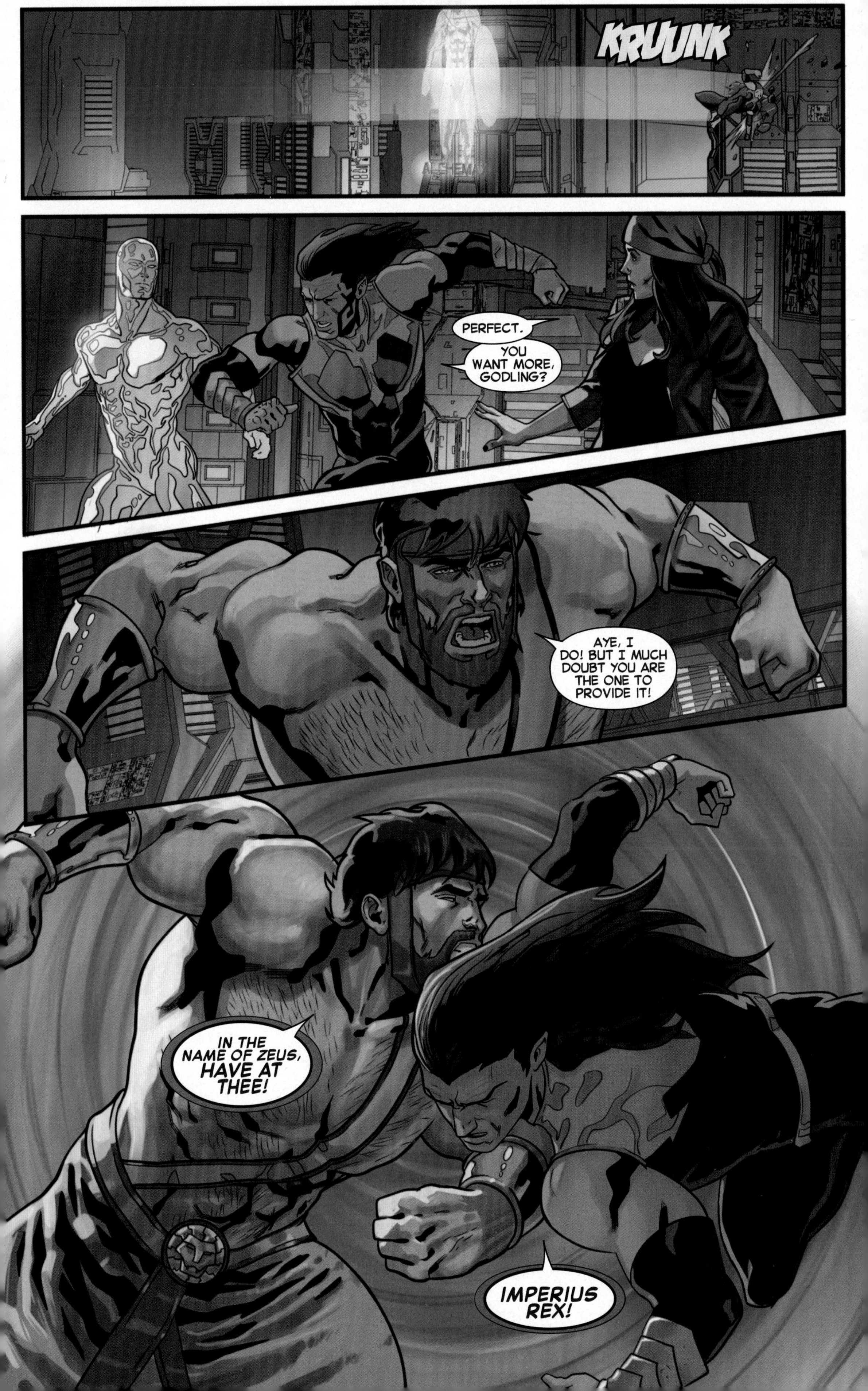
KRUUNK
ALCHEMAX
PERFECT.
YOU WANT MORE, GODLING?
AYE, I DO! BUT I MUCH DOUBT YOU ARE THE ONE TO PROVIDE IT!
IN THE NAME OF ZEUS, HAVE AT THEE!
IMPERIUS REX!

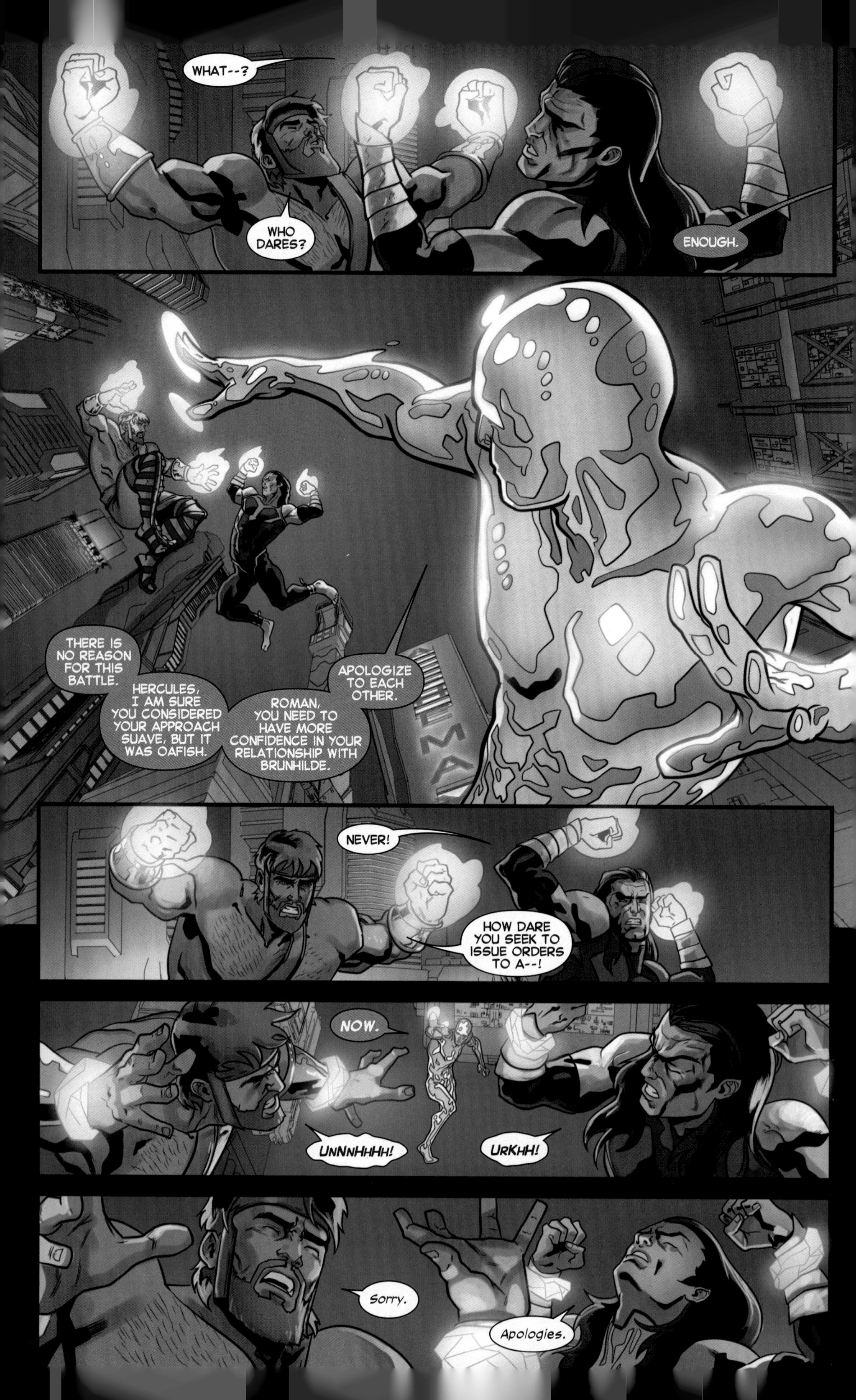
WHAT--?
WHO DARES?
ENOUGH.
THERE IS NO REASON FOR THIS BATTLE.
HERCULES, I AM SURE YOU CONSIDERED YOUR APPROACH SUAVE, BUT IT WAS OAFISH.
ROMAN, YOU NEED TO HAVE MORE CONFIDENCE IN YOUR RELATIONSHIP WITH BRUNHILDE.
APOLOGIZE TO EACH OTHER.
NEVER!
HOW DARE YOU SEEK TO ISSUE ORDERS TO A--!
NOW.
UNNNHHHH!
URKHH!
Sorry.
Apologies.

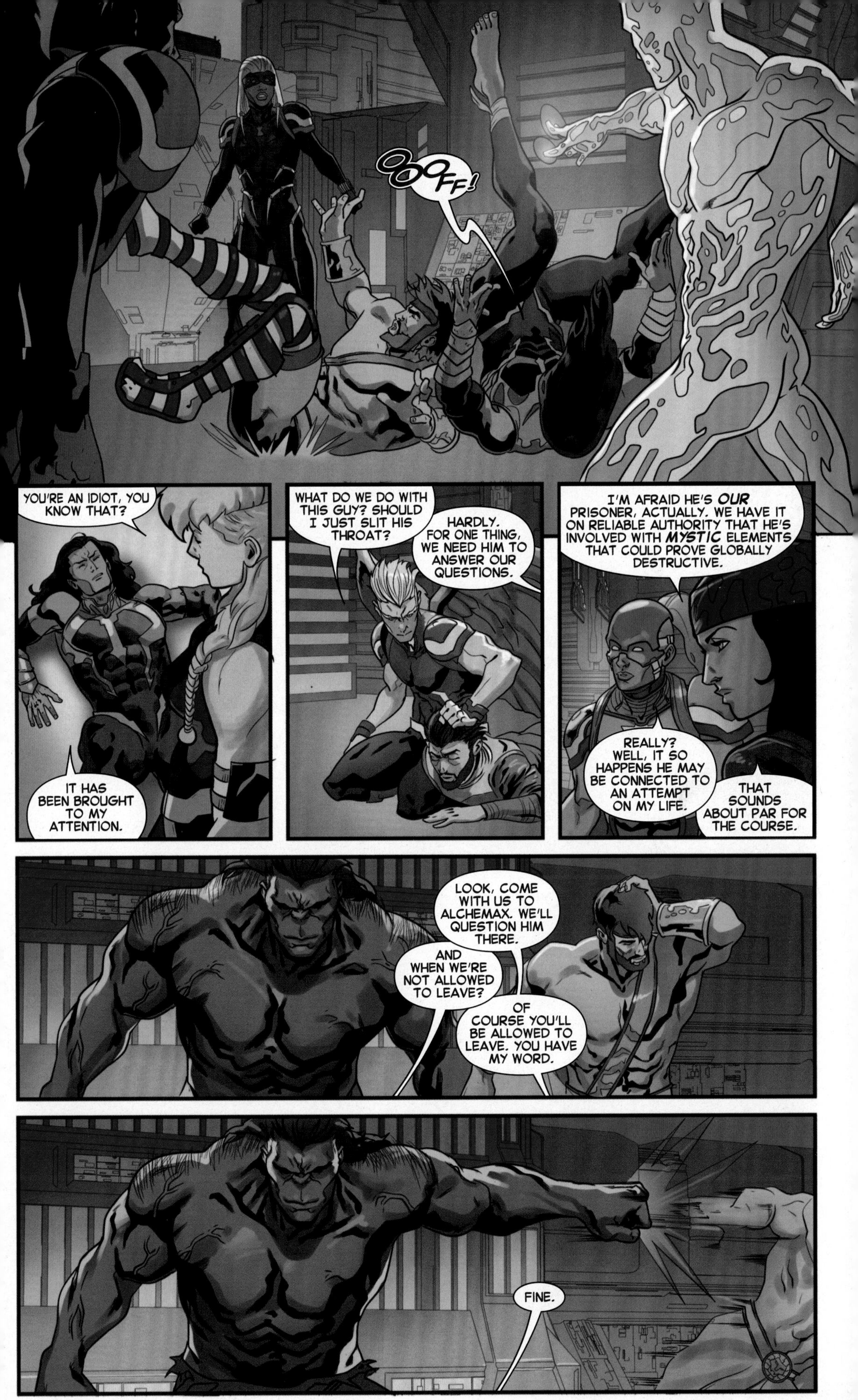
OOOFF!
YOU'RE AN IDIOT, YOU KNOW THAT?
IT HAS BEEN BROUGHT TO MY ATTENTION.
WHAT DO WE DO WITH THIS GUY? SHOULD I JUST SLIT HIS THROAT?
HARDLY. FOR ONE THING, WE NEED HIM TO ANSWER OUR QUESTIONS.
I'M AFRAID HE'S OUR PRISONER, ACTUALLY. WE HAVE IT ON RELIABLE AUTHORITY THAT HE'S INVOLVED WITH MYSTIC ELEMENTS THAT COULD PROVE GLOBALLY DESTRUCTIVE.
REALLY? WELL, IT SO HAPPENS HE MAY BE CONNECTED TO AN ATTEMPT ON MY LIFE.
THAT SOUNDS ABOUT PAR FOR THE COURSE.
LOOK, COME WITH US TO ALCHEMAX. WE'LL QUESTION HIM THERE.
AND WHEN WE'RE NOT ALLOWED TO LEAVE?
OF COURSE YOU'LL BE ALLOWED TO LEAVE. YOU HAVE MY WORD.
FINE.

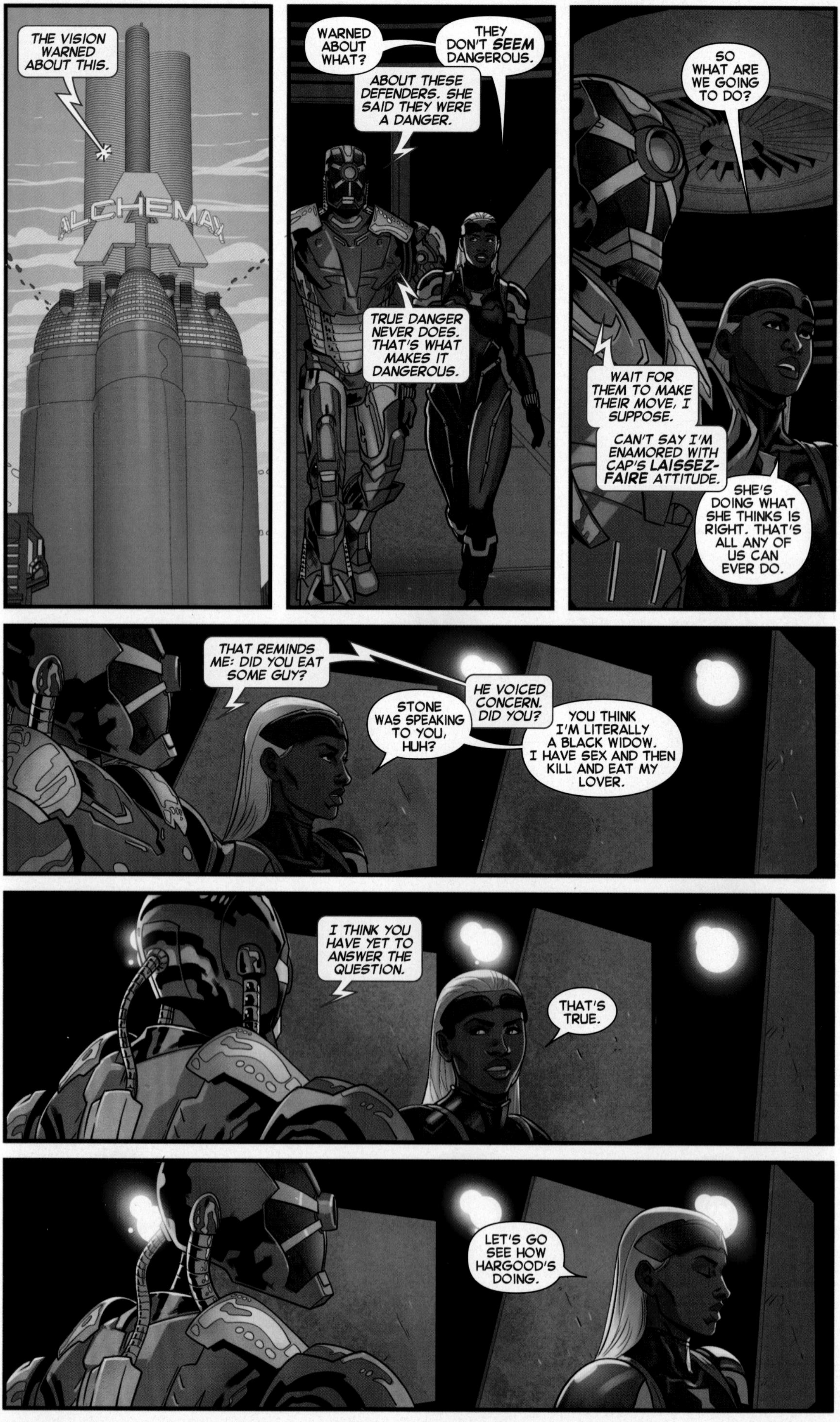
THE VISION WARNED ABOUT THIS.
WARNED ABOUT WHAT?
ABOUT THESE DEFENDERS. SHE SAID THEY WERE A DANGER.
THEY DON'T **SEEM** DANGEROUS.
TRUE DANGER NEVER DOES. THAT'S WHAT MAKES IT DANGEROUS.
SO WHAT ARE WE GOING TO DO?
WAIT FOR THEM TO MAKE THEIR MOVE, I SUPPOSE.
CAN'T SAY I'M ENAMORED WITH CAP'S **LAISSEZ-FAIRE** ATTITUDE.
SHE'S DOING WHAT SHE THINKS IS RIGHT. THAT'S ALL ANY OF US CAN EVER DO.
THAT REMINDS ME: DID YOU EAT SOME GUY?
STONE WAS SPEAKING TO YOU, HUH?
HE VOICED CONCERN. DID YOU?
YOU THINK I'M LITERALLY A BLACK WIDOW. I HAVE SEX AND THEN KILL AND EAT MY LOVER.
I THINK YOU HAVE YET TO ANSWER THE QUESTION.
THAT'S TRUE.
LET'S GO SEE HOW HARGOOD'S DOING.

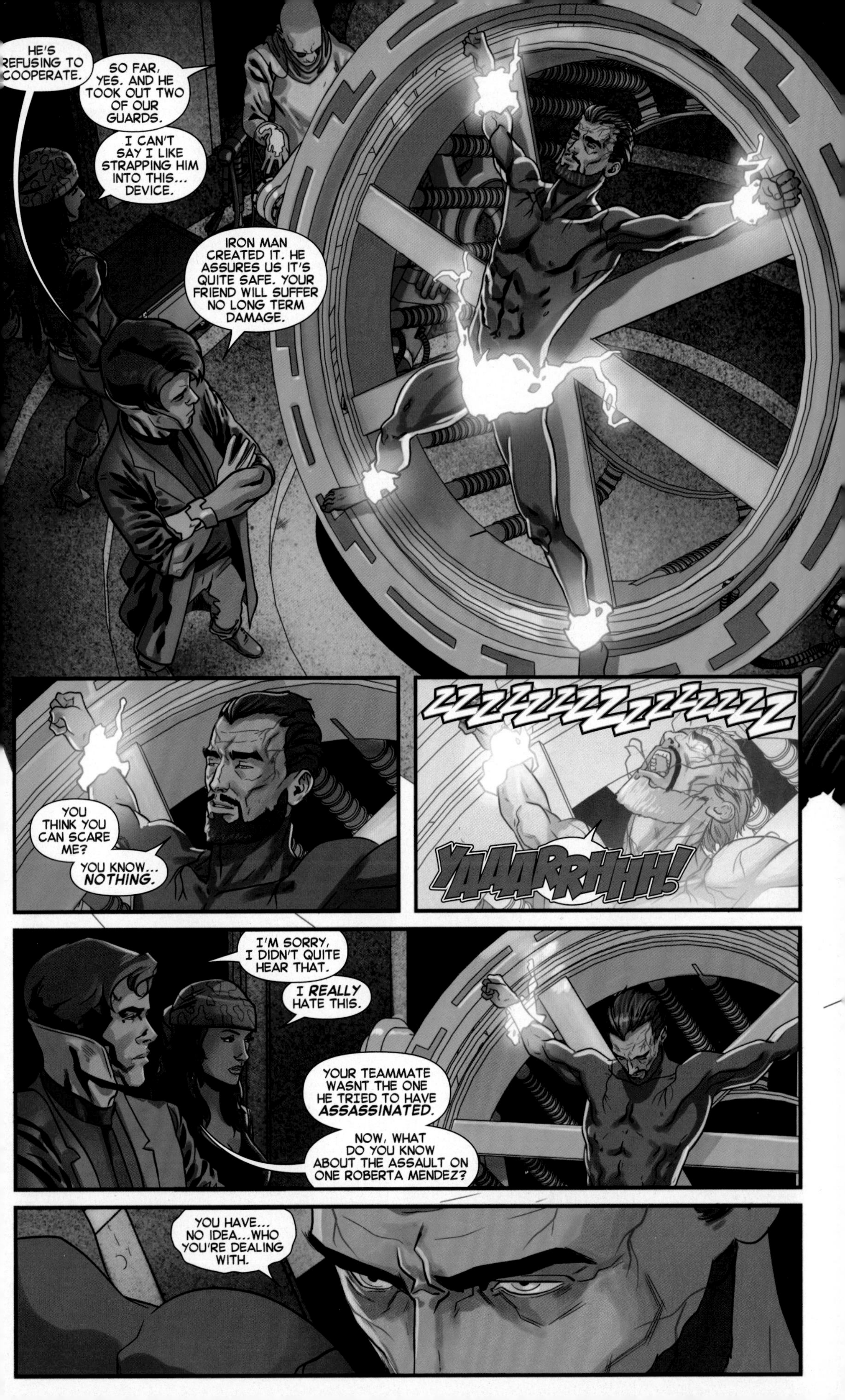
HE'S REFUSING TO COOPERATE.
SO FAR, YES. AND HE TOOK OUT TWO OF OUR GUARDS.
I CAN'T SAY I LIKE STRAPPING HIM INTO THIS... DEVICE.
IRON MAN CREATED IT. HE ASSURES US IT'S QUITE SAFE. YOUR FRIEND WILL SUFFER NO LONG TERM DAMAGE.
YOU THINK YOU CAN SCARE ME?
YOU KNOW... NOTHING.
ZZZZZZZZZZZZZZZZ
YAAARRHHH!
I'M SORRY, I DIDN'T QUITE HEAR THAT.
I REALLY HATE THIS.
YOUR TEAMMATE WASNT THE ONE HE TRIED TO HAVE ASSASSINATED.
NOW, WHAT DO YOU KNOW ABOUT THE ASSAULT ON ONE ROBERTA MENDEZ?
YOU HAVE... NO IDEA...WHO YOU'RE DEALING WITH.

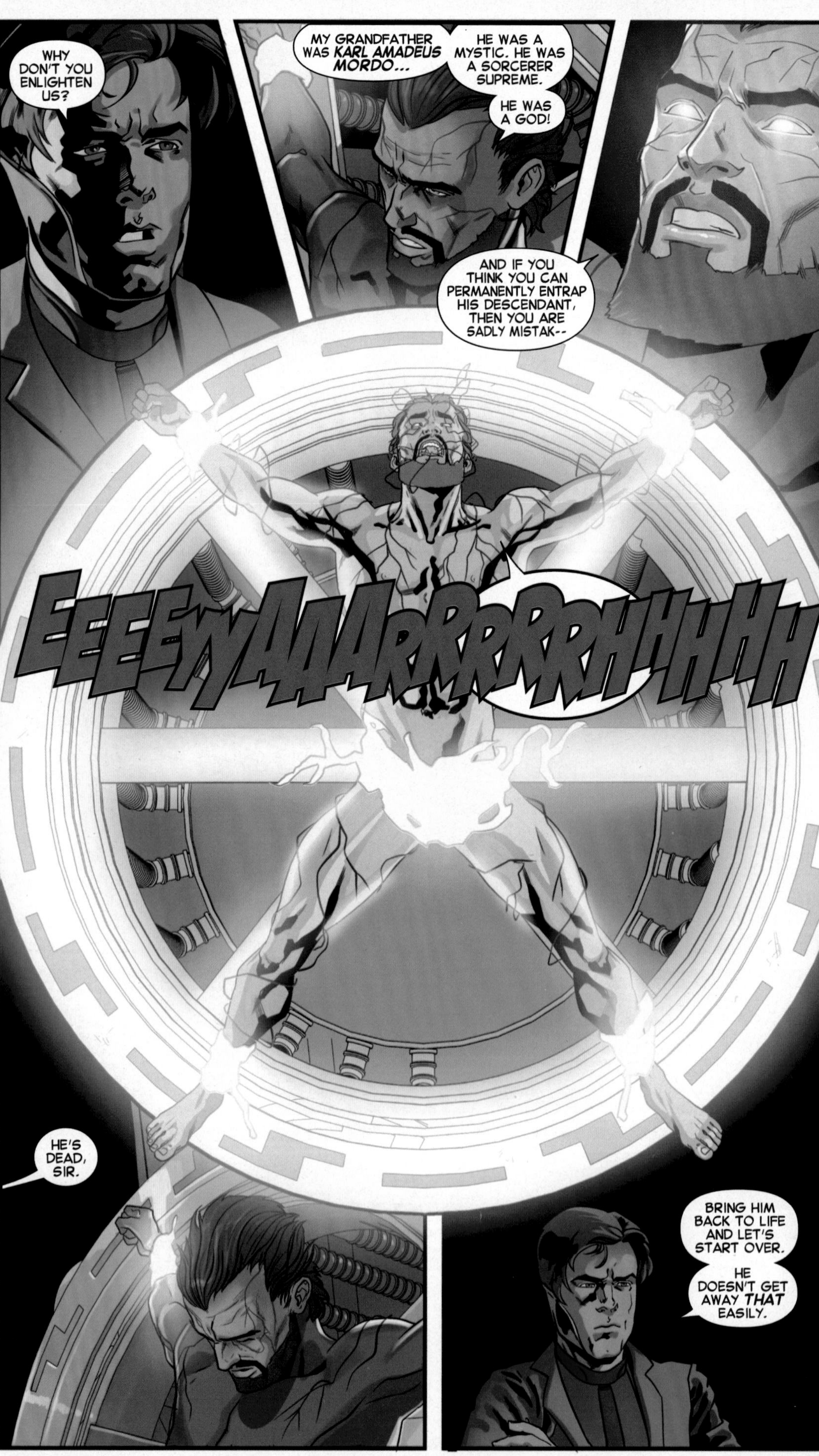
WHY DON'T YOU ENLIGHTEN US?
MY GRANDFATHER WAS KARL AMADEUS MORDO...
HE WAS A MYSTIC. HE WAS A SORCERER SUPREME.
HE WAS A GOD!
AND IF YOU THINK YOU CAN PERMANENTLY ENTRAP HIS DESCENDANT, THEN YOU ARE SADLY MISTAK--
EEEEYYAAARRRRRHHHHH
HE'S DEAD, SIR.
BRING HIM BACK TO LIFE AND LET'S START OVER.
HE DOESN'T GET AWAY THAT EASILY.

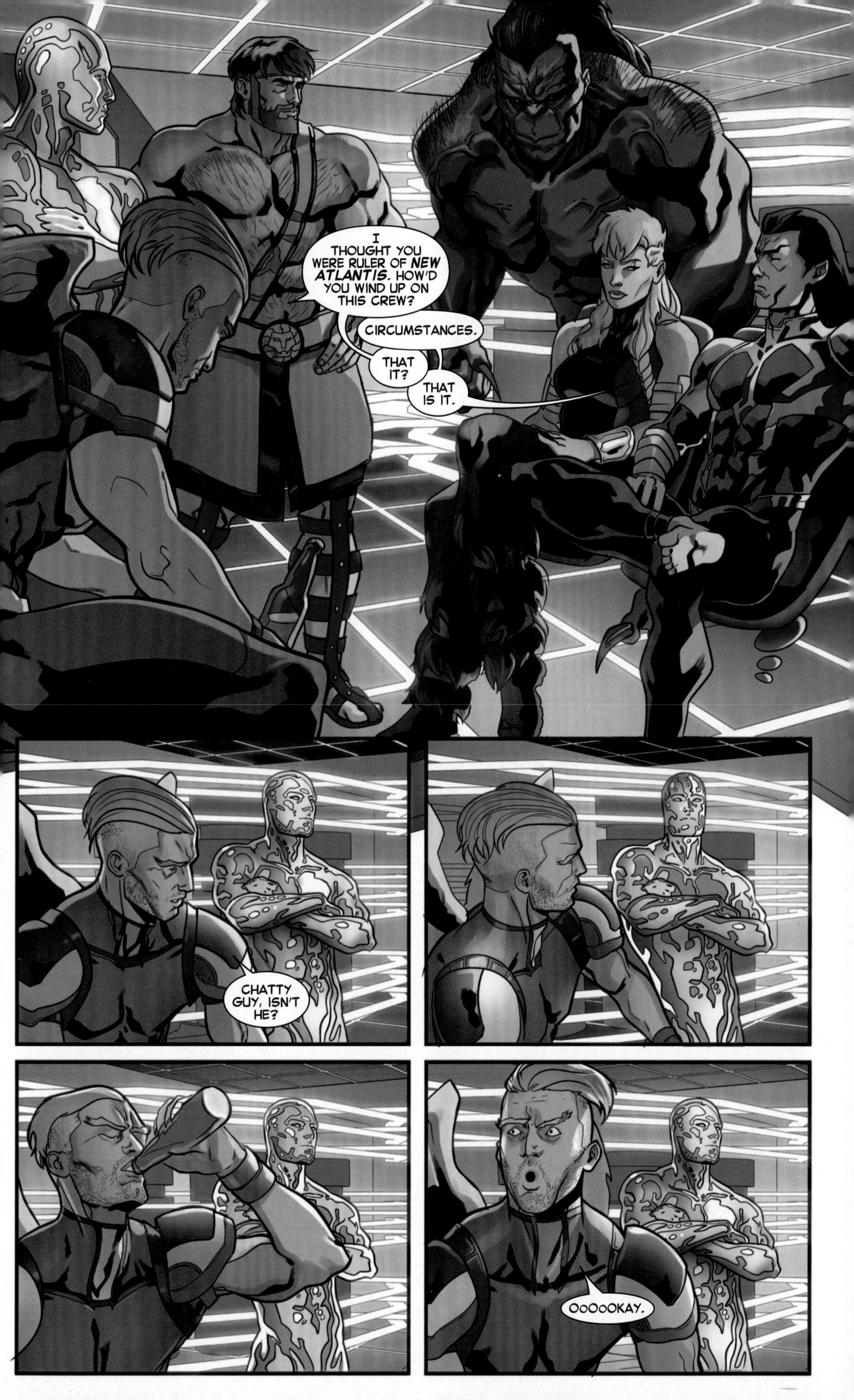
I THOUGHT YOU WERE RULER OF *NEW ATLANTIS*. HOW'D YOU WIND UP ON THIS CREW?
CIRCUMSTANCES.
THAT IT?
THAT IS IT.
CHATTY GUY, ISN'T HE?
OoOoOKAY.

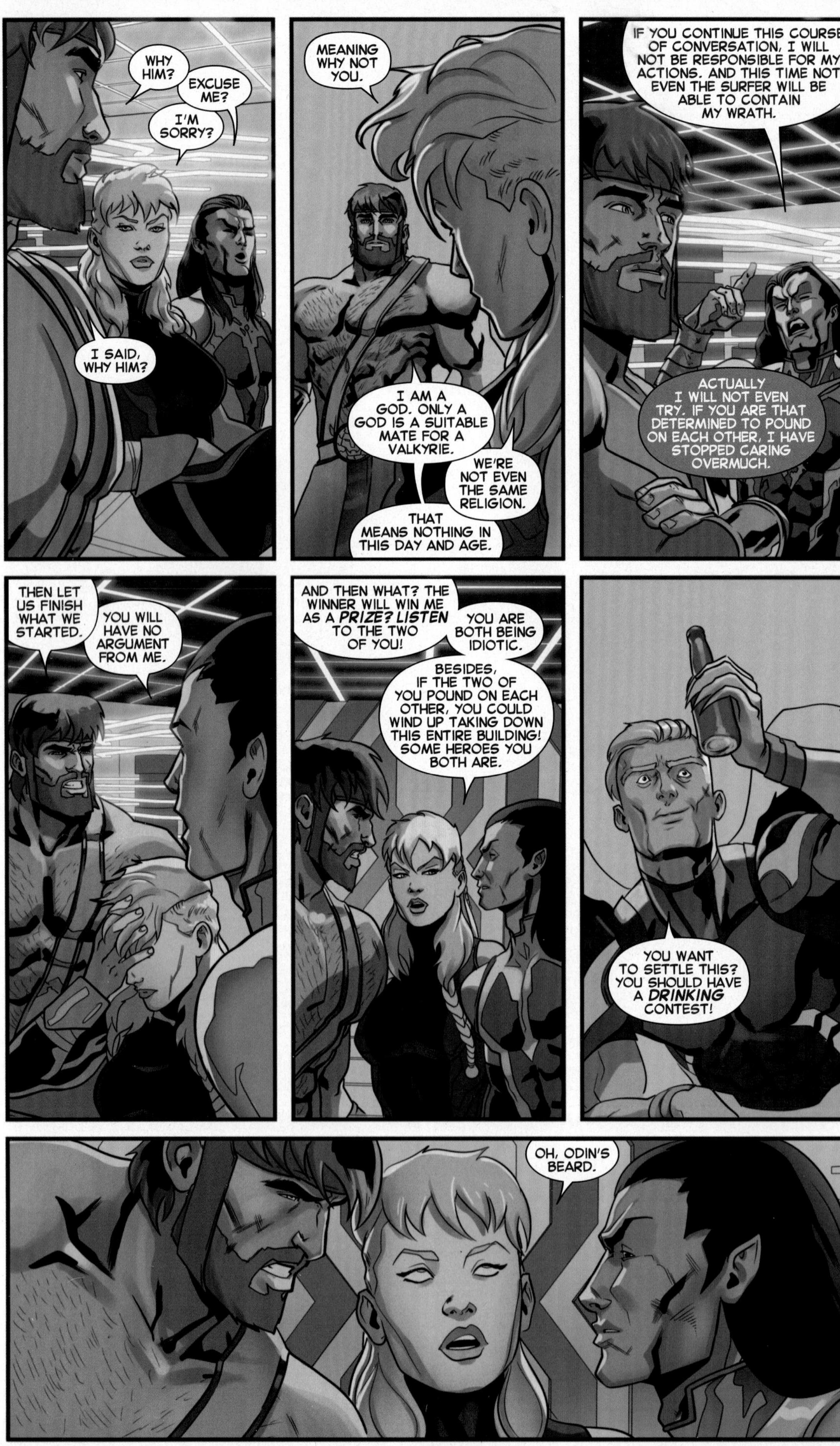
WHY HIM?
EXCUSE ME?
I'M SORRY?
I SAID, WHY HIM?
MEANING WHY NOT YOU.
I AM A GOD. ONLY A GOD IS A SUITABLE MATE FOR A VALKYRIE.
WE'RE NOT EVEN THE SAME RELIGION.
THAT MEANS NOTHING IN THIS DAY AND AGE.
IF YOU CONTINUE THIS COURSE OF CONVERSATION, I WILL NOT BE RESPONSIBLE FOR MY ACTIONS. AND THIS TIME NOT EVEN THE SURFER WILL BE ABLE TO CONTAIN MY WRATH.
ACTUALLY I WILL NOT EVEN TRY. IF YOU ARE THAT DETERMINED TO POUND ON EACH OTHER, I HAVE STOPPED CARING OVERMUCH.
THEN LET US FINISH WHAT WE STARTED.
YOU WILL HAVE NO ARGUMENT FROM ME.
AND THEN WHAT? THE WINNER WILL WIN ME AS A PRIZE? LISTEN TO THE TWO OF YOU!
YOU ARE BOTH BEING IDIOTIC.
BESIDES, IF THE TWO OF YOU POUND ON EACH OTHER, YOU COULD WIND UP TAKING DOWN THIS ENTIRE BUILDING! SOME HEROES YOU BOTH ARE.
YOU WANT TO SETTLE THIS? YOU SHOULD HAVE A DRINKING CONTEST!
OH, ODIN'S BEARD.

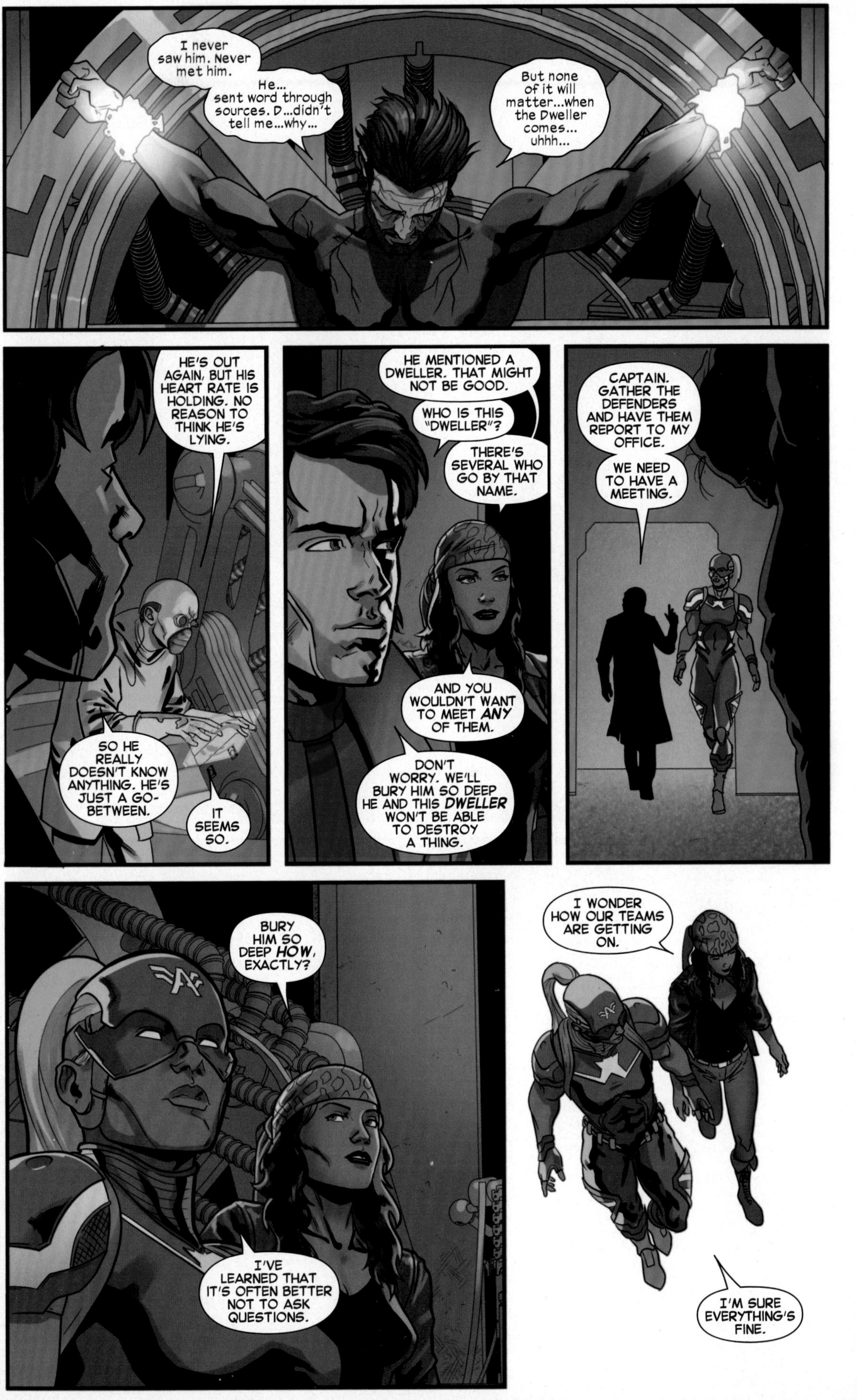
I never saw him. Never met him.
He... sent word through sources. D...didn't tell me...why...
But none of it will matter...when the Dweller comes... uhhh...
HE'S OUT AGAIN, BUT HIS HEART RATE IS HOLDING. NO REASON TO THINK HE'S LYING.
SO HE REALLY DOESN'T KNOW ANYTHING. HE'S JUST A GO-BETWEEN.
IT SEEMS SO.
HE MENTIONED A DWELLER. THAT MIGHT NOT BE GOOD.
WHO IS THIS "DWELLER"?
THERE'S SEVERAL WHO GO BY THAT NAME.
AND YOU WOULDN'T WANT TO MEET ANY OF THEM.
DON'T WORRY. WE'LL BURY HIM SO DEEP HE AND THIS DWELLER WON'T BE ABLE TO DESTROY A THING.
CAPTAIN. GATHER THE DEFENDERS AND HAVE THEM REPORT TO MY OFFICE.
WE NEED TO HAVE A MEETING.
BURY HIM SO DEEP HOW, EXACTLY?
I'VE LEARNED THAT IT'S OFTEN BETTER NOT TO ASK QUESTIONS.
I WONDER HOW OUR TEAMS ARE GETTING ON.
I'M SURE EVERYTHING'S FINE.

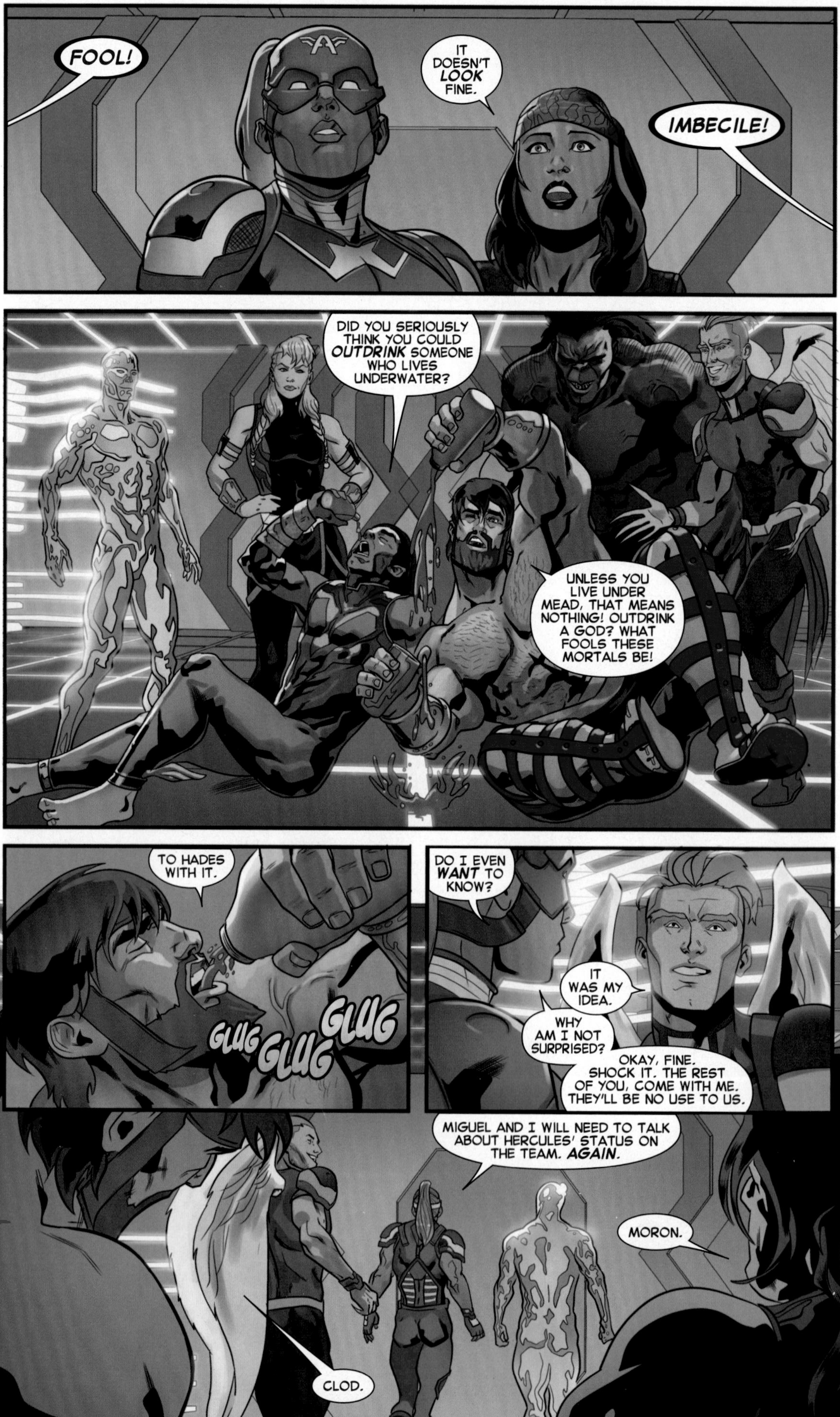
FOOL!
IT DOESN'T LOOK FINE.
IMBECILE!
DID YOU SERIOUSLY THINK YOU COULD OUTDRINK SOMEONE WHO LIVES UNDERWATER?
UNLESS YOU LIVE UNDER MEAD, THAT MEANS NOTHING! OUTDRINK A GOD? WHAT FOOLS THESE MORTALS BE!
TO HADES WITH IT.
GLUG GLUG GLUG
DO I EVEN WANT TO KNOW?
IT WAS MY IDEA.
WHY AM I NOT SURPRISED?
OKAY, FINE. SHOCK IT. THE REST OF YOU, COME WITH ME. THEY'LL BE NO USE TO US.
MIGUEL AND I WILL NEED TO TALK ABOUT HERCULES' STATUS ON THE TEAM. AGAIN.
MORON.
CLOD.

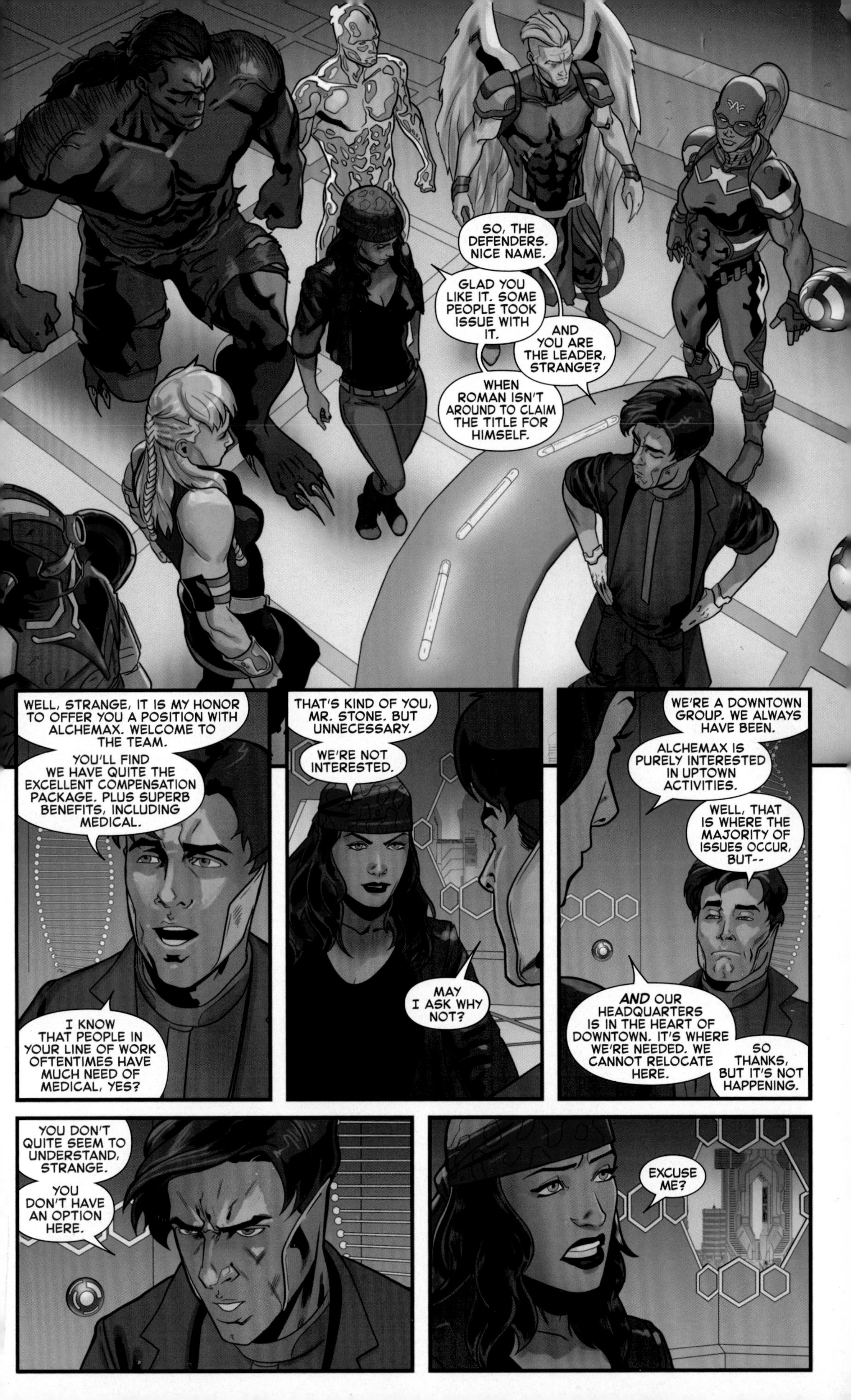
SO, THE DEFENDERS. NICE NAME.
GLAD YOU LIKE IT. SOME PEOPLE TOOK ISSUE WITH IT.
AND YOU ARE THE LEADER, STRANGE?
WHEN ROMAN ISN'T AROUND TO CLAIM THE TITLE FOR HIMSELF.
WELL, STRANGE, IT IS MY HONOR TO OFFER YOU A POSITION WITH ALCHEMAX. WELCOME TO THE TEAM.
YOU'LL FIND WE HAVE QUITE THE EXCELLENT COMPENSATION PACKAGE. PLUS SUPERB BENEFITS, INCLUDING MEDICAL.
I KNOW THAT PEOPLE IN YOUR LINE OF WORK OFTENTIMES HAVE MUCH NEED OF MEDICAL, YES?
THAT'S KIND OF YOU, MR. STONE. BUT UNNECESSARY.
WE'RE NOT INTERESTED.
MAY I ASK WHY NOT?
WE'RE A DOWNTOWN GROUP. WE ALWAYS HAVE BEEN.
ALCHEMAX IS PURELY INTERESTED IN UPTOWN ACTIVITIES.
WELL, THAT IS WHERE THE MAJORITY OF ISSUES OCCUR, BUT--
AND OUR HEADQUARTERS IS IN THE HEART OF DOWNTOWN. IT'S WHERE WE'RE NEEDED. WE CANNOT RELOCATE HERE.
SO THANKS, BUT IT'S NOT HAPPENING.
YOU DON'T QUITE SEEM TO UNDERSTAND, STRANGE.
YOU DON'T HAVE AN OPTION HERE.
EXCUSE ME?

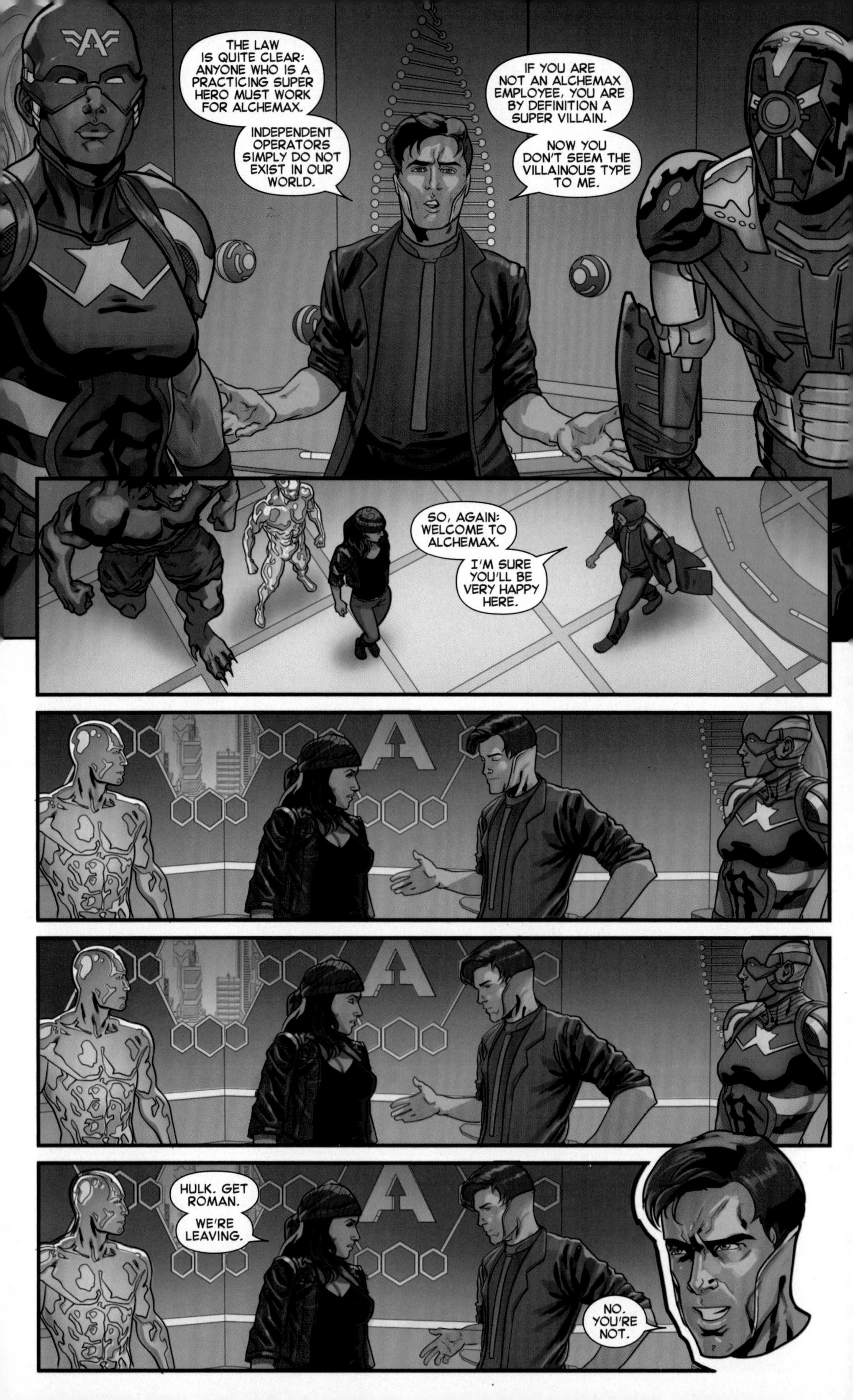
THE LAW IS QUITE CLEAR: ANYONE WHO IS A PRACTICING SUPER HERO MUST WORK FOR ALCHEMAX.
INDEPENDENT OPERATORS SIMPLY DO NOT EXIST IN OUR WORLD.
IF YOU ARE NOT AN ALCHEMAX EMPLOYEE, YOU ARE BY DEFINITION A SUPER VILLAIN.
NOW YOU DON'T SEEM THE VILLAINOUS TYPE TO ME.
SO, AGAIN: WELCOME TO ALCHEMAX.
I'M SURE YOU'LL BE VERY HAPPY HERE.
HULK. GET ROMAN.
WE'RE LEAVING.
NO. YOU'RE NOT.

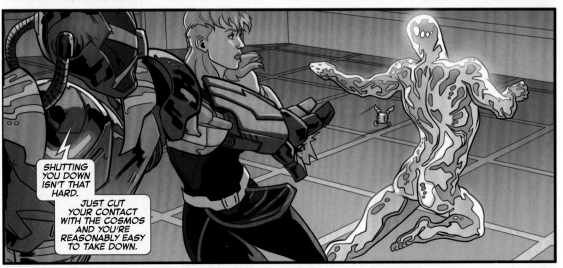

YOU DARE!

YES. WE DO.

SHUTTING YOU DOWN ISN'T THAT HARD.

JUST CUT YOUR CONTACT WITH THE COSMOS AND YOU'RE REASONABLY EASY TO TAKE DOWN.

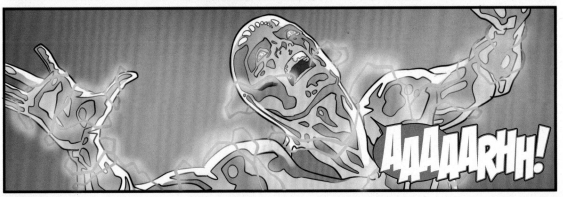

AAAAARHH!

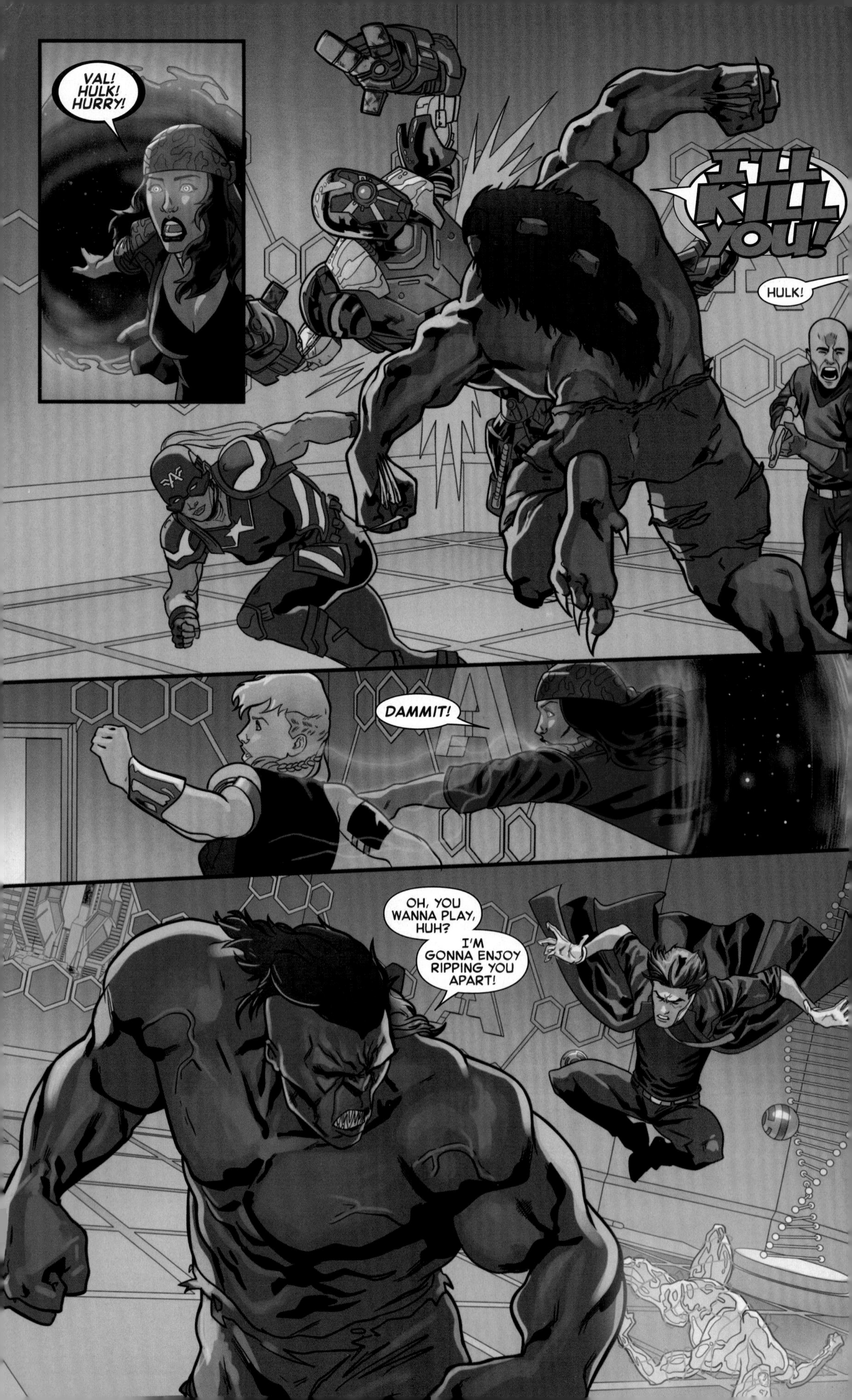
VAL! HULK! HURRY!
I'LL KILL YOU!
HULK!
DAMMIT!
OH, YOU WANNA PLAY, HUH?
I'M GONNA ENJOY RIPPING YOU APART!

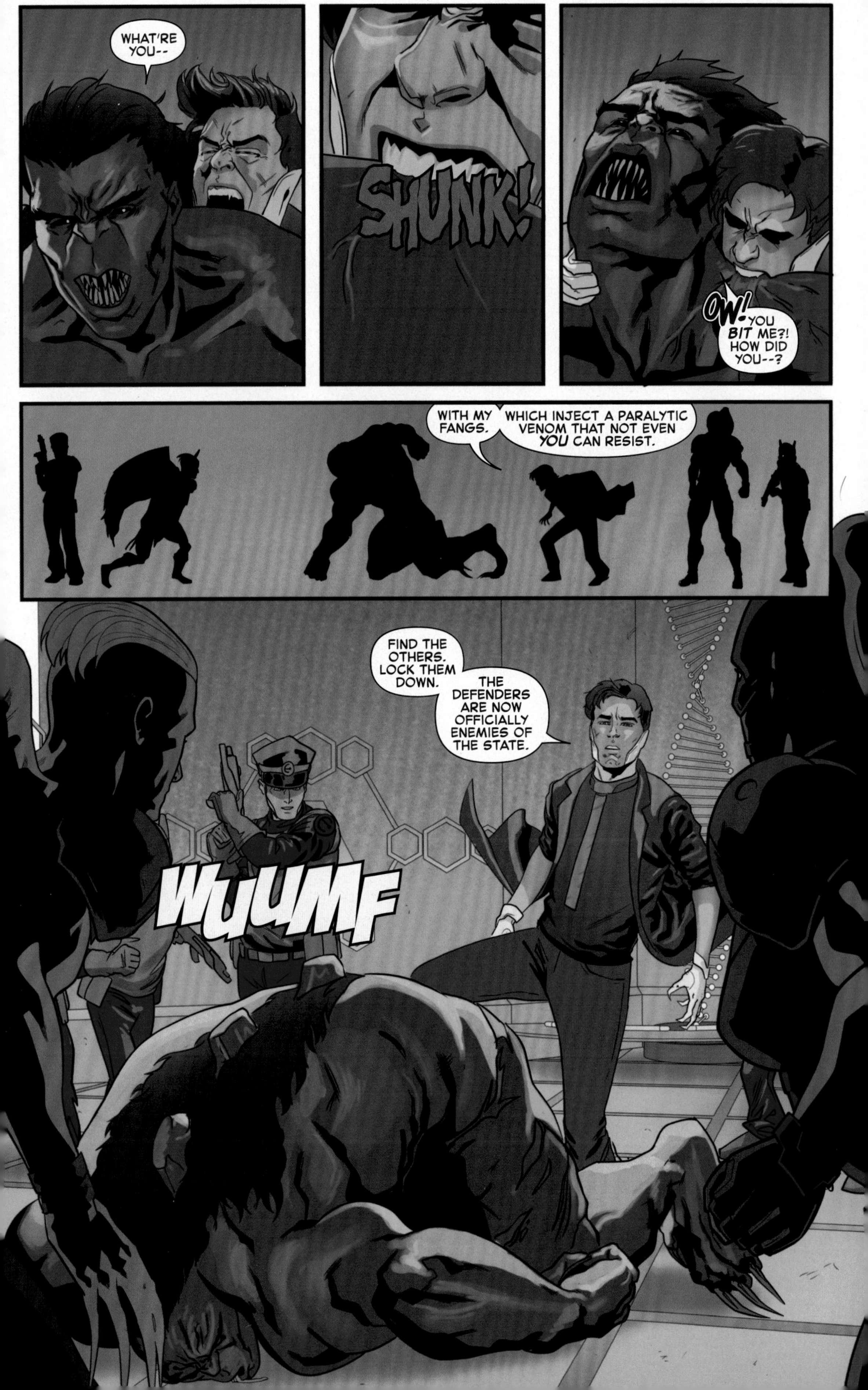
WHAT'RE YOU--
SHUNK!
OW! YOU BIT ME?! HOW DID YOU--?
WITH MY FANGS.
WHICH INJECT A PARALYTIC VENOM THAT NOT EVEN YOU CAN RESIST.
FIND THE OTHERS. LOCK THEM DOWN.
THE DEFENDERS ARE NOW OFFICIALLY ENEMIES OF THE STATE.
WUUMF

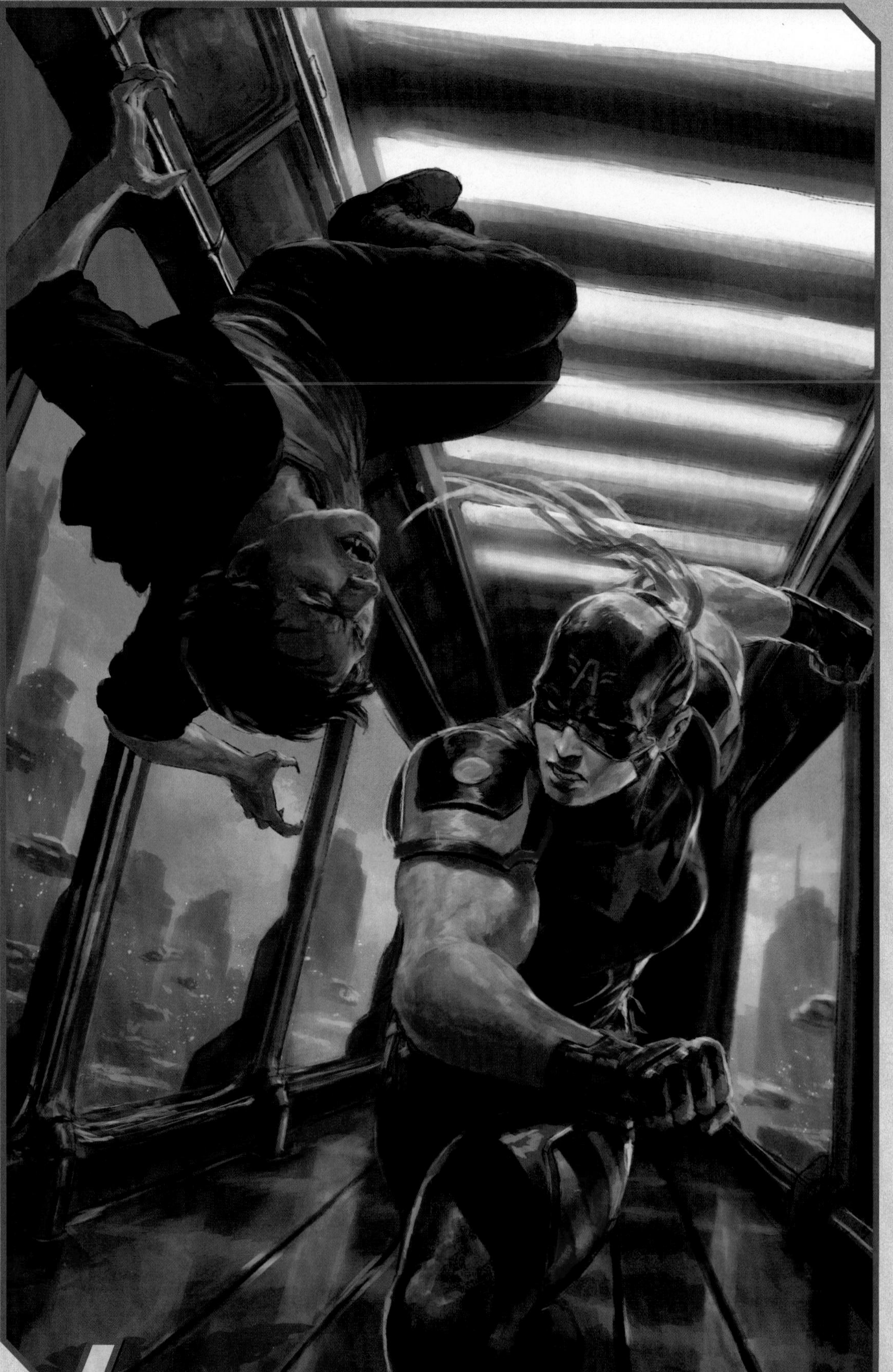

4

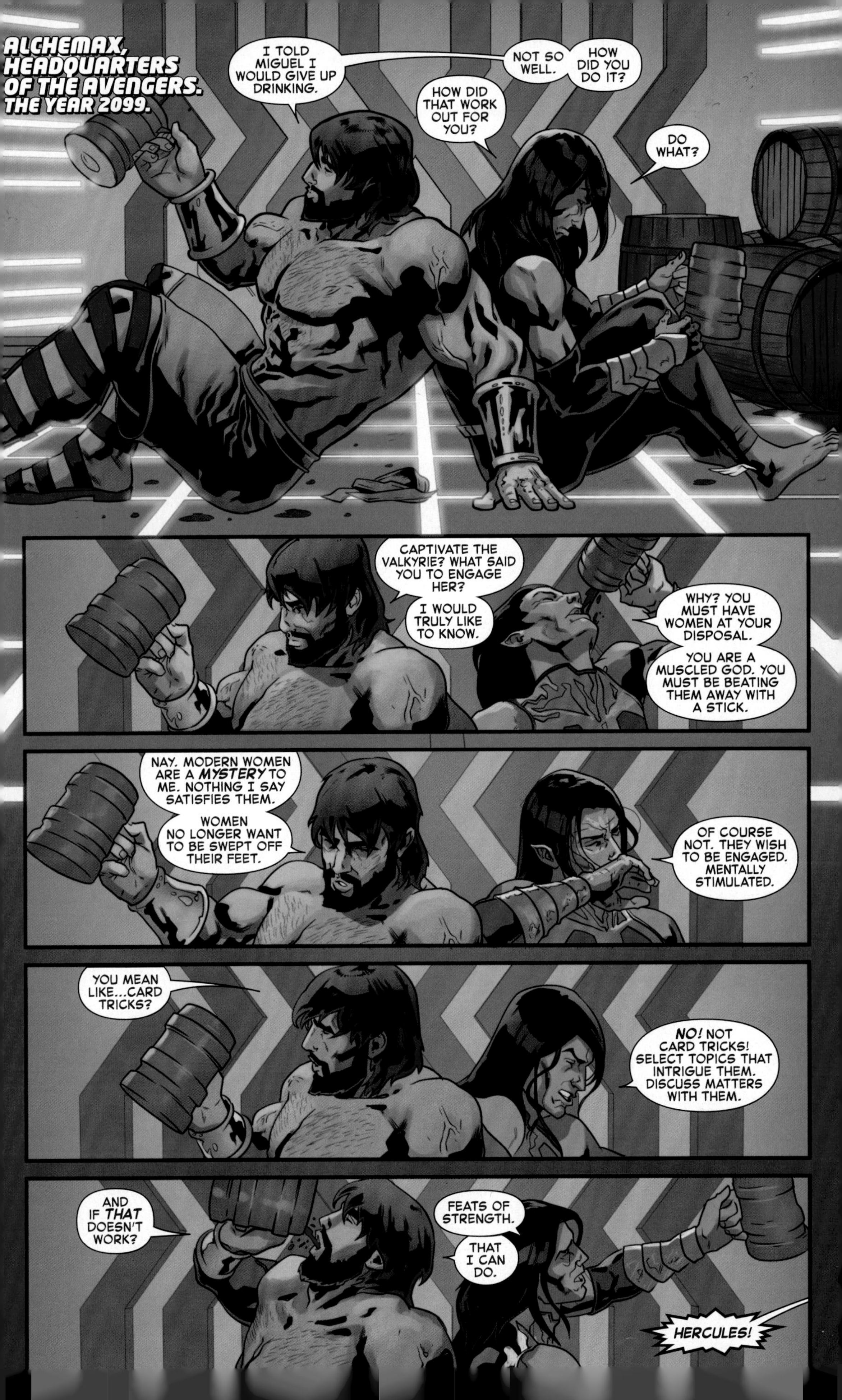
ALCHEMAX, HEADQUARTERS OF THE AVENGERS. THE YEAR 2099.
I TOLD MIGUEL I WOULD GIVE UP DRINKING.
HOW DID THAT WORK OUT FOR YOU?
NOT SO WELL.
HOW DID YOU DO IT?
DO WHAT?
CAPTIVATE THE VALKYRIE? WHAT SAID YOU TO ENGAGE HER?
I WOULD TRULY LIKE TO KNOW.
WHY? YOU MUST HAVE WOMEN AT YOUR DISPOSAL.
YOU ARE A MUSCLED GOD. YOU MUST BE BEATING THEM AWAY WITH A STICK.
NAY. MODERN WOMEN ARE A MYSTERY TO ME. NOTHING I SAY SATISFIES THEM.
WOMEN NO LONGER WANT TO BE SWEPT OFF THEIR FEET.
OF COURSE NOT. THEY WISH TO BE ENGAGED. MENTALLY STIMULATED.
YOU MEAN LIKE...CARD TRICKS?
NO! NOT CARD TRICKS! SELECT TOPICS THAT INTRIGUE THEM. DISCUSS MATTERS WITH THEM.
AND IF THAT DOESN'T WORK?
FEATS OF STRENGTH.
THAT I CAN DO.
HERCULES!

ONE SIDE. WE'RE HERE TO ARREST THE SUB-MARINER.

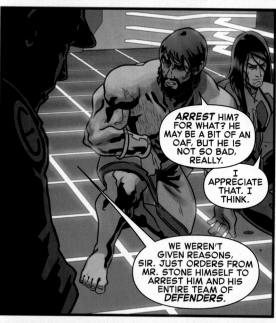

ARREST HIM? FOR WHAT? HE MAY BE A BIT OF AN OAF, BUT HE IS NOT SO BAD, REALLY.

I APPRECIATE THAT. I THINK.

WE WEREN'T GIVEN REASONS, SIR. JUST ORDERS FROM MR. STONE HIMSELF TO ARREST HIM AND HIS ENTIRE TEAM OF DEFENDERS.

WELL... THAT MAKES SENSE.

STEP ASIDE, SIR. WE DON'T WANT TO HAVE TO BRING YOU IN T--

KRAAAAASH

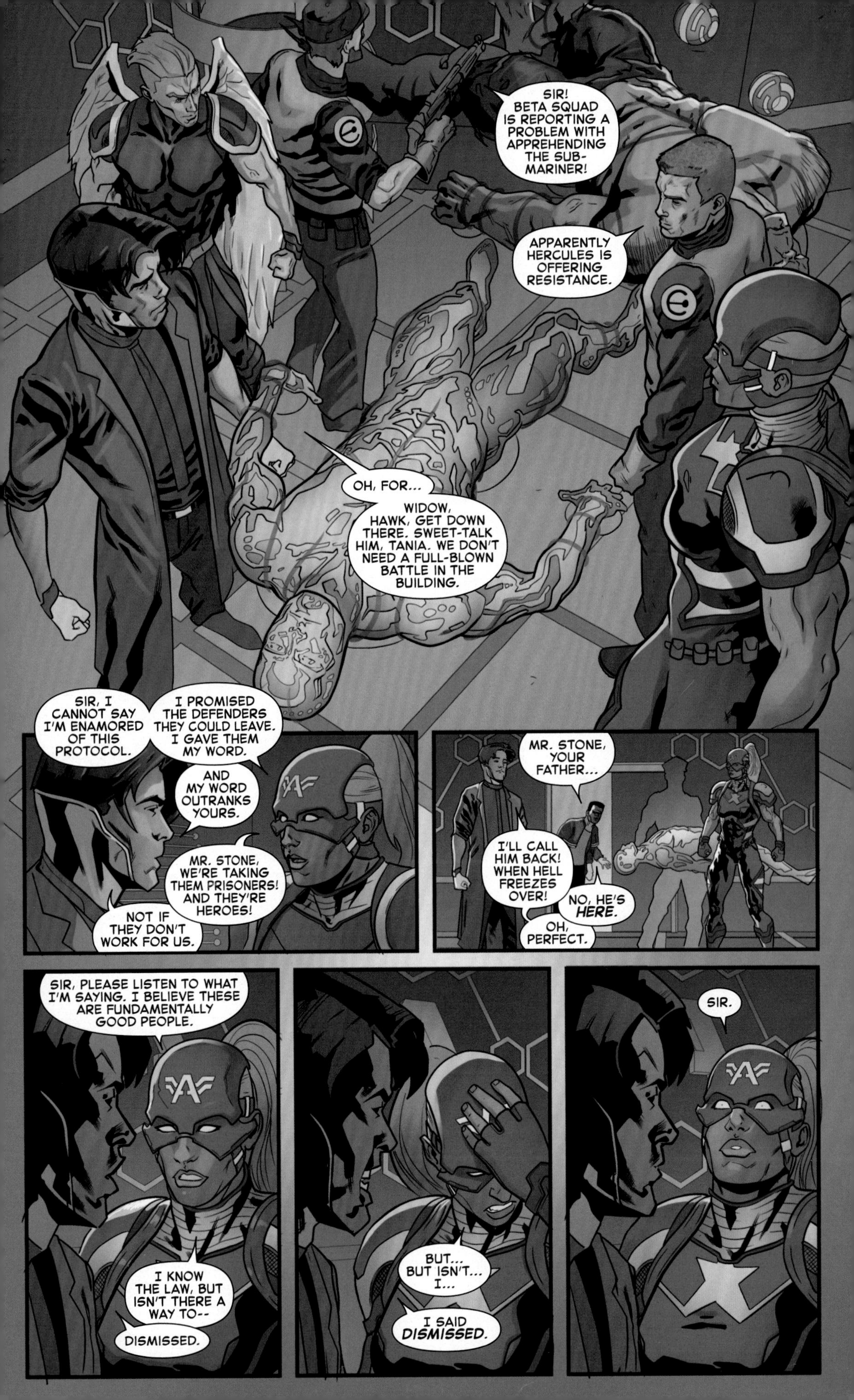
SIR! BETA SQUAD IS REPORTING A PROBLEM WITH APPREHENDING THE SUB-MARINER!
APPARENTLY HERCULES IS OFFERING RESISTANCE.
OH, FOR...
WIDOW, HAWK, GET DOWN THERE. SWEET-TALK HIM, TANIA. WE DON'T NEED A FULL-BLOWN BATTLE IN THE BUILDING.
SIR, I CANNOT SAY I'M ENAMORED OF THIS PROTOCOL.
I PROMISED THE DEFENDERS THEY COULD LEAVE. I GAVE THEM MY WORD.
AND MY WORD OUTRANKS YOURS.
MR. STONE, WE'RE TAKING THEM PRISONERS! AND THEY'RE HEROES!
NOT IF THEY DON'T WORK FOR US.
MR. STONE, YOUR FATHER...
I'LL CALL HIM BACK! WHEN HELL FREEZES OVER!
NO, HE'S *HERE.*
OH, PERFECT.
SIR, PLEASE LISTEN TO WHAT I'M SAYING. I BELIEVE THESE ARE FUNDAMENTALLY GOOD PEOPLE.
I KNOW THE LAW, BUT ISN'T THERE A WAY TO--
DISMISSED.
BUT... BUT ISN'T... I...
I SAID *DISMISSED.*
SIR.

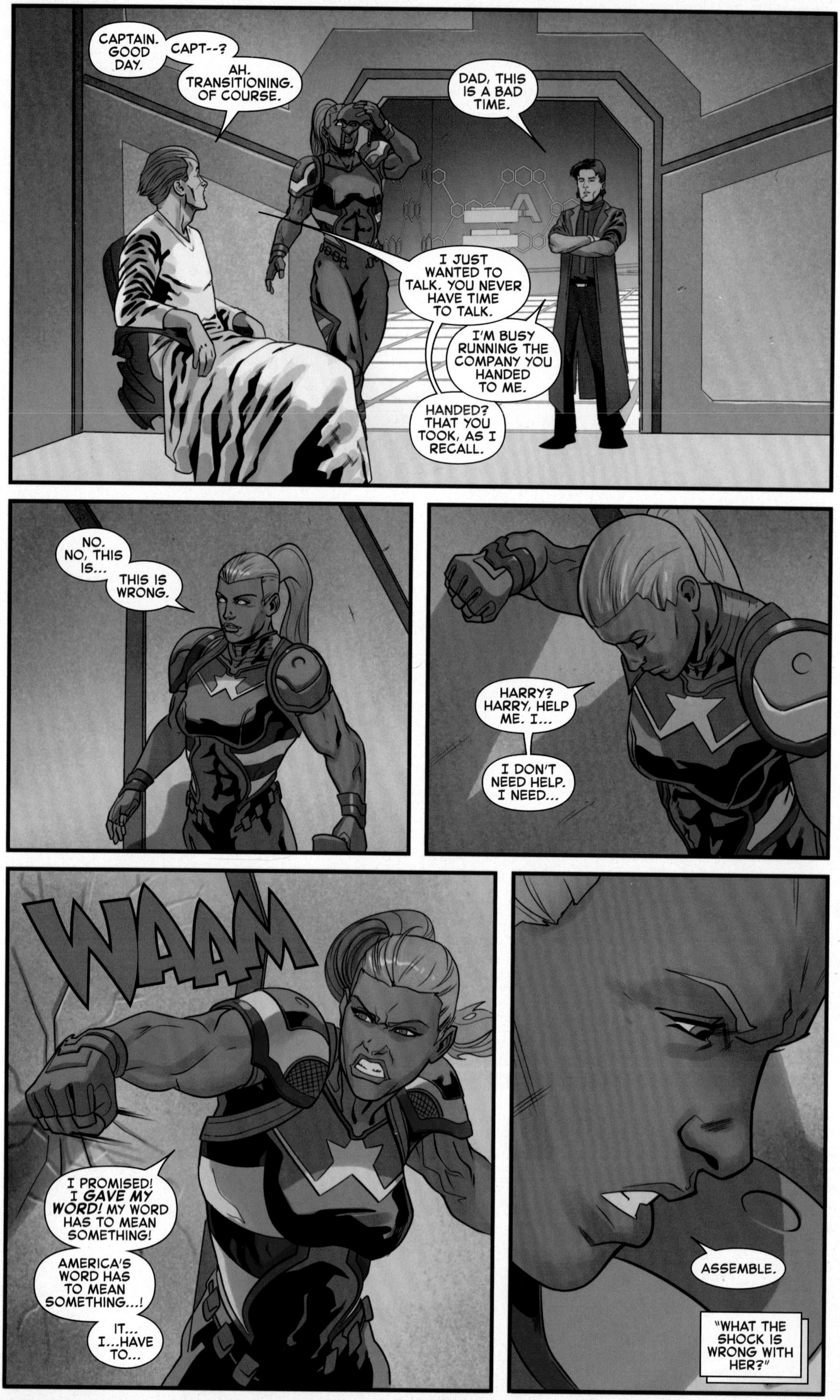
CAPTAIN. GOOD DAY.
CAPT--?
AH. TRANSITIONING. OF COURSE.
DAD, THIS IS A BAD TIME.
I JUST WANTED TO TALK. YOU NEVER HAVE TIME TO TALK.
I'M BUSY RUNNING THE COMPANY YOU HANDED TO ME.
HANDED? THAT YOU TOOK, AS I RECALL.
NO. NO, THIS IS...
THIS IS WRONG.
HARRY? HARRY, HELP ME. I...
I DON'T NEED HELP. I NEED...
WAAM
I PROMISED! I GAVE MY WORD! MY WORD HAS TO MEAN SOMETHING!
AMERICA'S WORD HAS TO MEAN SOMETHING...!
IT... I...HAVE TO...
ASSEMBLE.
"WHAT THE SHOCK IS WRONG WITH HER?"

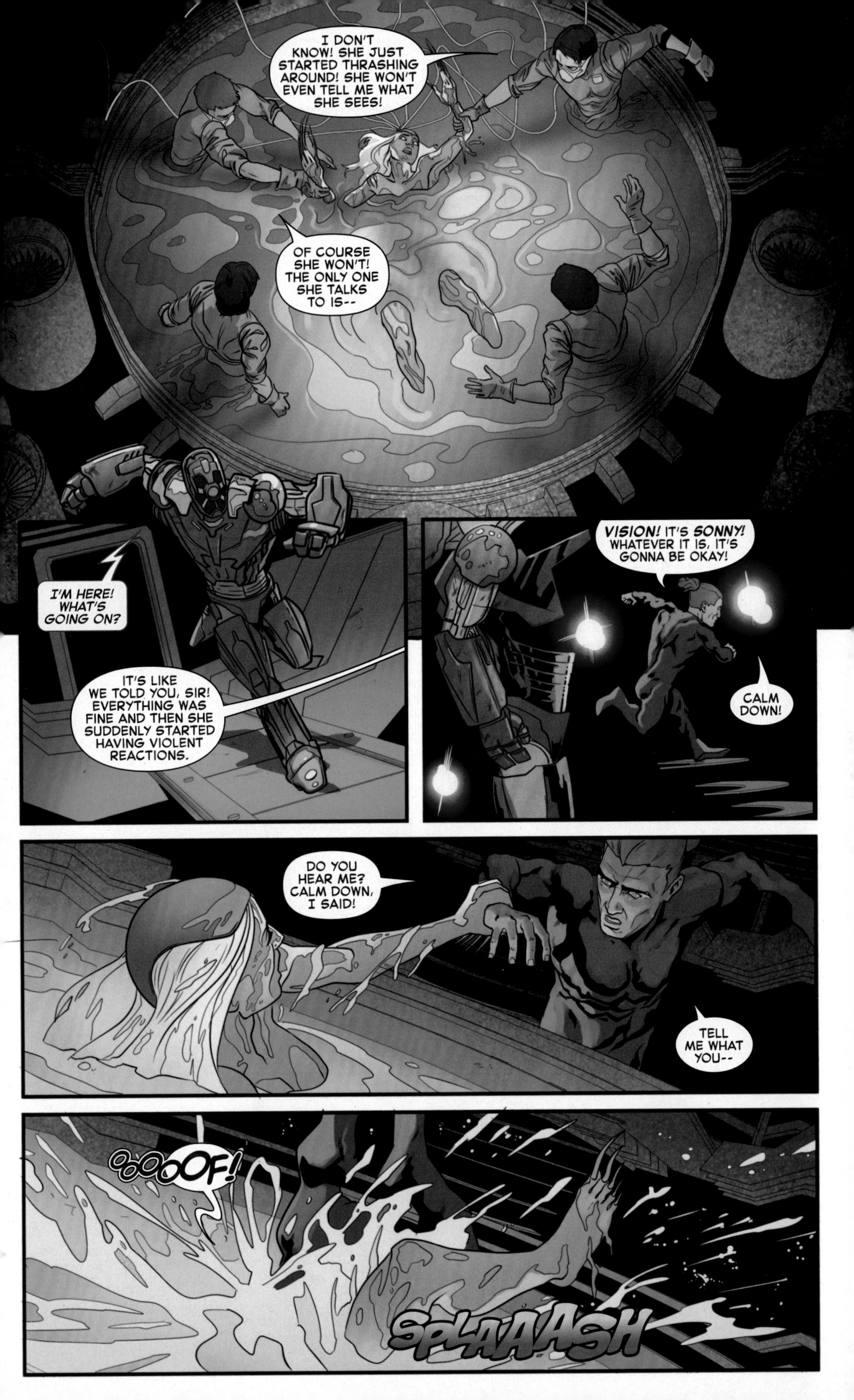
I DON'T KNOW! SHE JUST STARTED THRASHING AROUND! SHE WON'T EVEN TELL ME WHAT SHE SEES!
OF COURSE SHE WON'T! THE ONLY ONE SHE TALKS TO IS--
I'M HERE! WHAT'S GOING ON?
IT'S LIKE WE TOLD YOU, SIR! EVERYTHING WAS FINE AND THEN SHE SUDDENLY STARTED HAVING VIOLENT REACTIONS.
VISION! IT'S SONNY! WHATEVER IT IS, IT'S GONNA BE OKAY!
CALM DOWN!
DO YOU HEAR ME? CALM DOWN, I SAID!
TELL ME WHAT YOU--
OOOOOF!
SPLAAASH

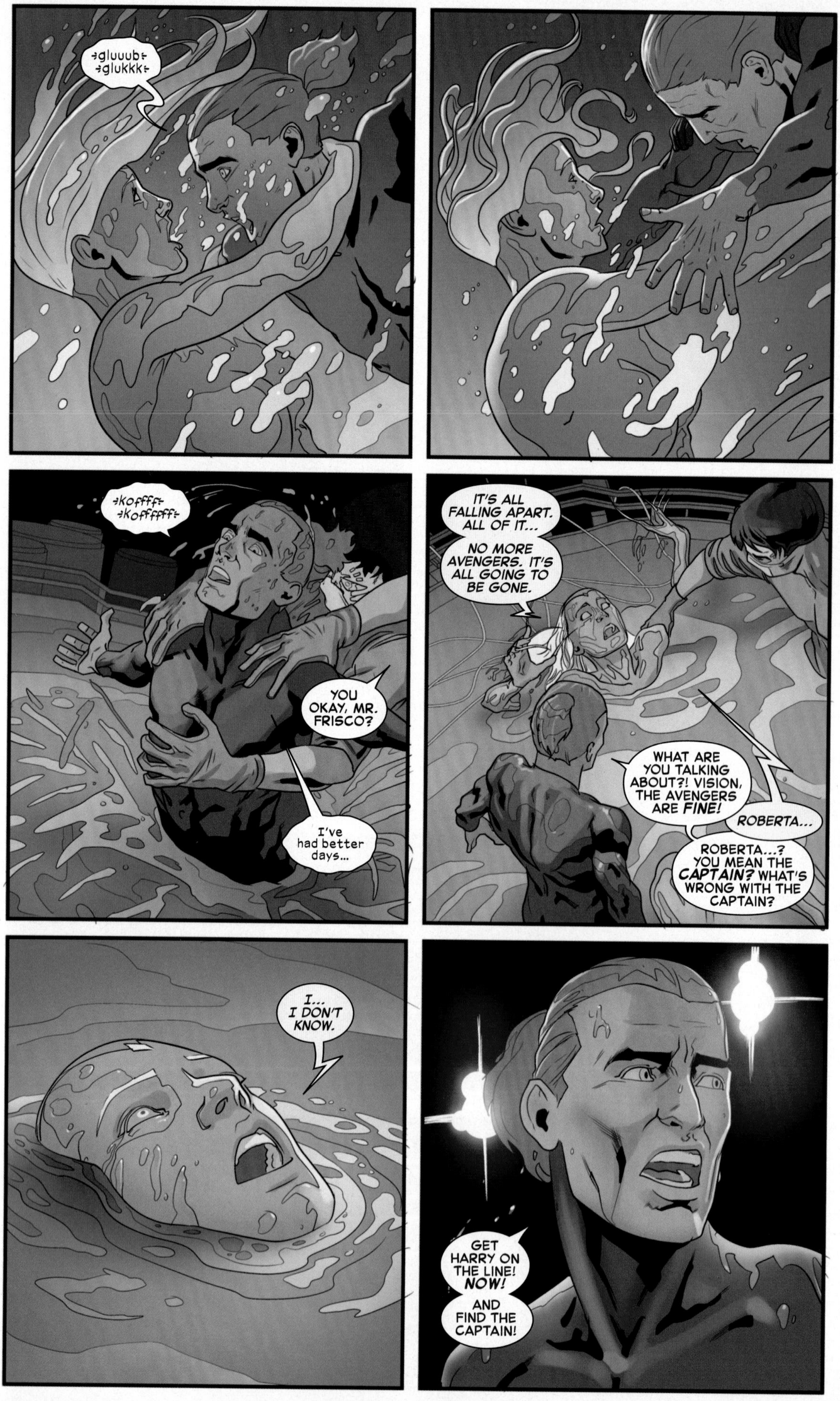

gluuub glukkk
koffff kofffffff
YOU OKAY, MR. FRISCO?
I've had better days...
IT'S ALL FALLING APART. ALL OF IT...
NO MORE AVENGERS. IT'S ALL GOING TO BE GONE.
WHAT ARE YOU TALKING ABOUT?! VISION, THE AVENGERS ARE FINE!
ROBERTA...
ROBERTA...? YOU MEAN THE CAPTAIN? WHAT'S WRONG WITH THE CAPTAIN?
I... I DON'T KNOW.
GET HARRY ON THE LINE! NOW!
AND FIND THE CAPTAIN!

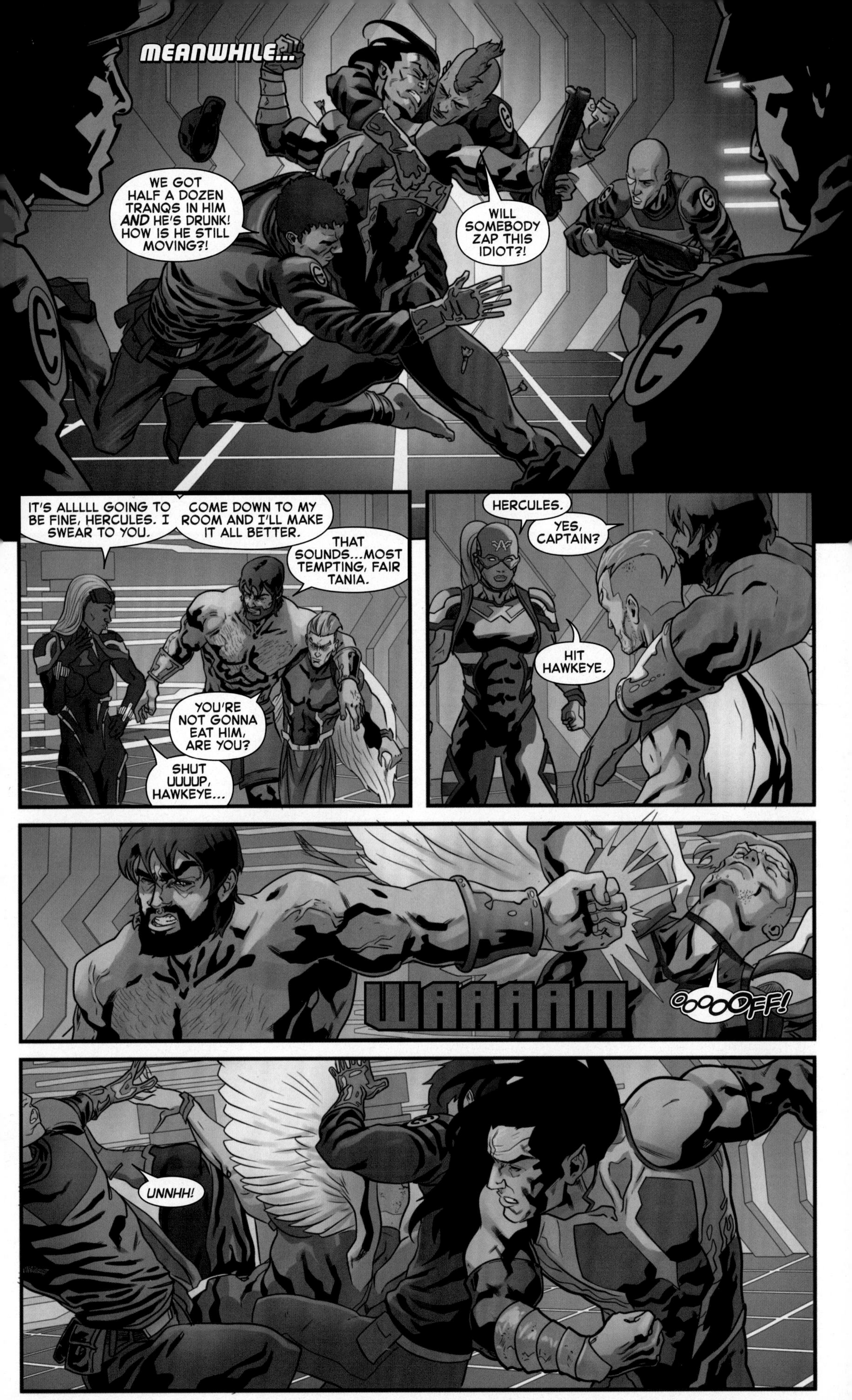
MEANWHILE...
WE GOT HALF A DOZEN TRANQS IN HIM AND HE'S DRUNK! HOW IS HE STILL MOVING?!
WILL SOMEBODY ZAP THIS IDIOT?!
IT'S ALLLLL GOING TO BE FINE, HERCULES. I SWEAR TO YOU.
COME DOWN TO MY ROOM AND I'LL MAKE IT ALL BETTER.
THAT SOUNDS...MOST TEMPTING, FAIR TANIA.
YOU'RE NOT GONNA EAT HIM, ARE YOU?
SHUT UUUUP, HAWKEYE...
HERCULES.
YES, CAPTAIN?
HIT HAWKEYE.
WAAAAM
OOOOOFF!
UNNHH!

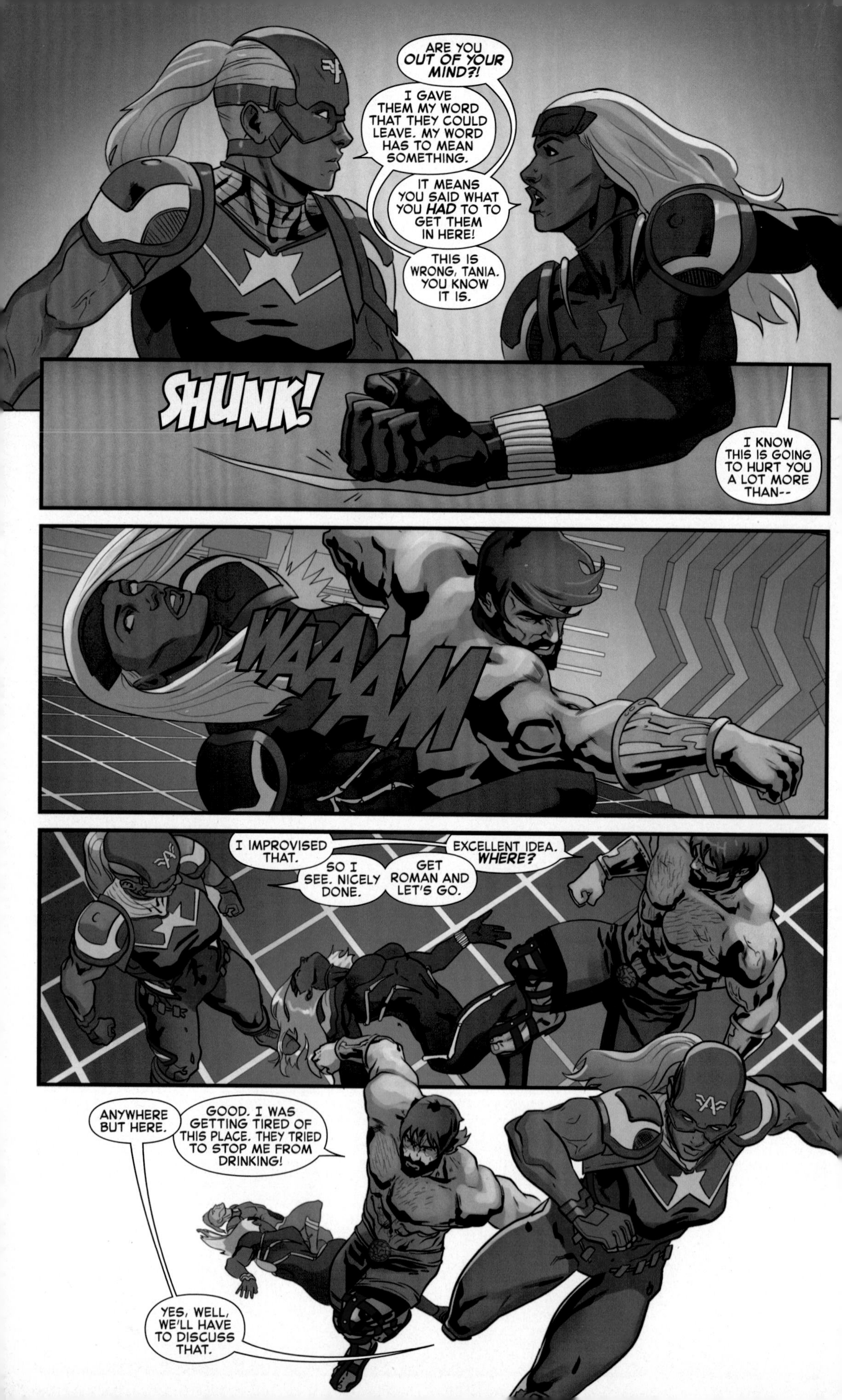

ARE YOU OUT OF YOUR MIND?!
I GAVE THEM MY WORD THAT THEY COULD LEAVE. MY WORD HAS TO MEAN SOMETHING.
IT MEANS YOU SAID WHAT YOU HAD TO TO GET THEM IN HERE!
THIS IS WRONG, TANIA. YOU KNOW IT IS.
SHUNK!
I KNOW THIS IS GOING TO HURT YOU A LOT MORE THAN--
WAAAM
I IMPROVISED THAT.
SO I SEE. NICELY DONE.
EXCELLENT IDEA. WHERE?
GET ROMAN AND LET'S GO.
ANYWHERE BUT HERE.
GOOD. I WAS GETTING TIRED OF THIS PLACE. THEY TRIED TO STOP ME FROM DRINKING!
YES, WELL, WE'LL HAVE TO DISCUSS THAT.

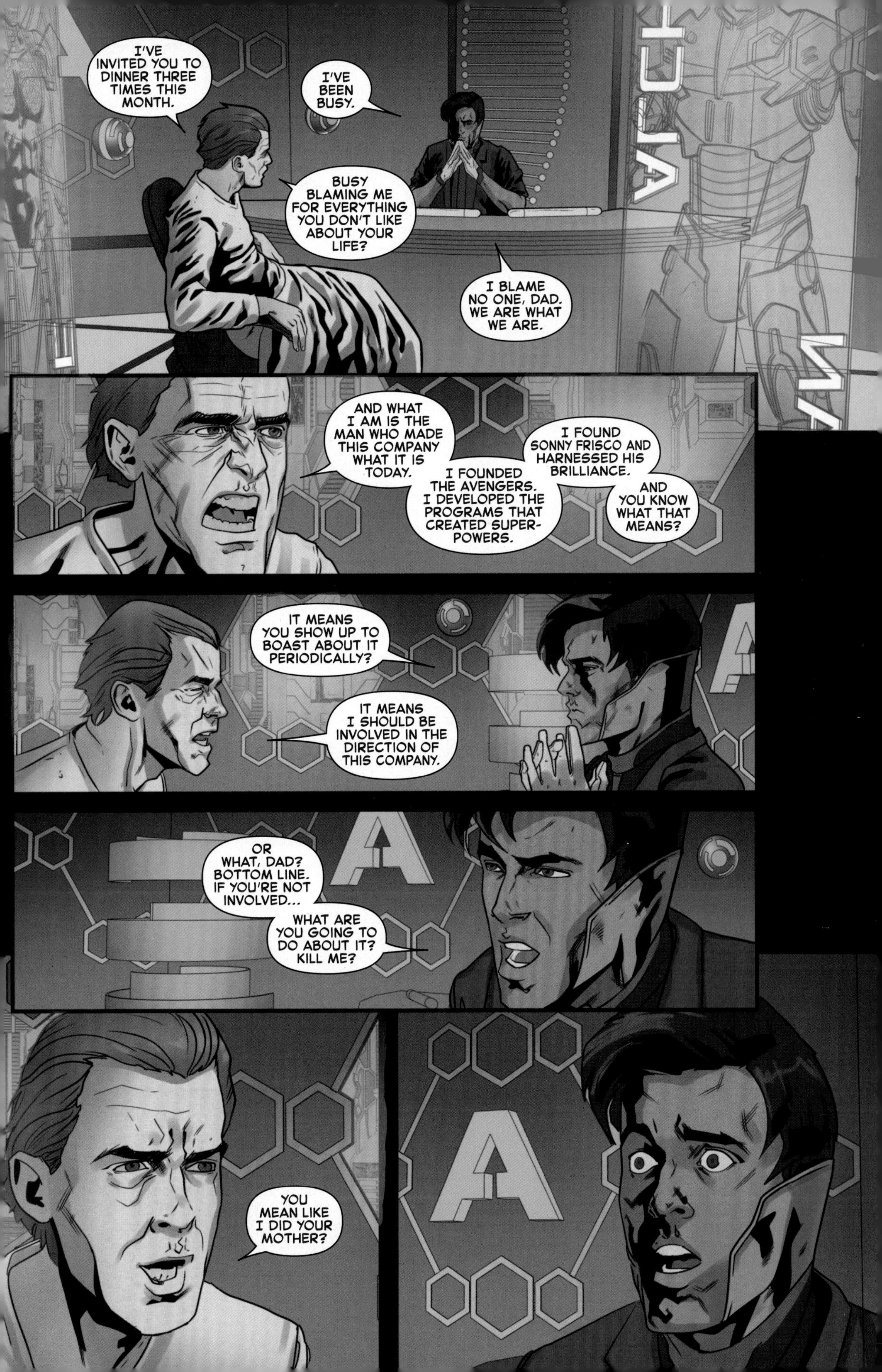

I'VE INVITED YOU TO DINNER THREE TIMES THIS MONTH.
I'VE BEEN BUSY.
BUSY BLAMING ME FOR EVERYTHING YOU DON'T LIKE ABOUT YOUR LIFE?
I BLAME NO ONE, DAD. WE ARE WHAT WE ARE.
AND WHAT I AM IS THE MAN WHO MADE THIS COMPANY WHAT IT IS TODAY.
I FOUNDED THE AVENGERS. I DEVELOPED THE PROGRAMS THAT CREATED SUPER-POWERS.
I FOUND SONNY FRISCO AND HARNESSED HIS BRILLIANCE.
AND YOU KNOW WHAT THAT MEANS?
IT MEANS YOU SHOW UP TO BOAST ABOUT IT PERIODICALLY?
IT MEANS I SHOULD BE INVOLVED IN THE DIRECTION OF THIS COMPANY.
OR WHAT, DAD? BOTTOM LINE. IF YOU'RE NOT INVOLVED...
WHAT ARE YOU GOING TO DO ABOUT IT? KILL ME?
YOU MEAN LIKE I DID YOUR MOTHER?

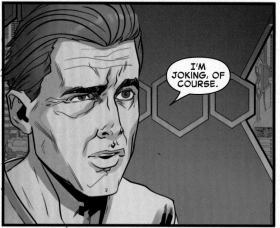

I'M JOKING, OF COURSE.

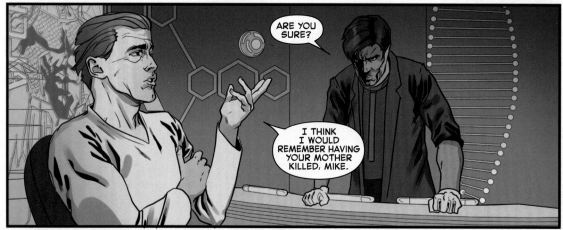

ARE YOU SURE?

I THINK I WOULD REMEMBER HAVING YOUR MOTHER KILLED, MIKE.

SORRY, MR. STONE, I COULDN'T STOP HIM FROM--

QUIET.

MIGUEL, WE HAVE A SITUATION. SOMETHING'S WRONG WITH CAPTAIN AMERICA.

THAT WAS INEVITABLE. YOU GAVE HER A *CONSCIENCE*, MIKE. I ALWAYS *WARNED* YOU ABOUT--

SHUT UP, DAD. SONNY, WHAT ARE YOU TALKING ABOUT?

I JUST CHECKED. SHE HELPED HERCULES AND SUB-MARINER AVOID CAPTURE.

GET DOWN TO THE HOLDING LEVEL!

ALREADY ON IT.

MOVE QUICKLY...

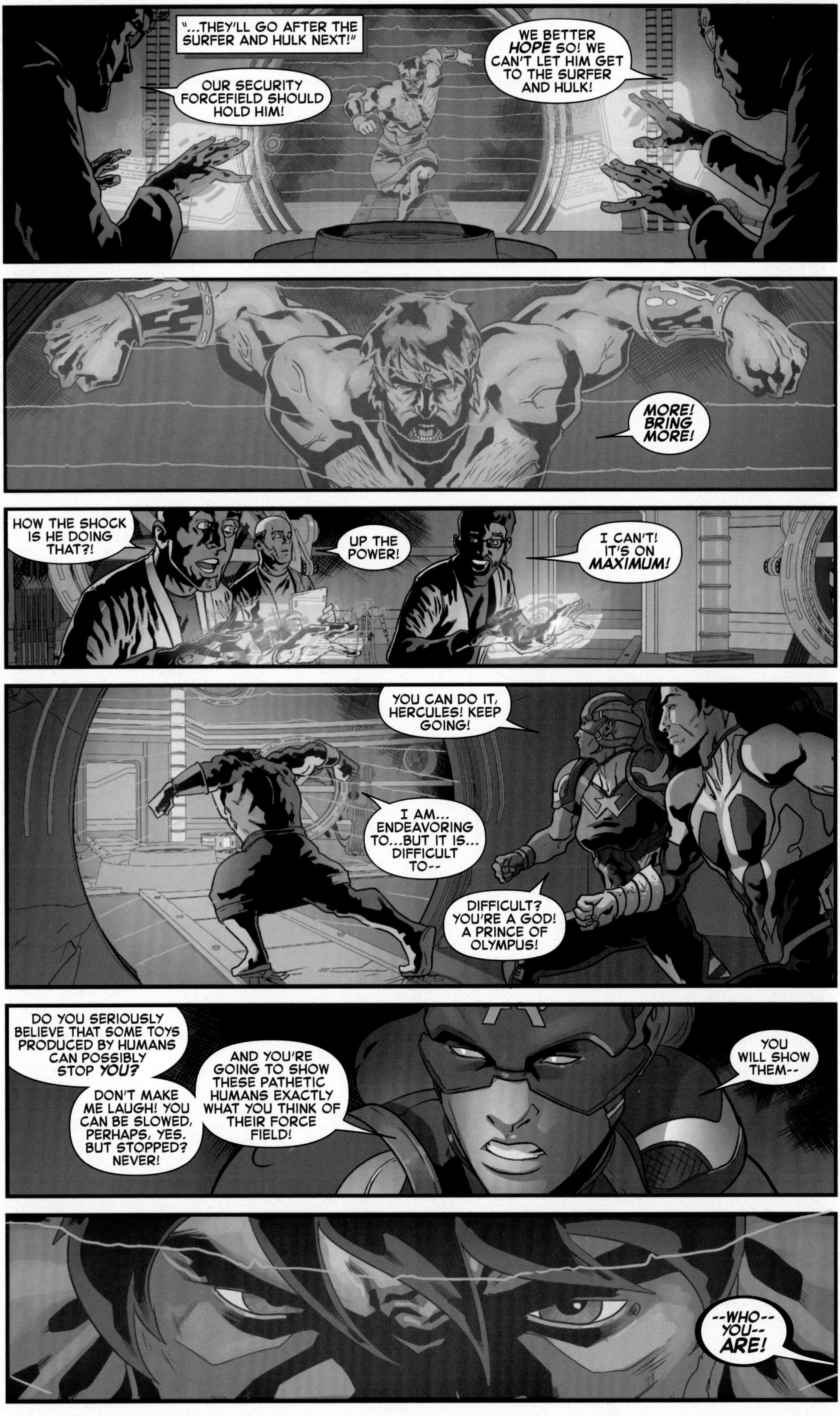
"...THEY'LL GO AFTER THE SURFER AND HULK NEXT!"
OUR SECURITY FORCEFIELD SHOULD HOLD HIM!
WE BETTER *HOPE* SO! WE CAN'T LET HIM GET TO THE SURFER AND HULK!
MORE! BRING MORE!
HOW THE SHOCK IS HE DOING THAT?!
UP THE POWER!
I CAN'T! IT'S ON *MAXIMUM!*
YOU CAN DO IT, HERCULES! KEEP GOING!
I AM... ENDEAVORING TO...BUT IT IS... DIFFICULT TO--
DIFFICULT? YOU'RE A GOD! A PRINCE OF OLYMPUS!
DO YOU SERIOUSLY BELIEVE THAT SOME TOYS PRODUCED BY HUMANS CAN POSSIBLY STOP *YOU?*
DON'T MAKE ME LAUGH! YOU CAN BE SLOWED, PERHAPS, YES. BUT STOPPED? NEVER!
AND YOU'RE GOING TO SHOW THESE PATHETIC HUMANS EXACTLY WHAT YOU THINK OF THEIR FORCE FIELD!
YOU WILL SHOW THEM--
--WHO-- YOU-- *ARE!*

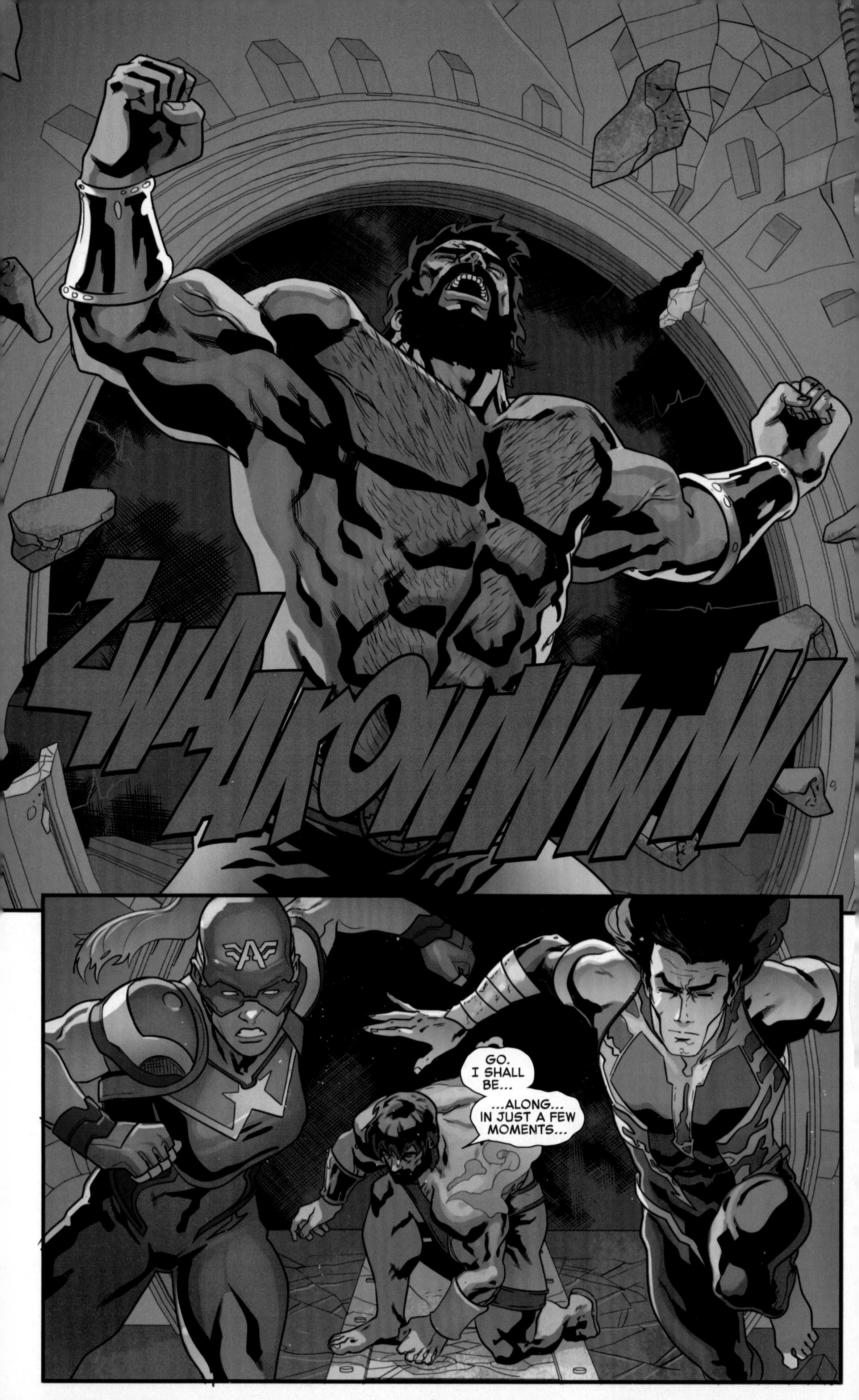
GO. I SHALL BE...
...ALONG... IN JUST A FEW MOMENTS...

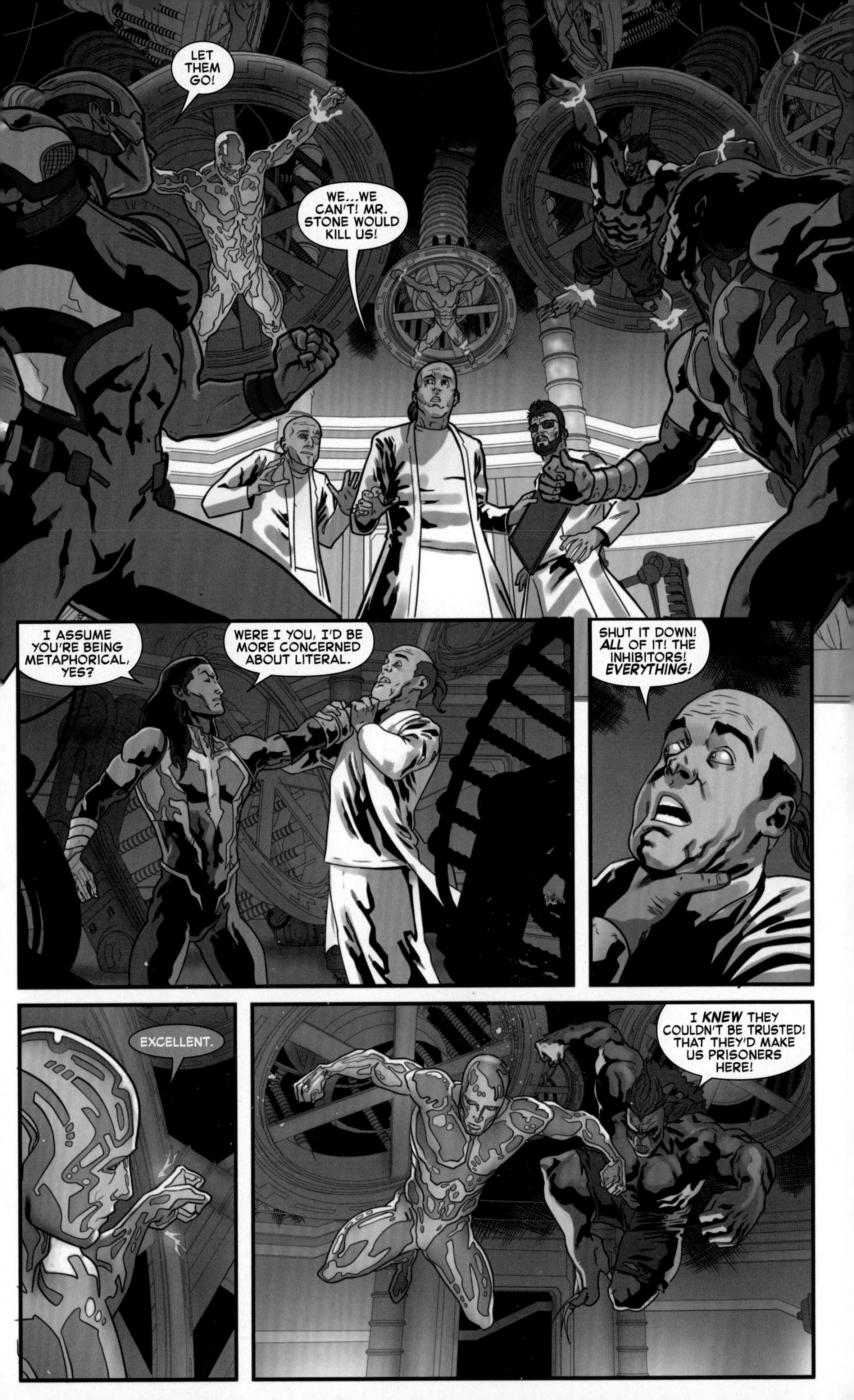

LET THEM GO!
WE...WE CAN'T! MR. STONE WOULD KILL US!
I ASSUME YOU'RE BEING METAPHORICAL, YES?
WERE I YOU, I'D BE MORE CONCERNED ABOUT LITERAL.
SHUT IT DOWN! ALL OF IT! THE INHIBITORS! EVERYTHING!
EXCELLENT.
I KNEW THEY COULDN'T BE TRUSTED! THAT THEY'D MAKE US PRISONERS HERE!

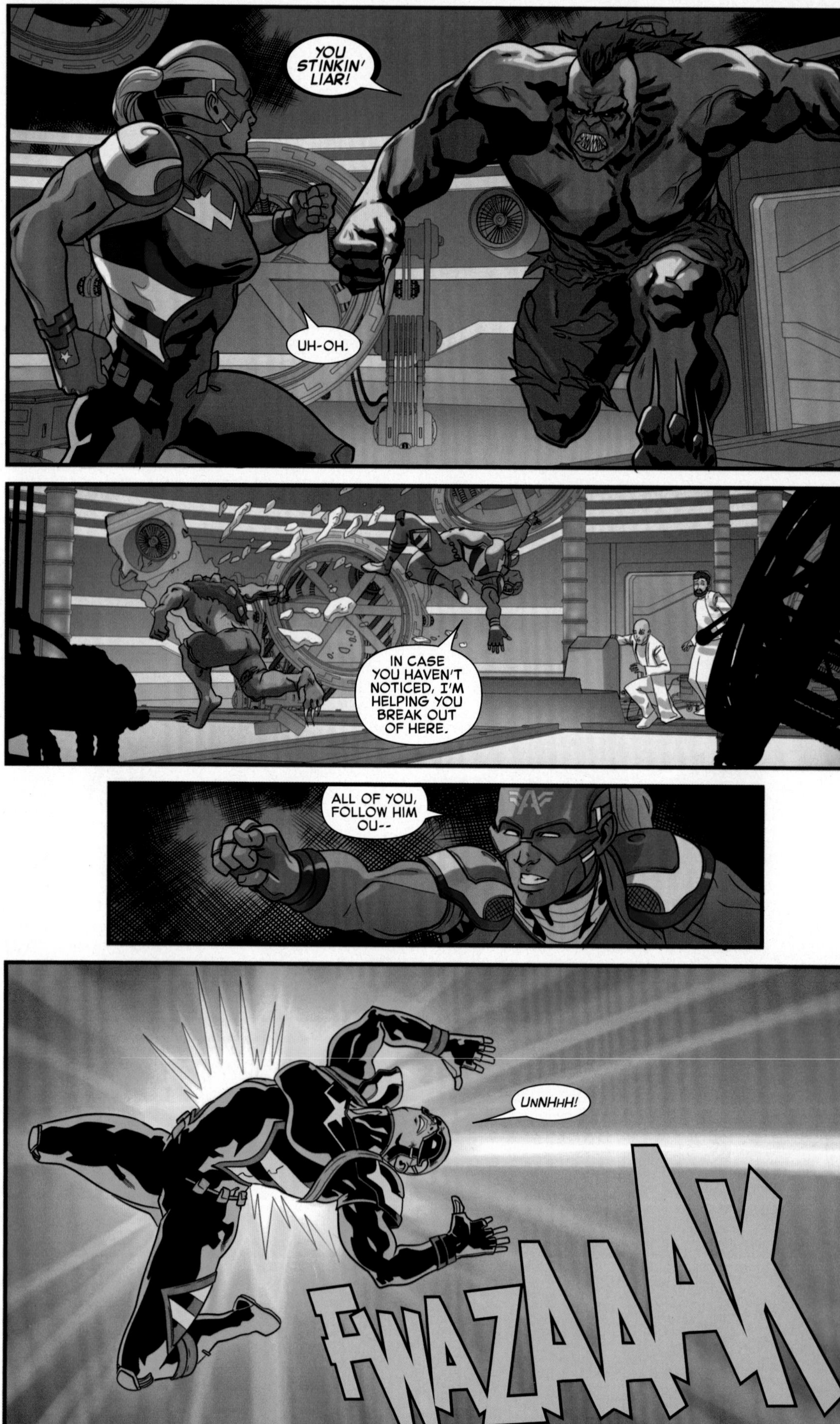
YOU STINKIN' LIAR!
UH-OH.
IN CASE YOU HAVEN'T NOTICED, I'M HELPING YOU BREAK OUT OF HERE.
ALL OF YOU, FOLLOW HIM OU--
UNNHHH!
FWAZAAAK

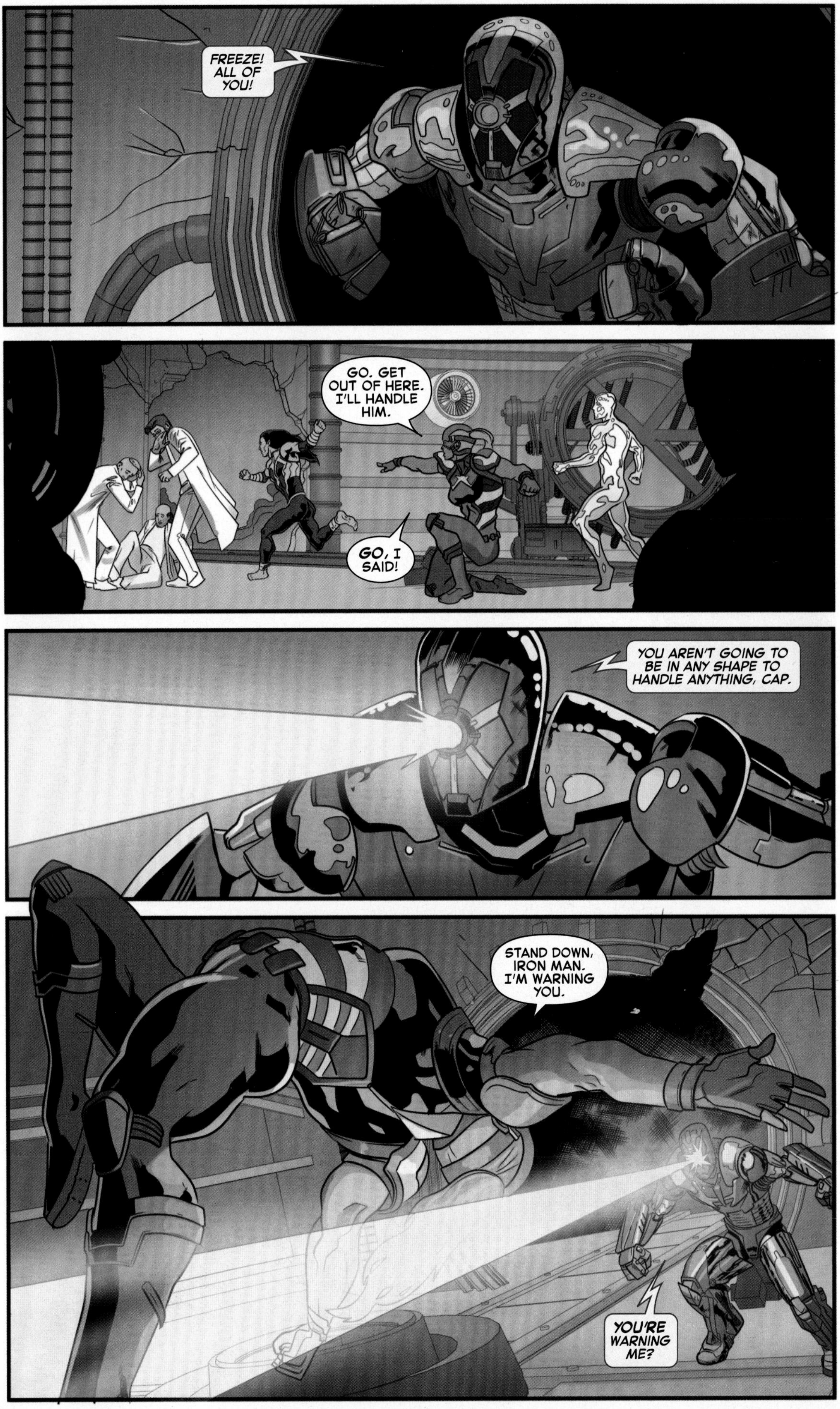
FREEZE! ALL OF YOU!
GO. GET OUT OF HERE. I'LL HANDLE HIM.
GO, I SAID!
YOU AREN'T GOING TO BE IN ANY SHAPE TO HANDLE ANYTHING, CAP.
STAND DOWN, IRON MAN. I'M WARNING YOU.
YOU'RE WARNING ME?

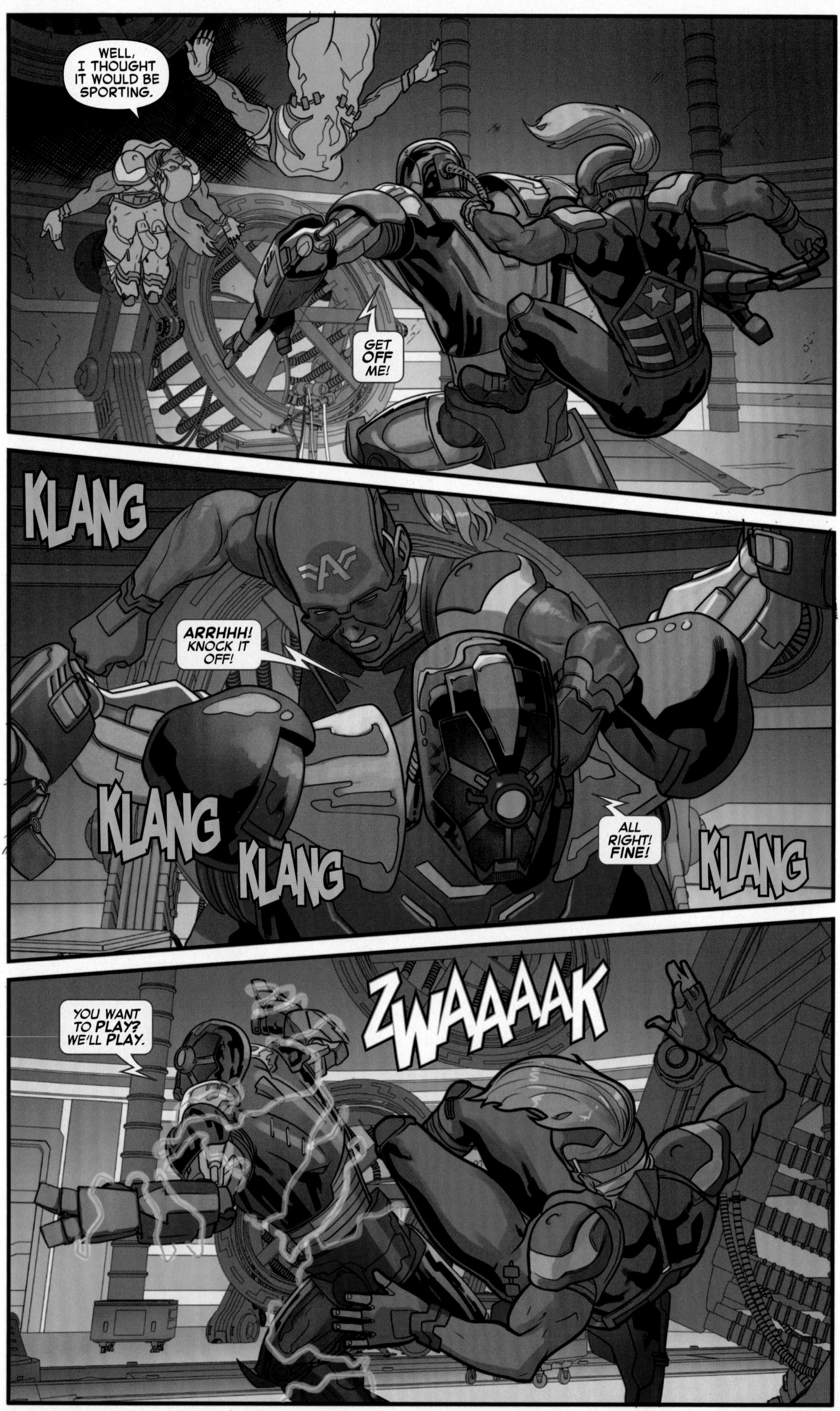
WELL, I THOUGHT IT WOULD BE SPORTING.
GET OFF ME!
KLANG
ARRHHH! KNOCK IT OFF!
KLANG
KLANG
ALL RIGHT! FINE!
KLANG
YOU WANT TO PLAY? WE'LL PLAY.
ZWAAAAK

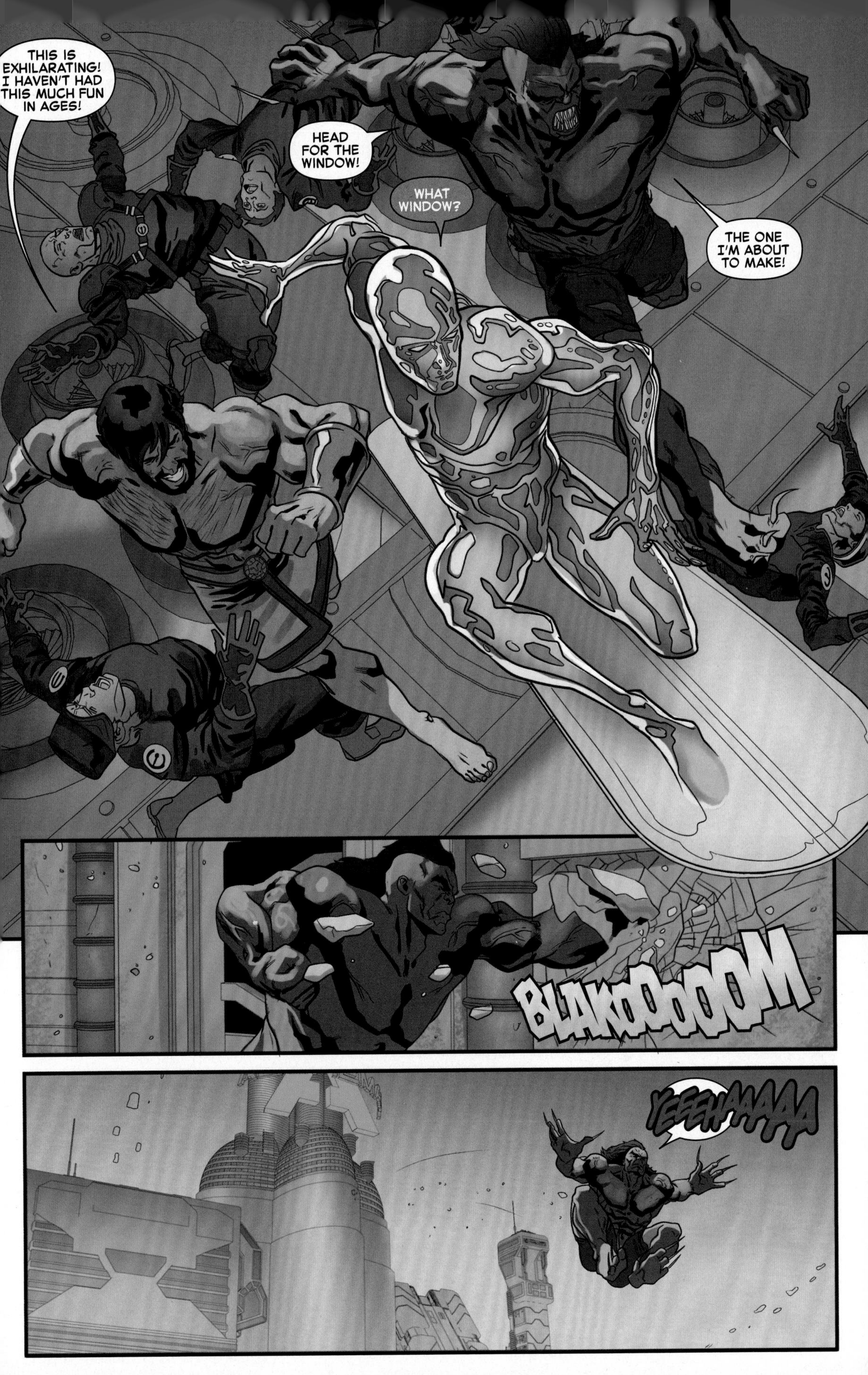
THIS IS EXHILARATING! I HAVEN'T HAD THIS MUCH FUN IN AGES!
HEAD FOR THE WINDOW!
WHAT WINDOW?
THE ONE I'M ABOUT TO MAKE!
BLAKOOOOOOM
YEEEHAAAAA

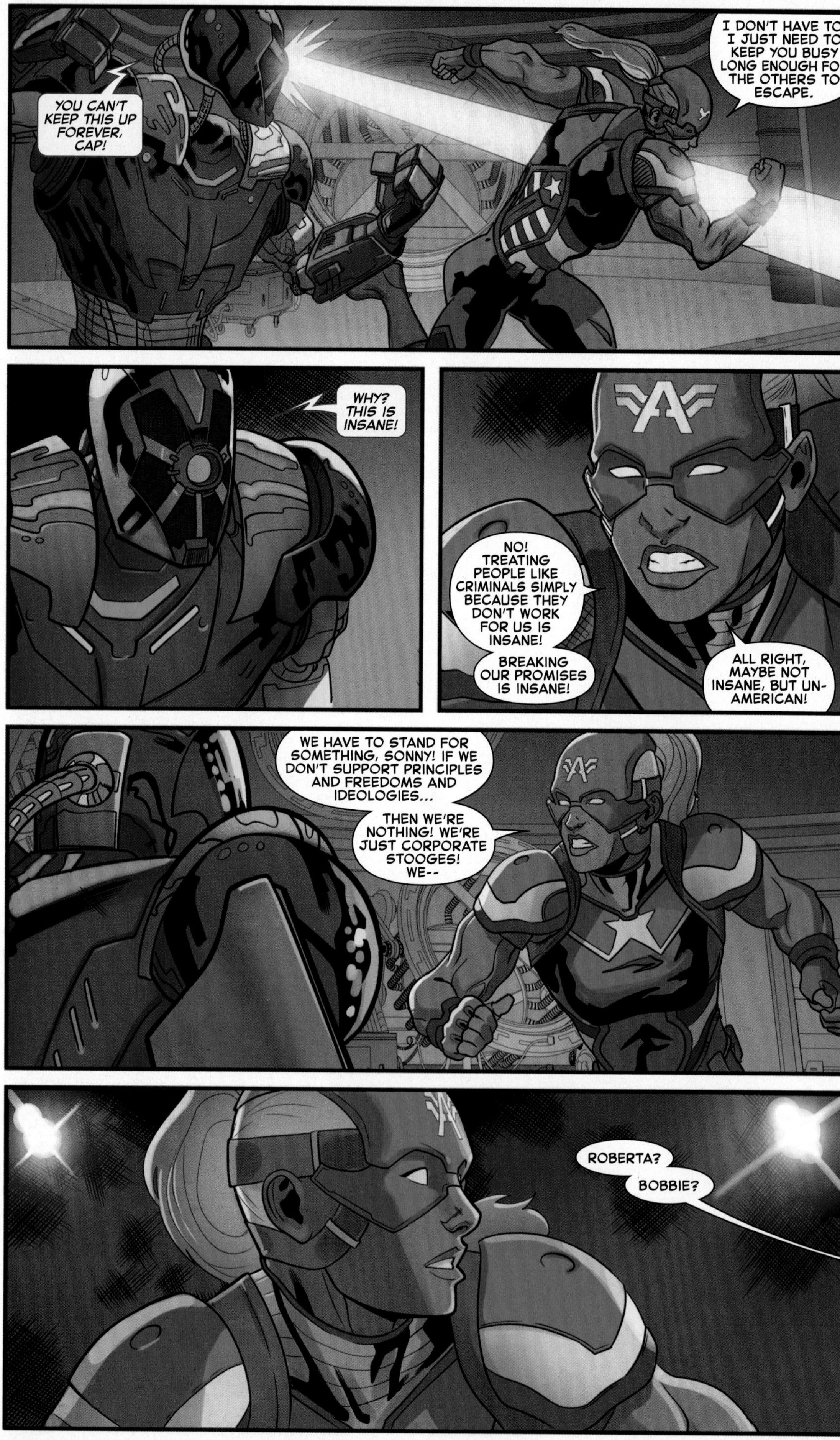

YOU CAN'T KEEP THIS UP FOREVER, CAP!
I DON'T HAVE TO! I JUST NEED TO KEEP YOU BUSY LONG ENOUGH FOR THE OTHERS TO ESCAPE.
WHY? THIS IS INSANE!
NO! TREATING PEOPLE LIKE CRIMINALS SIMPLY BECAUSE THEY DON'T WORK FOR US IS INSANE!
BREAKING OUR PROMISES IS INSANE!
ALL RIGHT, MAYBE NOT INSANE, BUT UN-AMERICAN!
WE HAVE TO STAND FOR SOMETHING, SONNY! IF WE DON'T SUPPORT PRINCIPLES AND FREEDOMS AND IDEOLOGIES...
THEN WE'RE NOTHING! WE'RE JUST CORPORATE STOOGES! WE--
ROBERTA?
BOBBIE?

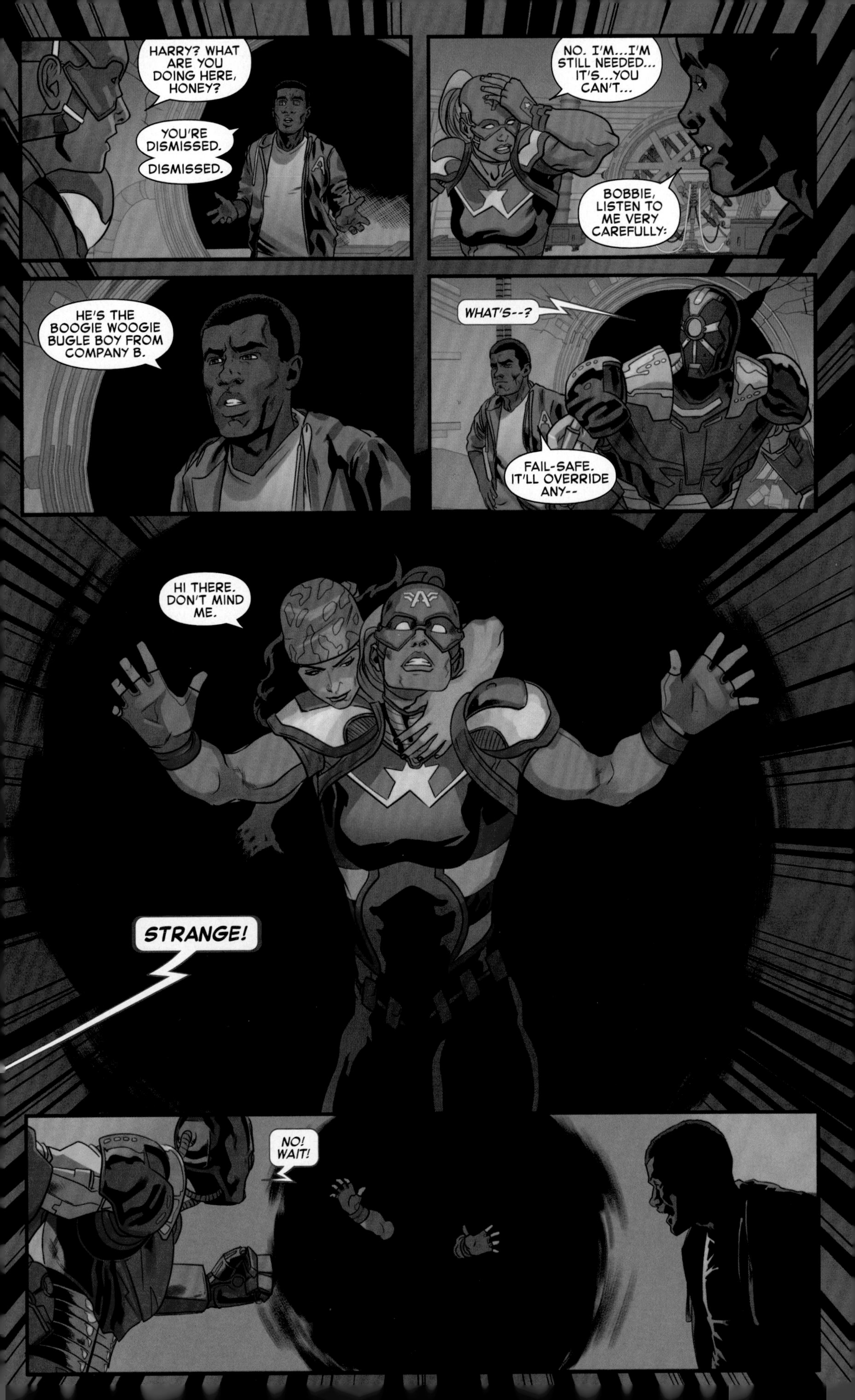
HARRY? WHAT ARE YOU DOING HERE, HONEY?
YOU'RE DISMISSED.
DISMISSED.
NO. I'M...I'M STILL NEEDED... IT'S...YOU CAN'T...
BOBBIE, LISTEN TO ME VERY CAREFULLY:
HE'S THE BOOGIE WOOGIE BUGLE BOY FROM COMPANY B.
WHAT'S--?
FAIL-SAFE. IT'LL OVERRIDE ANY--
HI THERE. DON'T MIND ME.
STRANGE!
NO! WAIT!

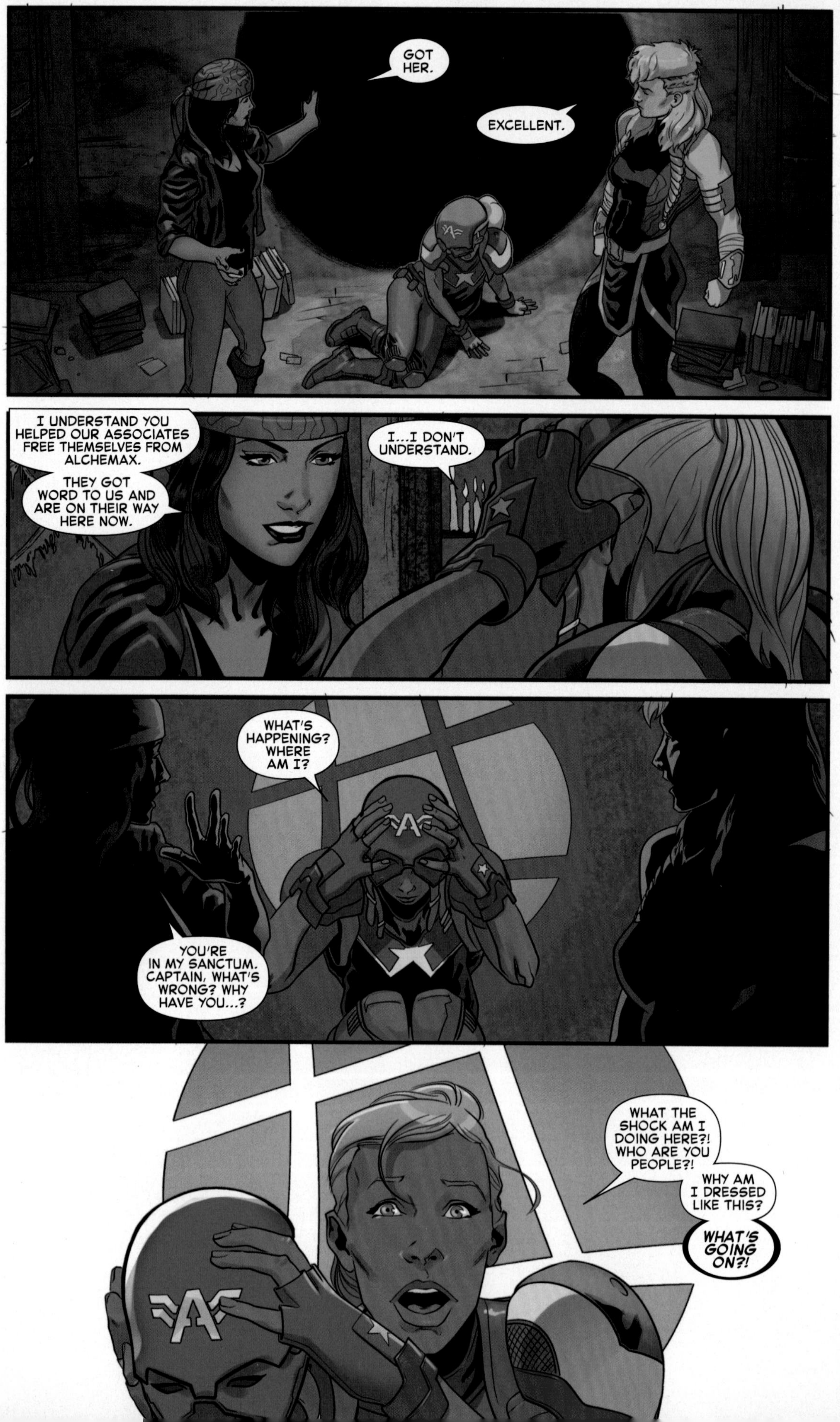
GOT HER.
EXCELLENT.
I UNDERSTAND YOU HELPED OUR ASSOCIATES FREE THEMSELVES FROM ALCHEMAX.
THEY GOT WORD TO US AND ARE ON THEIR WAY HERE NOW.
I...I DON'T UNDERSTAND.
WHAT'S HAPPENING? WHERE AM I?
YOU'RE IN MY SANCTUM. CAPTAIN, WHAT'S WRONG? WHY HAVE YOU...?
WHAT THE SHOCK AM I DOING HERE?! WHO ARE YOU PEOPLE?!
WHY AM I DRESSED LIKE THIS?
WHAT'S GOING ON?!

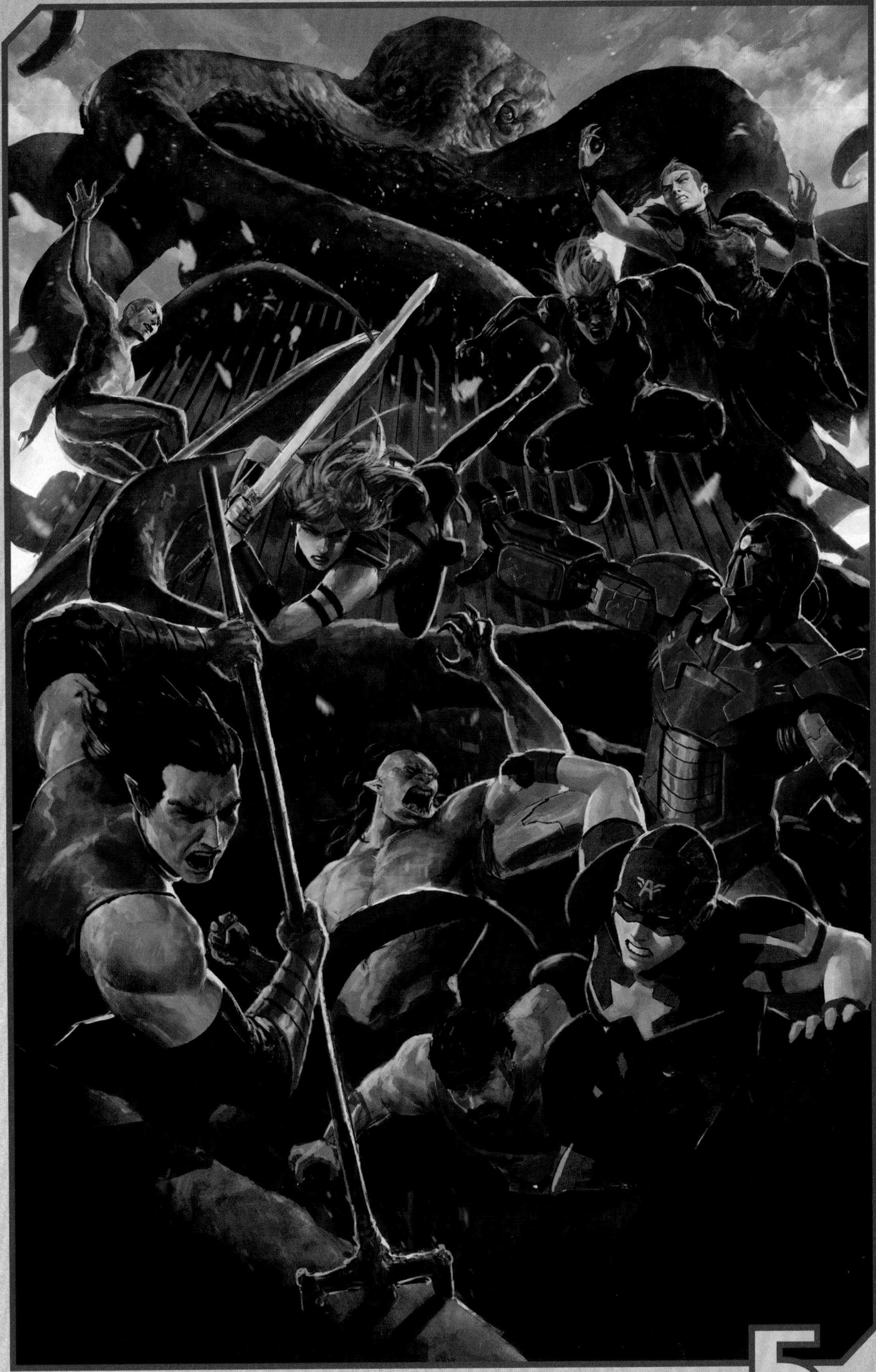

5

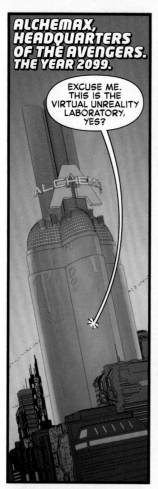

ALCHEMAX, HEADQUARTERS OF THE AVENGERS. THE YEAR 2099.

EXCUSE ME. THIS IS THE VIRTUAL UNREALITY LABORATORY, YES?

WHAT ARE YOU DOING...? YOU'RE NOT PERMITTED IN HERE!

AND YET HERE I AM. APPARENTLY SOMEONE SHUT DOWN THE POWER TO THE DEVICE THAT WAS HOLDING ME IN PLACE.

AND I THOUGHT I WOULD USE MY PROXIMITY TO THIS DEVICE TO GOOD EFFECT.

WHO ARE YOU?!

MY NAME IS MARTIN HARGOOD. BUT I BELIEVE I SHALL HENCEFORTH GO BY THE NAME OF MY ANCESTOR...

BARON MORDO.

AND THIS GATEWAY WILL PROVIDE ME ACCESS TO THE BEING THAT I HAVE BEEN ENDEAVORING TO BRING HERE.

DOWN ON YOUR KNEES, GENTLEMEN! BE PREPARED TO GREET HIM!

AND THEN BE DEVOURED BY HIM!

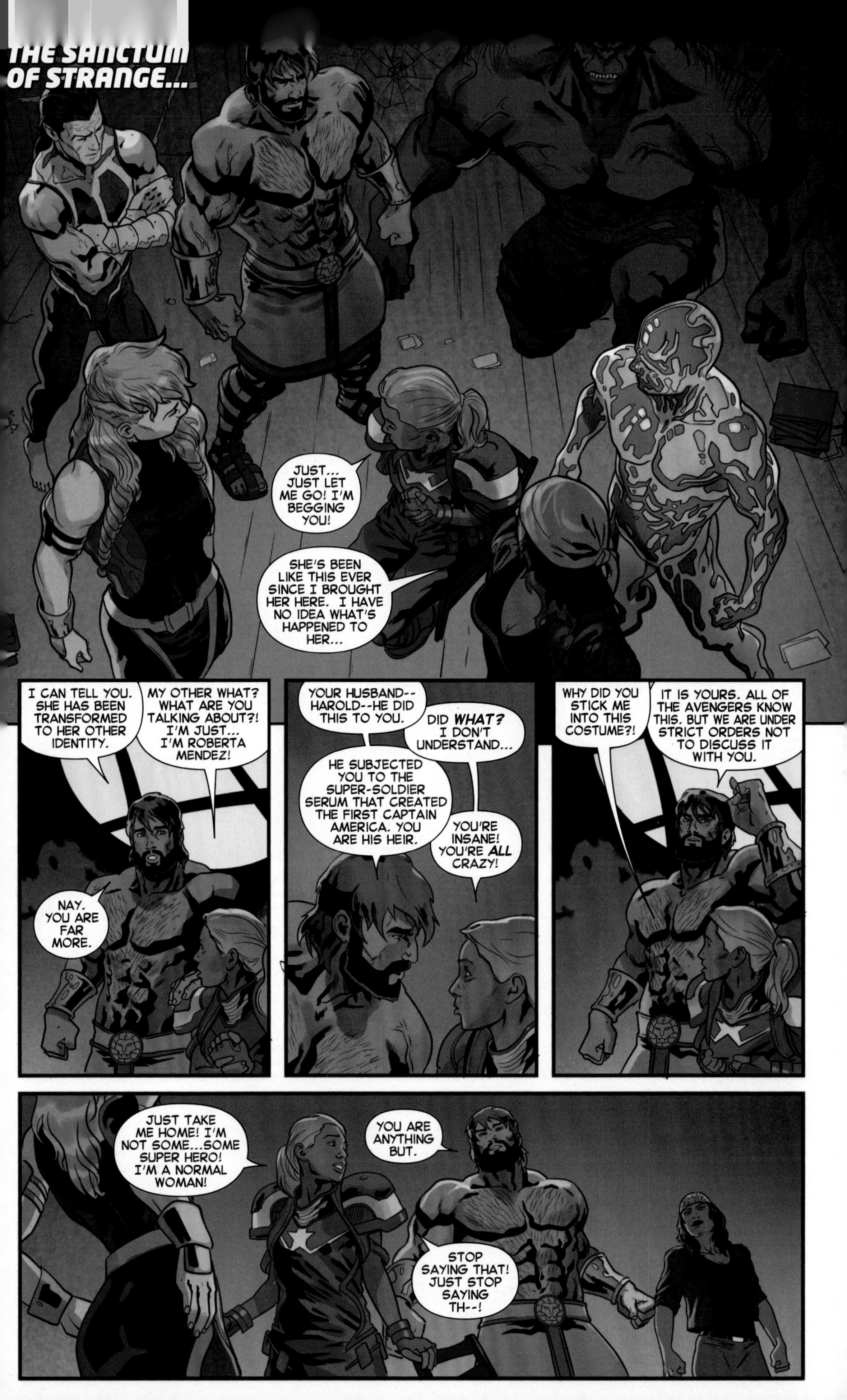
THE SANCTUM OF STRANGE...
JUST... JUST LET ME GO! I'M BEGGING YOU!
SHE'S BEEN LIKE THIS EVER SINCE I BROUGHT HER HERE. I HAVE NO IDEA WHAT'S HAPPENED TO HER...
I CAN TELL YOU. SHE HAS BEEN TRANSFORMED TO HER OTHER IDENTITY.
MY OTHER WHAT? WHAT ARE YOU TALKING ABOUT?! I'M JUST... I'M ROBERTA MENDEZ!
NAY. YOU ARE FAR MORE.
YOUR HUSBAND-- HAROLD--HE DID THIS TO YOU.
DID WHAT? I DON'T UNDERSTAND...
HE SUBJECTED YOU TO THE SUPER-SOLDIER SERUM THAT CREATED THE FIRST CAPTAIN AMERICA. YOU ARE HIS HEIR.
YOU'RE INSANE! YOU'RE ALL CRAZY!
WHY DID YOU STICK ME INTO THIS COSTUME?!
IT IS YOURS. ALL OF THE AVENGERS KNOW THIS. BUT WE ARE UNDER STRICT ORDERS NOT TO DISCUSS IT WITH YOU.
JUST TAKE ME HOME! I'M NOT SOME...SOME SUPER HERO! I'M A NORMAL WOMAN!
YOU ARE ANYTHING BUT.
STOP SAYING THAT! JUST STOP SAYING TH--!

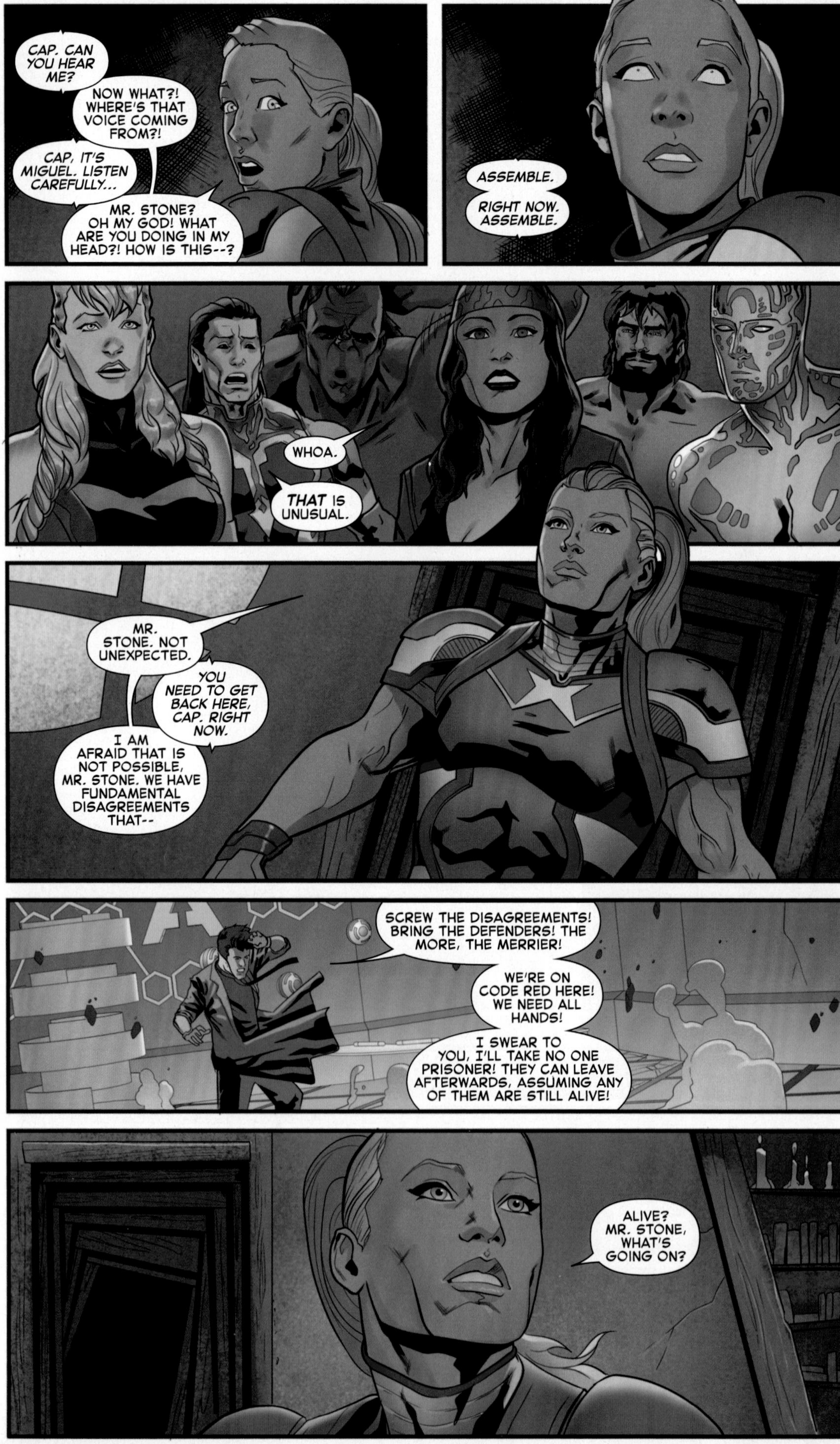
CAP. CAN YOU HEAR ME?
NOW WHAT?! WHERE'S THAT VOICE COMING FROM?!
CAP, IT'S MIGUEL. LISTEN CAREFULLY...
MR. STONE? OH MY GOD! WHAT ARE YOU DOING IN MY HEAD?! HOW IS THIS--?
ASSEMBLE.
RIGHT NOW. ASSEMBLE.
WHOA.
THAT IS UNUSUAL.
MR. STONE. NOT UNEXPECTED.
YOU NEED TO GET BACK HERE, CAP. RIGHT NOW.
I AM AFRAID THAT IS NOT POSSIBLE, MR. STONE. WE HAVE FUNDAMENTAL DISAGREEMENTS THAT--
SCREW THE DISAGREEMENTS! BRING THE DEFENDERS! THE MORE, THE MERRIER!
WE'RE ON CODE RED HERE! WE NEED ALL HANDS!
I SWEAR TO YOU, I'LL TAKE NO ONE PRISONER! THEY CAN LEAVE AFTERWARDS, ASSUMING ANY OF THEM ARE STILL ALIVE!
ALIVE? MR. STONE, WHAT'S GOING ON?

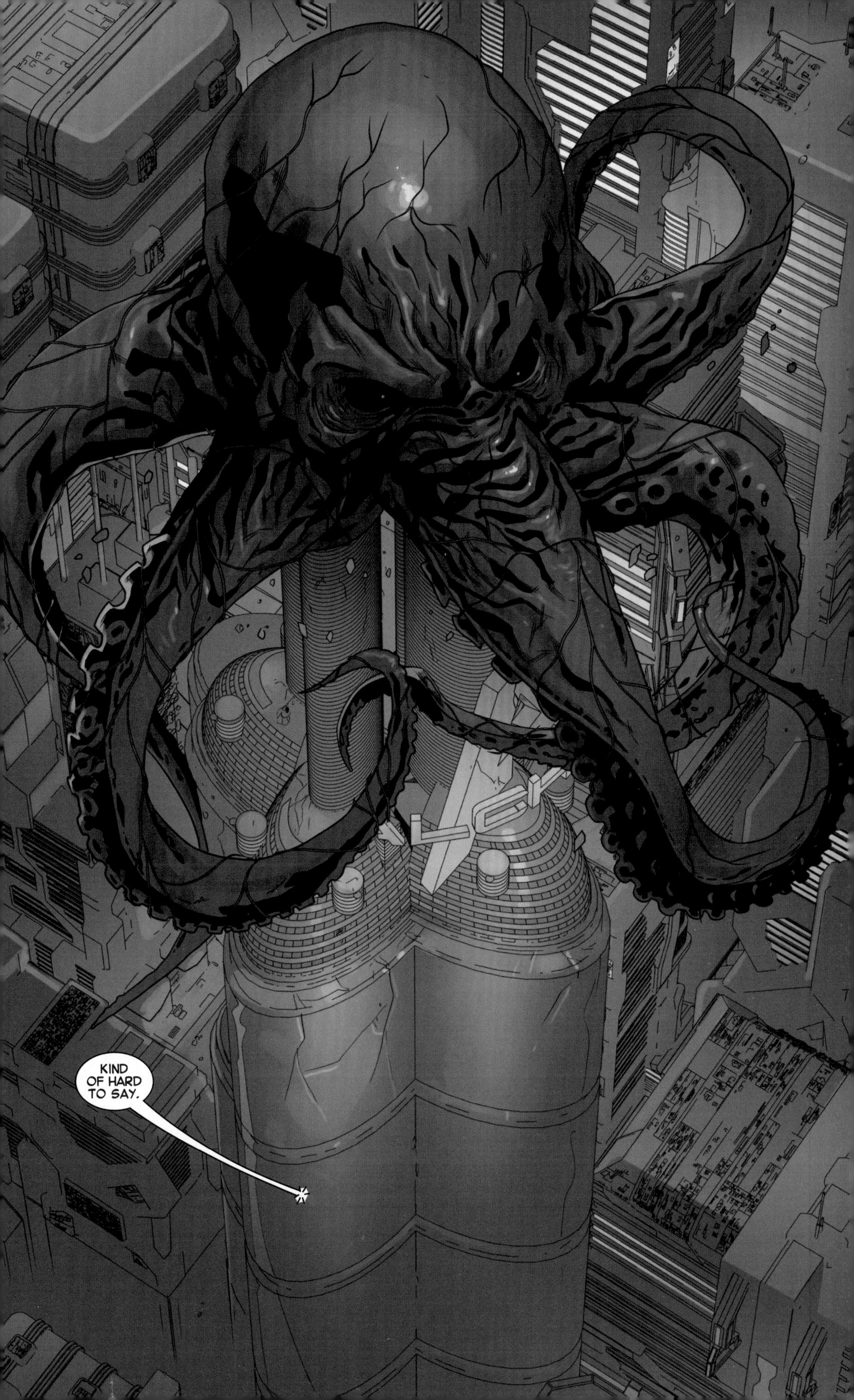
KIND OF HARD TO SAY.

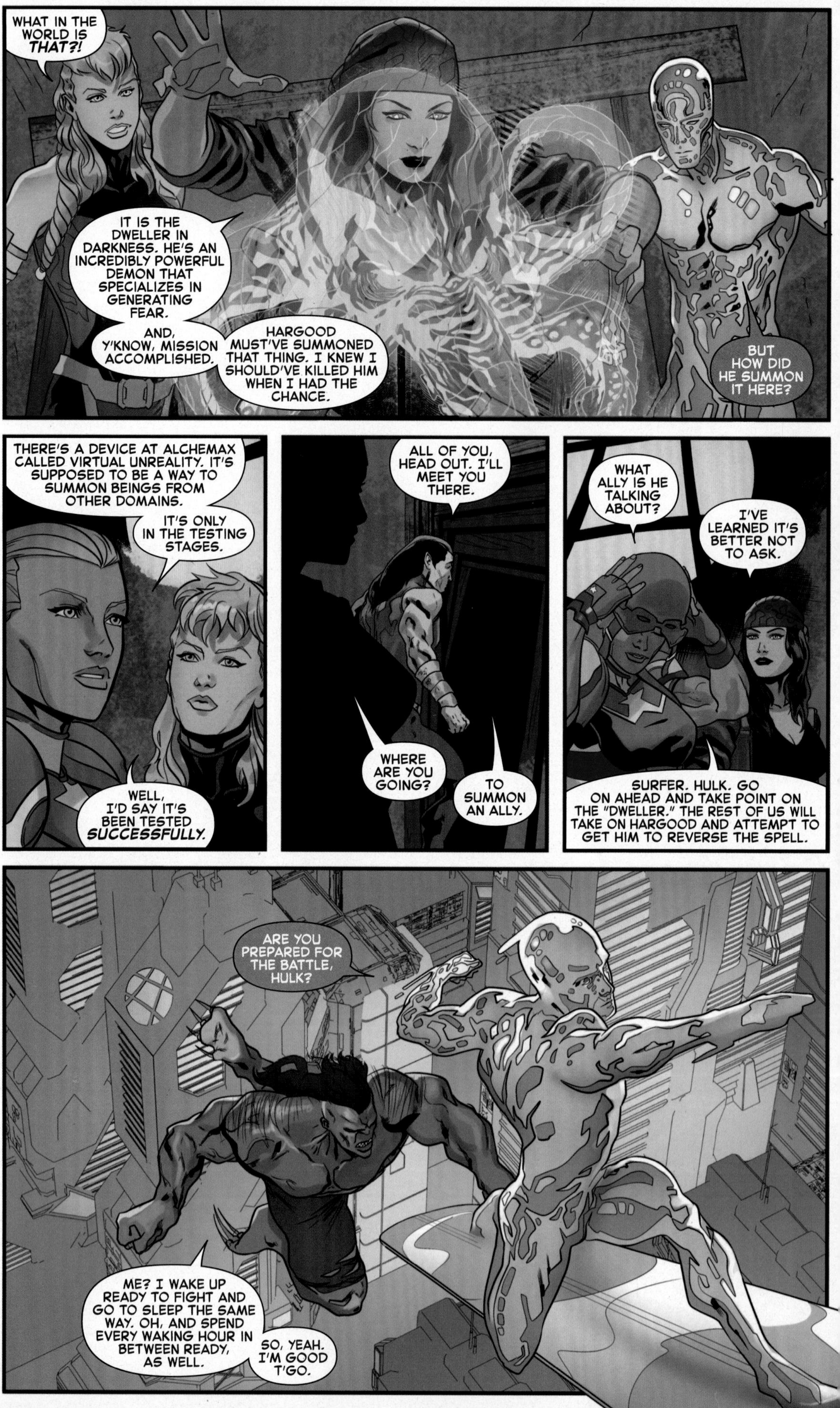
WHAT IN THE WORLD IS THAT?!
IT IS THE DWELLER IN DARKNESS. HE'S AN INCREDIBLY POWERFUL DEMON THAT SPECIALIZES IN GENERATING FEAR.
AND, Y'KNOW, MISSION ACCOMPLISHED.
HARGOOD MUST'VE SUMMONED THAT THING. I KNEW I SHOULD'VE KILLED HIM WHEN I HAD THE CHANCE.
BUT HOW DID HE SUMMON IT HERE?
THERE'S A DEVICE AT ALCHEMAX CALLED VIRTUAL UNREALITY. IT'S SUPPOSED TO BE A WAY TO SUMMON BEINGS FROM OTHER DOMAINS.
IT'S ONLY IN THE TESTING STAGES.
WELL, I'D SAY IT'S BEEN TESTED SUCCESSFULLY.
ALL OF YOU, HEAD OUT. I'LL MEET YOU THERE.
WHERE ARE YOU GOING?
TO SUMMON AN ALLY.
WHAT ALLY IS HE TALKING ABOUT?
I'VE LEARNED IT'S BETTER NOT TO ASK.
SURFER. HULK. GO ON AHEAD AND TAKE POINT ON THE "DWELLER." THE REST OF US WILL TAKE ON HARGOOD AND ATTEMPT TO GET HIM TO REVERSE THE SPELL.
ARE YOU PREPARED FOR THE BATTLE, HULK?
ME? I WAKE UP READY TO FIGHT AND GO TO SLEEP THE SAME WAY. OH, AND SPEND EVERY WAKING HOUR IN BETWEEN READY, AS WELL.
SO, YEAH. I'M GOOD T'GO.

YOU TRULY THINK TO DUEL WITH ME? ARE YOU MAD?
WHAT I AM IS SOMEONE WHO BELONGS HERE! THAT'S SURE AS HELL NOT YOU!
TELL ME, HUMAN...WHAT FEARS DO YOU HAVE, EH? SOME, CERTAINLY.
AHHH... WHAT A TINY MAN YOU ARE. HOW YOU WERE TORMENTED IN YOUR YOUTH.
AND ALL THAT YOU HAVE CREATED WAS DESIGNED TO PROTECT YOU FROM ABUSE.
YOUR FEARS ARE NOT AT ALL BURIED, ARE THEY?
HOW TRULY PATHETIC, TO THINK THAT *THIS* IS THE BEST YOUR WORLD HAS TO OFFER.

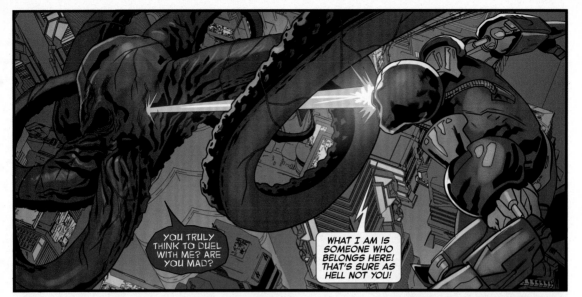

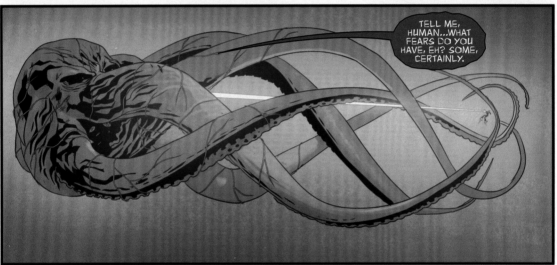

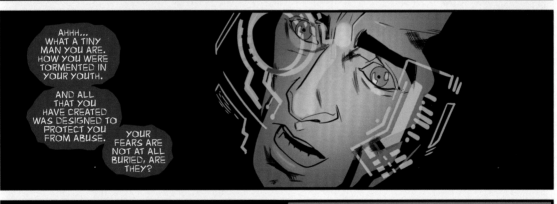

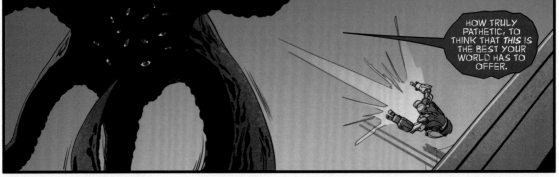

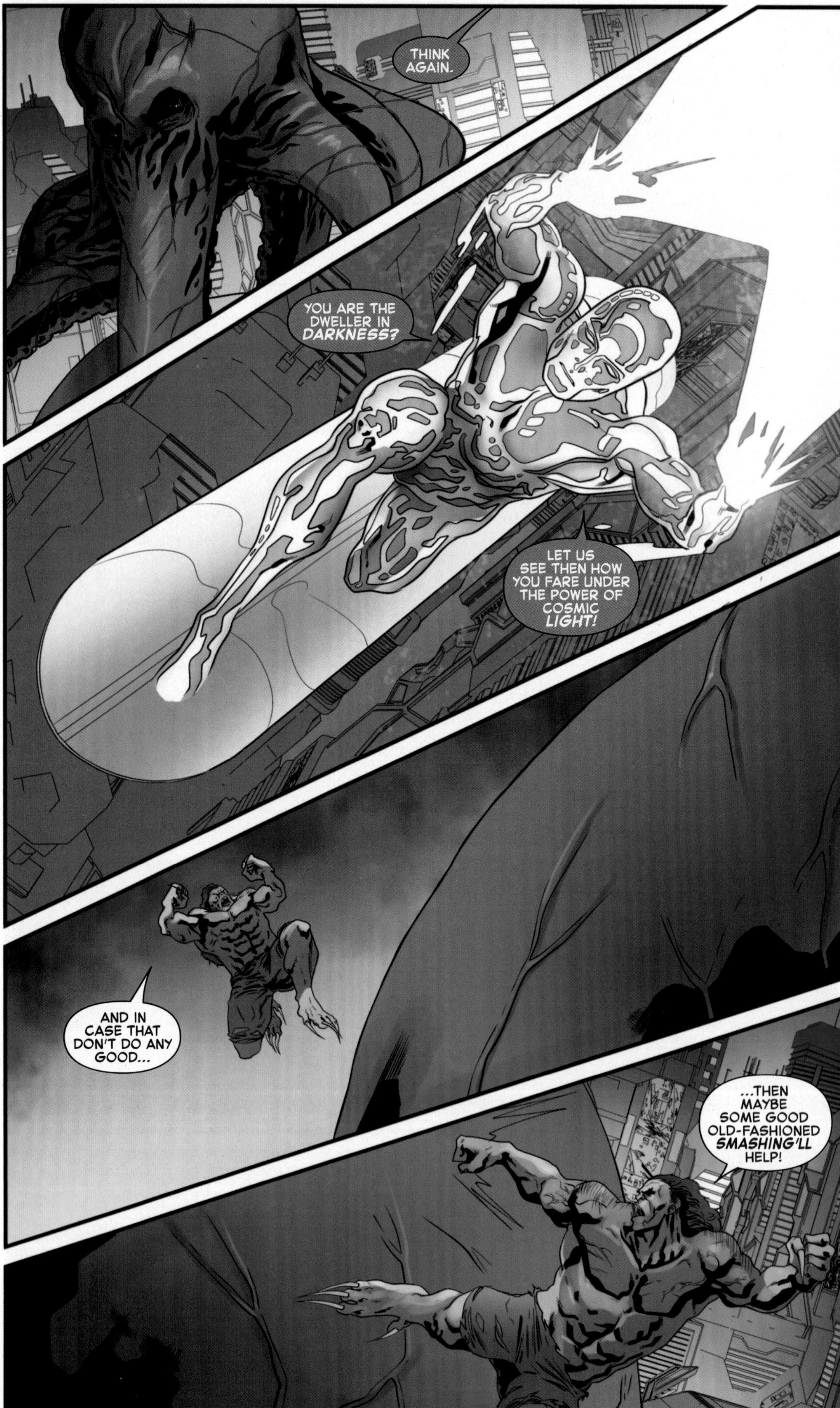
THINK AGAIN.
YOU ARE THE DWELLER IN DARKNESS?
LET US SEE THEN HOW YOU FARE UNDER THE POWER OF COSMIC LIGHT!
AND IN CASE THAT DON'T DO ANY GOOD...
...THEN MAYBE SOME GOOD OLD-FASHIONED SMASHING'LL HELP!

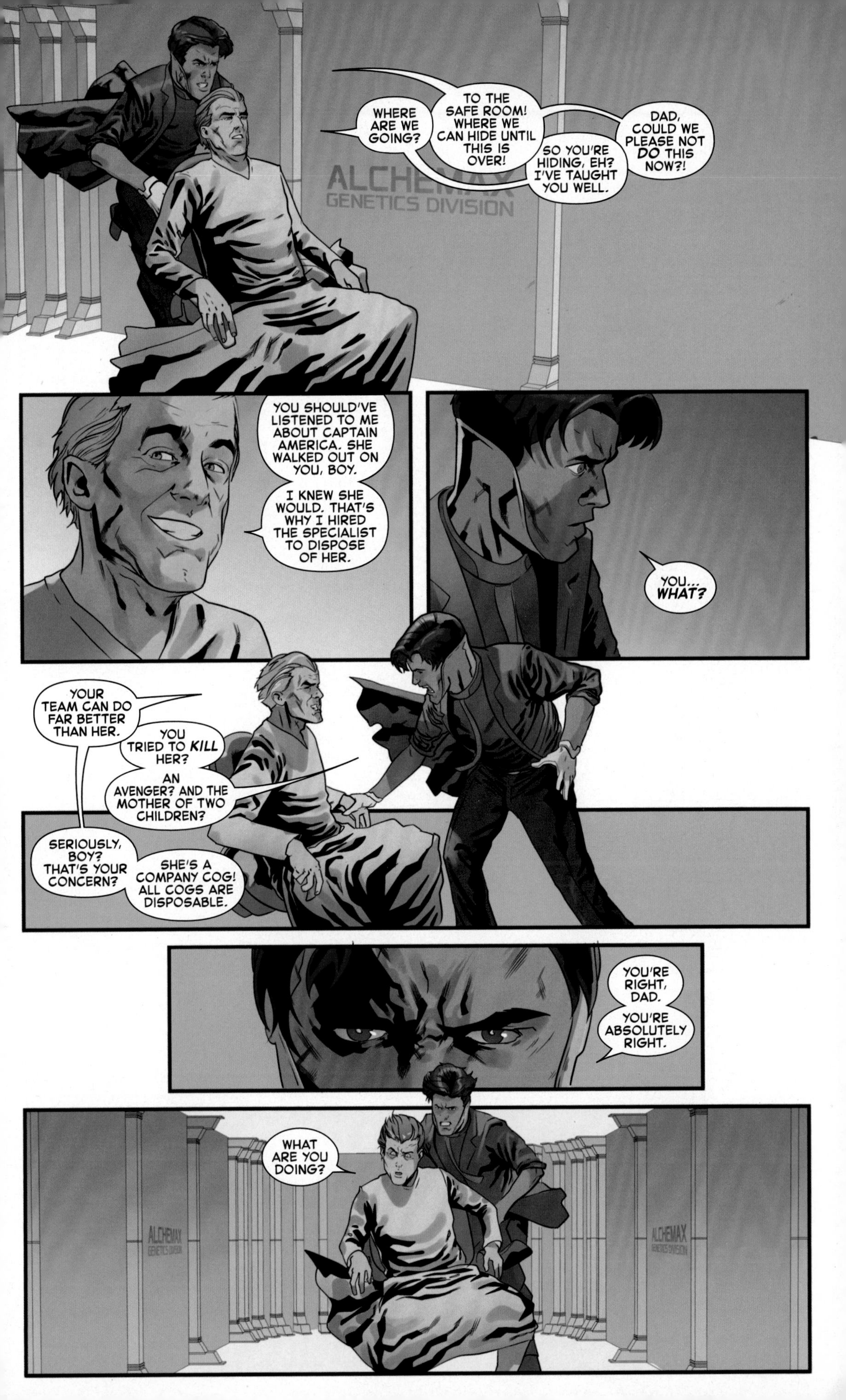
WHERE ARE WE GOING?
TO THE SAFE ROOM! WHERE WE CAN HIDE UNTIL THIS IS OVER!
SO YOU'RE HIDING, EH? I'VE TAUGHT YOU WELL.
DAD, COULD WE PLEASE NOT DO THIS NOW?!
ALCHEMAX GENETICS DIVISION
YOU SHOULD'VE LISTENED TO ME ABOUT CAPTAIN AMERICA. SHE WALKED OUT ON YOU, BOY.
I KNEW SHE WOULD. THAT'S WHY I HIRED THE SPECIALIST TO DISPOSE OF HER.
YOU... WHAT?
YOUR TEAM CAN DO FAR BETTER THAN HER.
YOU TRIED TO KILL HER?
AN AVENGER? AND THE MOTHER OF TWO CHILDREN?
SERIOUSLY, BOY? THAT'S YOUR CONCERN?
SHE'S A COMPANY COG! ALL COGS ARE DISPOSABLE.
YOU'RE RIGHT, DAD.
YOU'RE ABSOLUTELY RIGHT.
WHAT ARE YOU DOING?

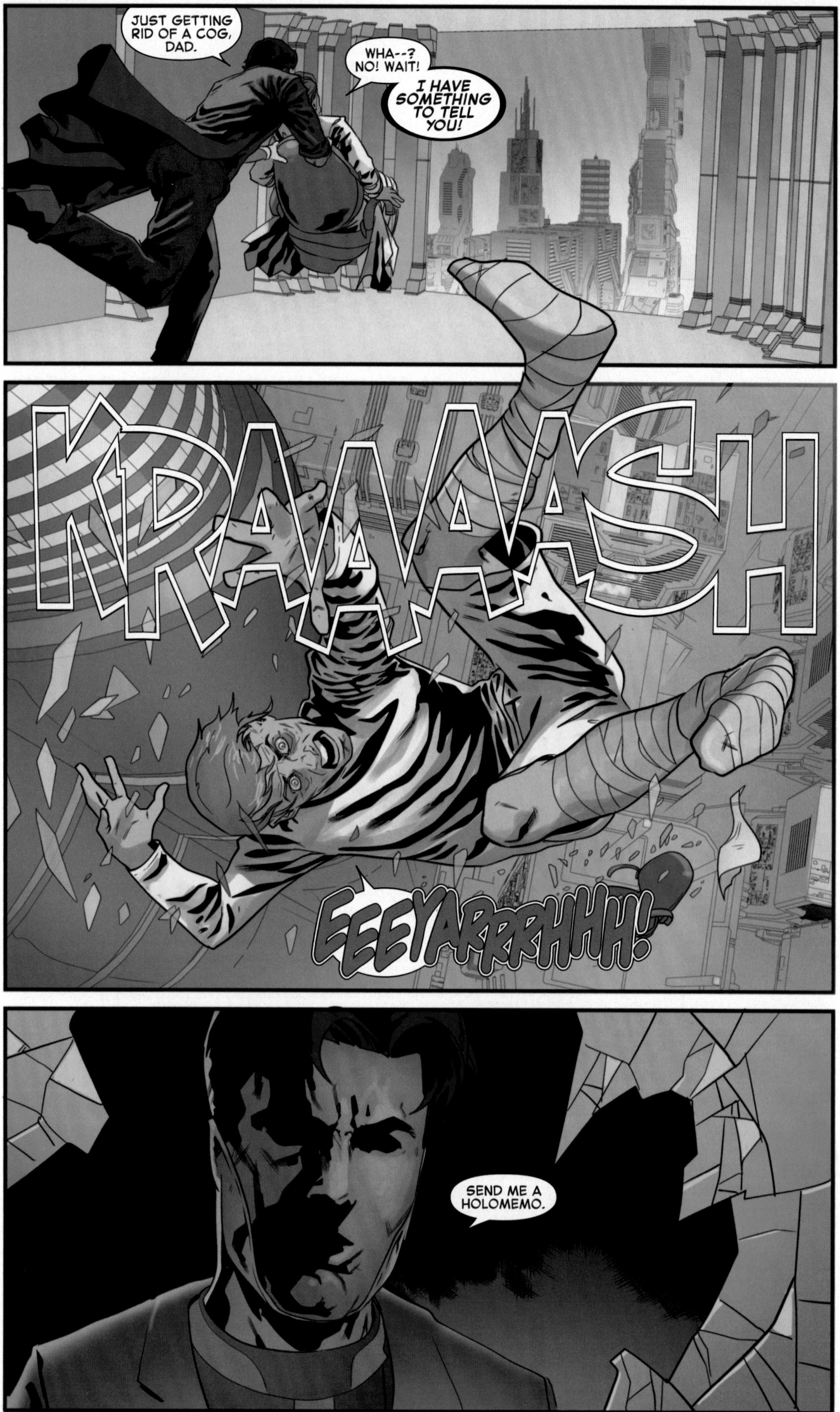
JUST GETTING RID OF A COG, DAD.
WHA--? NO! WAIT!
I HAVE SOMETHING TO TELL YOU!
KRAAASH
EEEYARRRHHH!
SEND ME A HOLOMEMO.

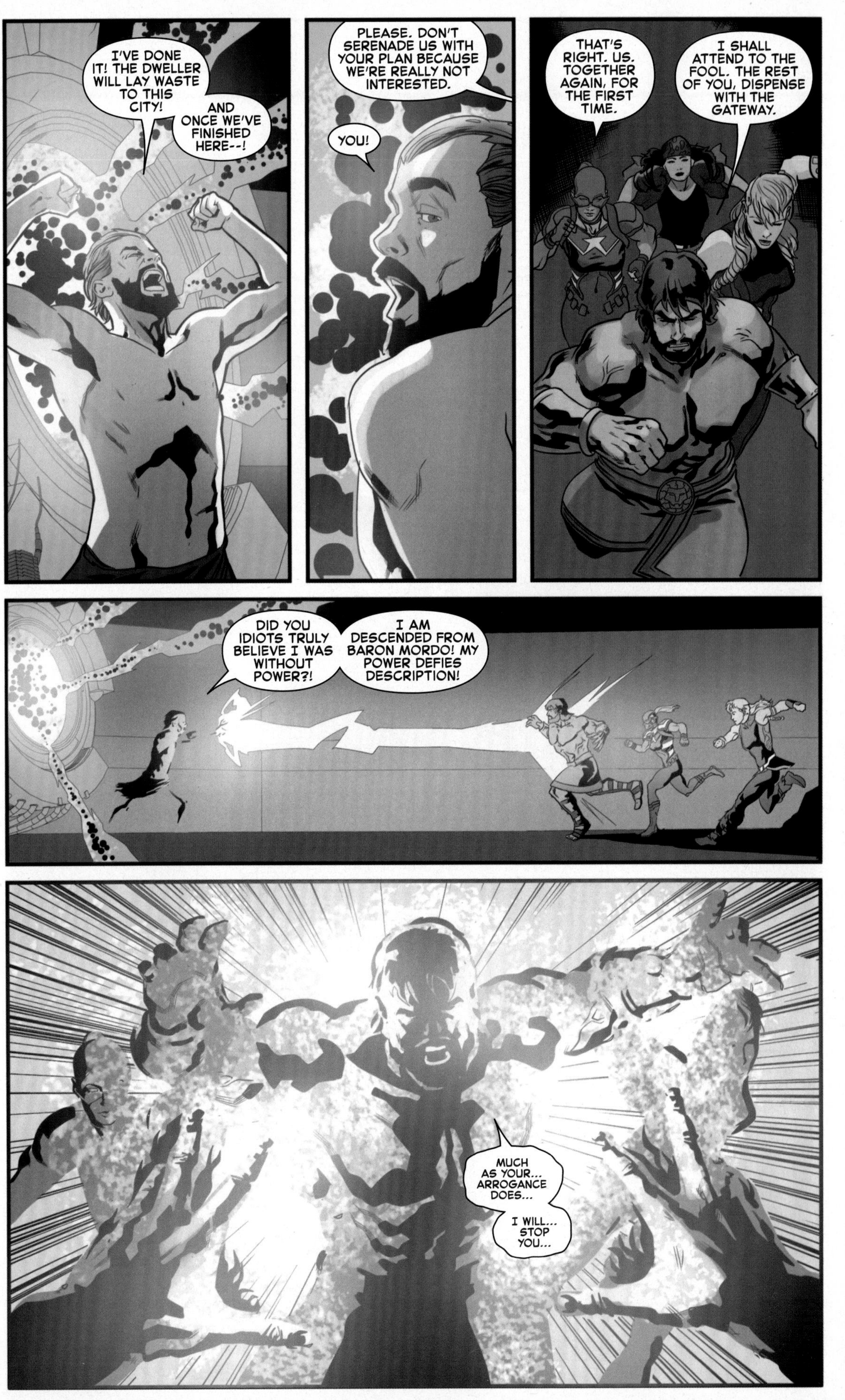
I'VE DONE IT! THE DWELLER WILL LAY WASTE TO THIS CITY!
AND ONCE WE'VE FINISHED HERE--!
PLEASE. DON'T SERENADE US WITH YOUR PLAN BECAUSE WE'RE REALLY NOT INTERESTED.
YOU!
THAT'S RIGHT. US. TOGETHER AGAIN, FOR THE FIRST TIME.
I SHALL ATTEND TO THE FOOL. THE REST OF YOU, DISPENSE WITH THE GATEWAY.
DID YOU IDIOTS TRULY BELIEVE I WAS WITHOUT POWER?!
I AM DESCENDED FROM BARON MORDO! MY POWER DEFIES DESCRIPTION!
MUCH AS YOUR... ARROGANCE DOES...
I WILL... STOP YOU...

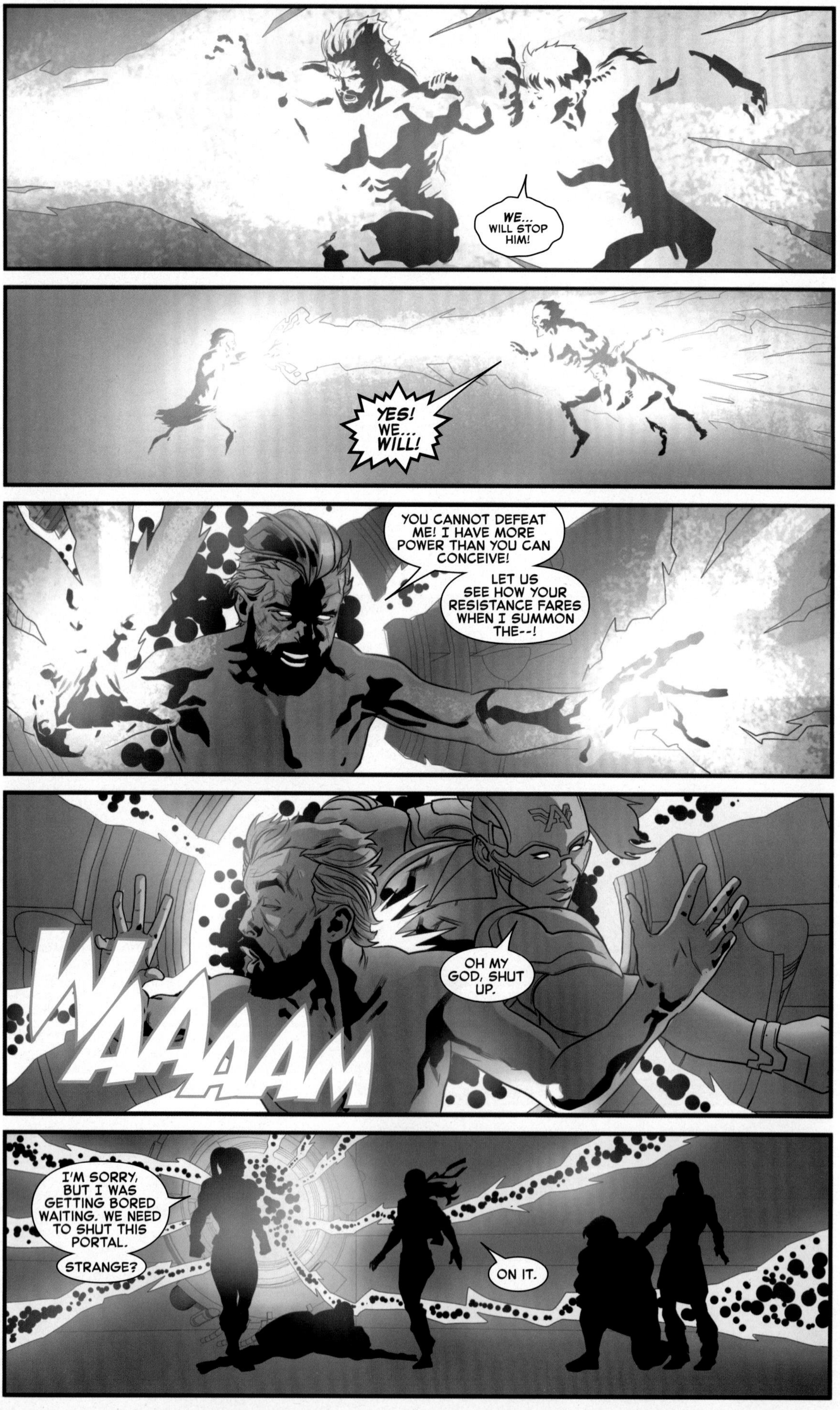
WE... WILL STOP HIM!
YES! WE... WILL!
YOU CANNOT DEFEAT ME! I HAVE MORE POWER THAN YOU CAN CONCEIVE!
LET US SEE HOW YOUR RESISTANCE FARES WHEN I SUMMON THE--!
WAAAAAM
OH MY GOD, SHUT UP.
I'M SORRY, BUT I WAS GETTING BORED WAITING. WE NEED TO SHUT THIS PORTAL.
STRANGE?
ON IT.

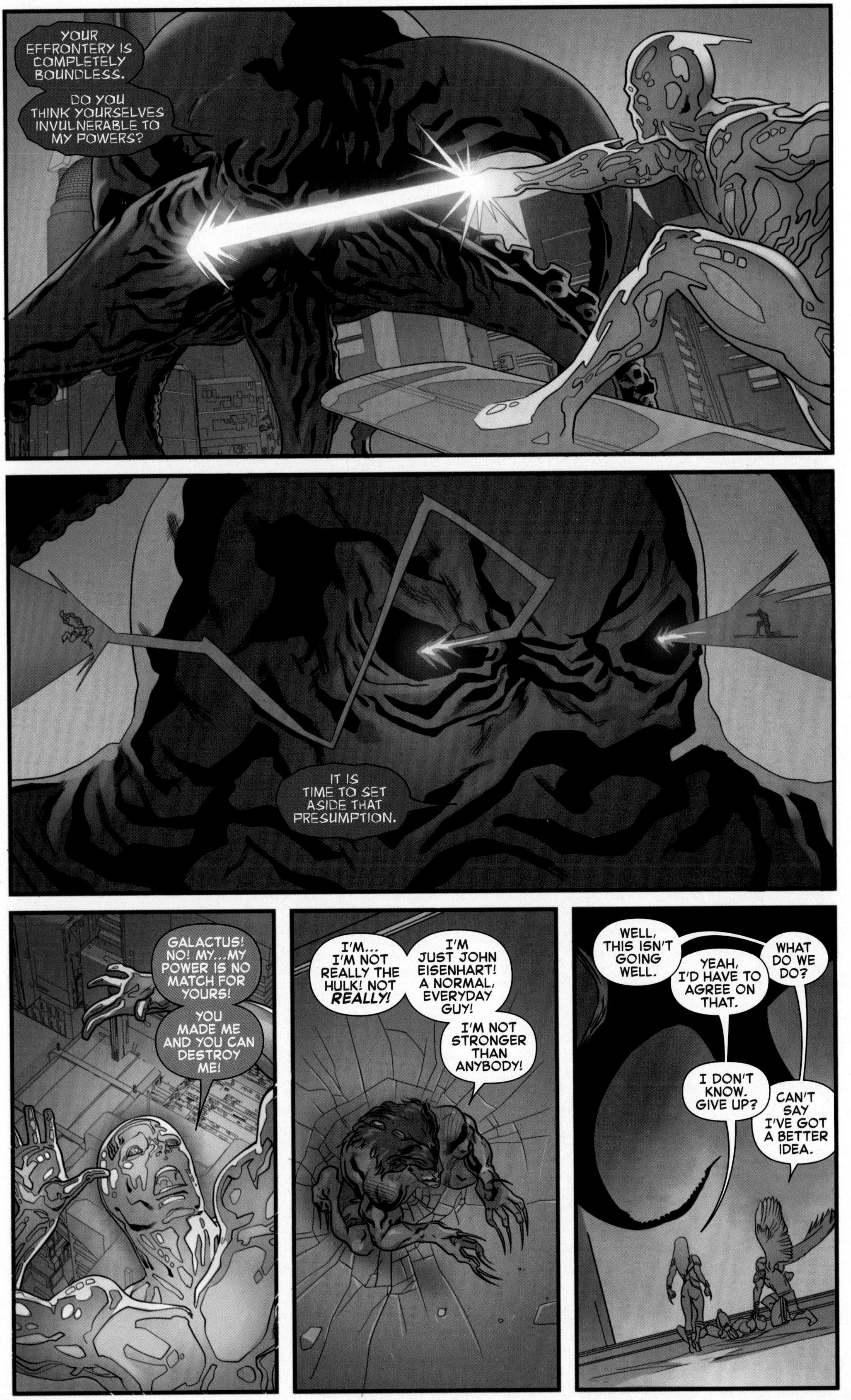
YOUR EFFRONTERY IS COMPLETELY BOUNDLESS.
DO YOU THINK YOURSELVES INVULNERABLE TO MY POWERS?
IT IS TIME TO SET ASIDE THAT PRESUMPTION.
GALACTUS! NO! MY...MY POWER IS NO MATCH FOR YOURS!
YOU MADE ME AND YOU CAN DESTROY ME!
I'M... I'M NOT REALLY THE HULK! NOT REALLY!
I'M JUST JOHN EISENHART! A NORMAL, EVERYDAY GUY!
I'M NOT STRONGER THAN ANYBODY!
WELL, THIS ISN'T GOING WELL.
YEAH, I'D HAVE TO AGREE ON THAT.
WHAT DO WE DO?
I DON'T KNOW. GIVE UP?
CAN'T SAY I'VE GOT A BETTER IDEA.

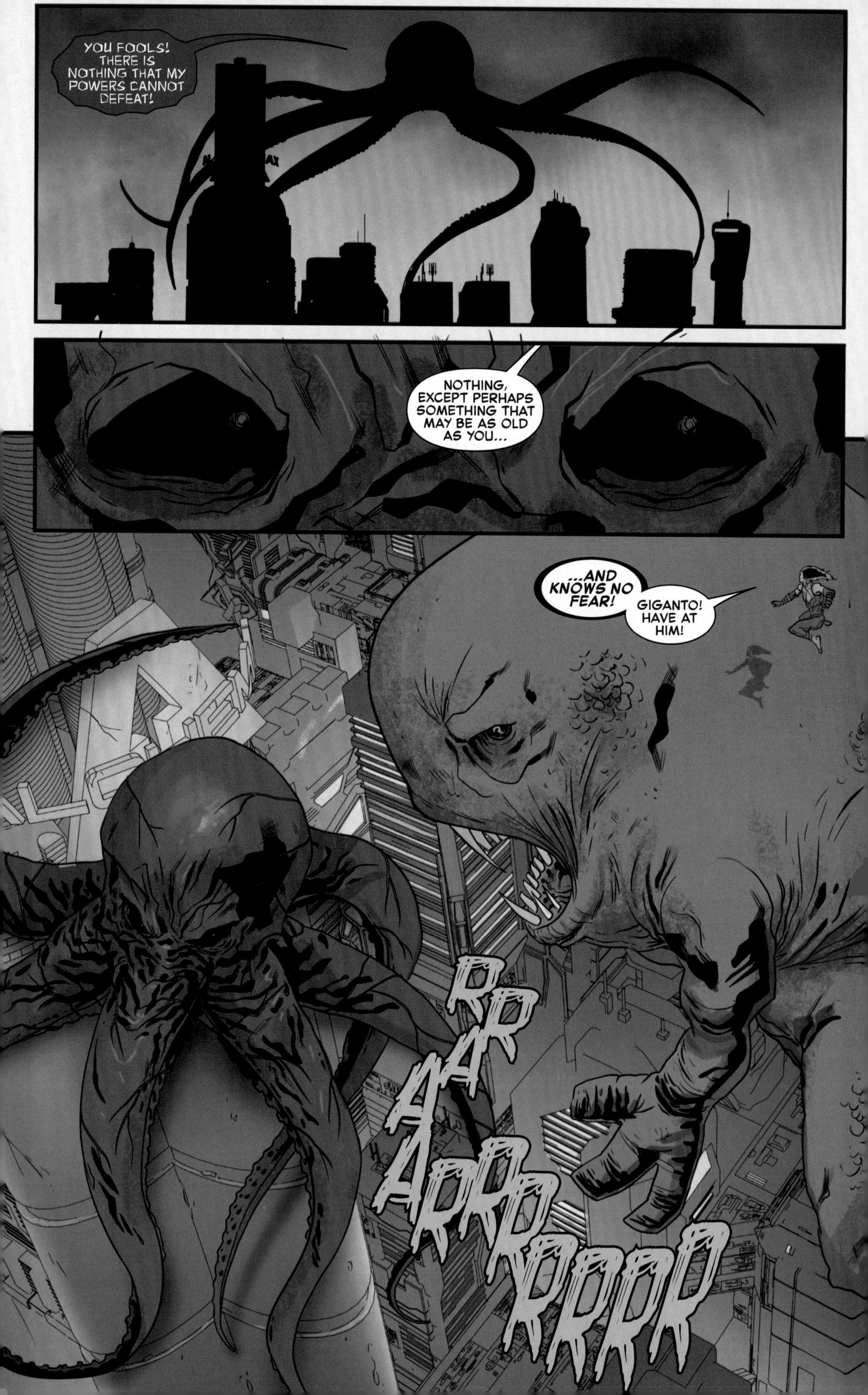
YOU FOOLS! THERE IS NOTHING THAT MY POWERS CANNOT DEFEAT!
NOTHING, EXCEPT PERHAPS SOMETHING THAT MAY BE AS OLD AS YOU...
...AND KNOWS NO FEAR!
GIGANTO! HAVE AT HIM!
RRAAARRRRRRR

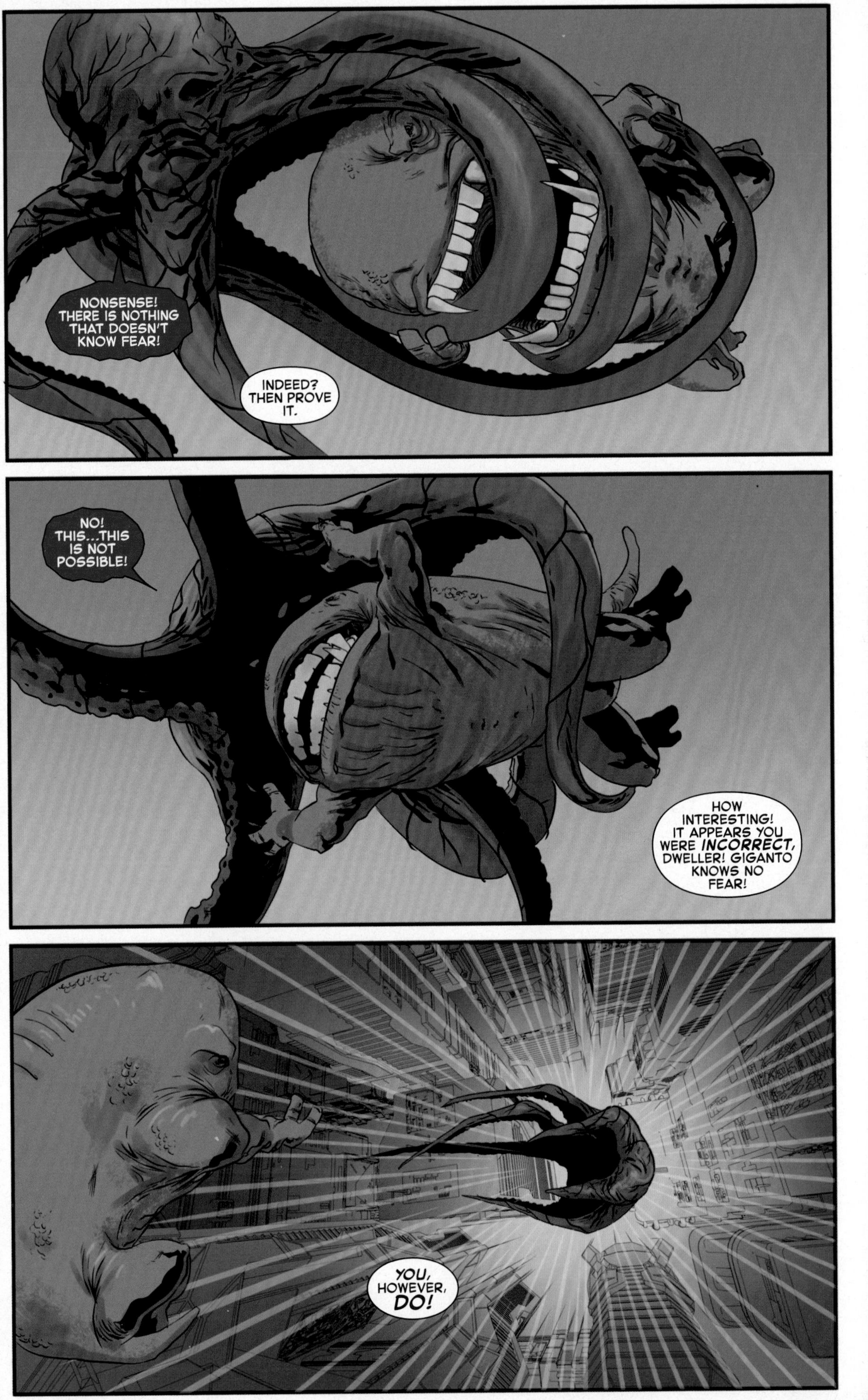
NONSENSE! THERE IS NOTHING THAT DOESN'T KNOW FEAR!
INDEED? THEN PROVE IT.
NO! THIS...THIS IS NOT POSSIBLE!
HOW INTERESTING! IT APPEARS YOU WERE *INCORRECT*, DWELLER! GIGANTO KNOWS NO FEAR!
YOU, HOWEVER, *DO!*

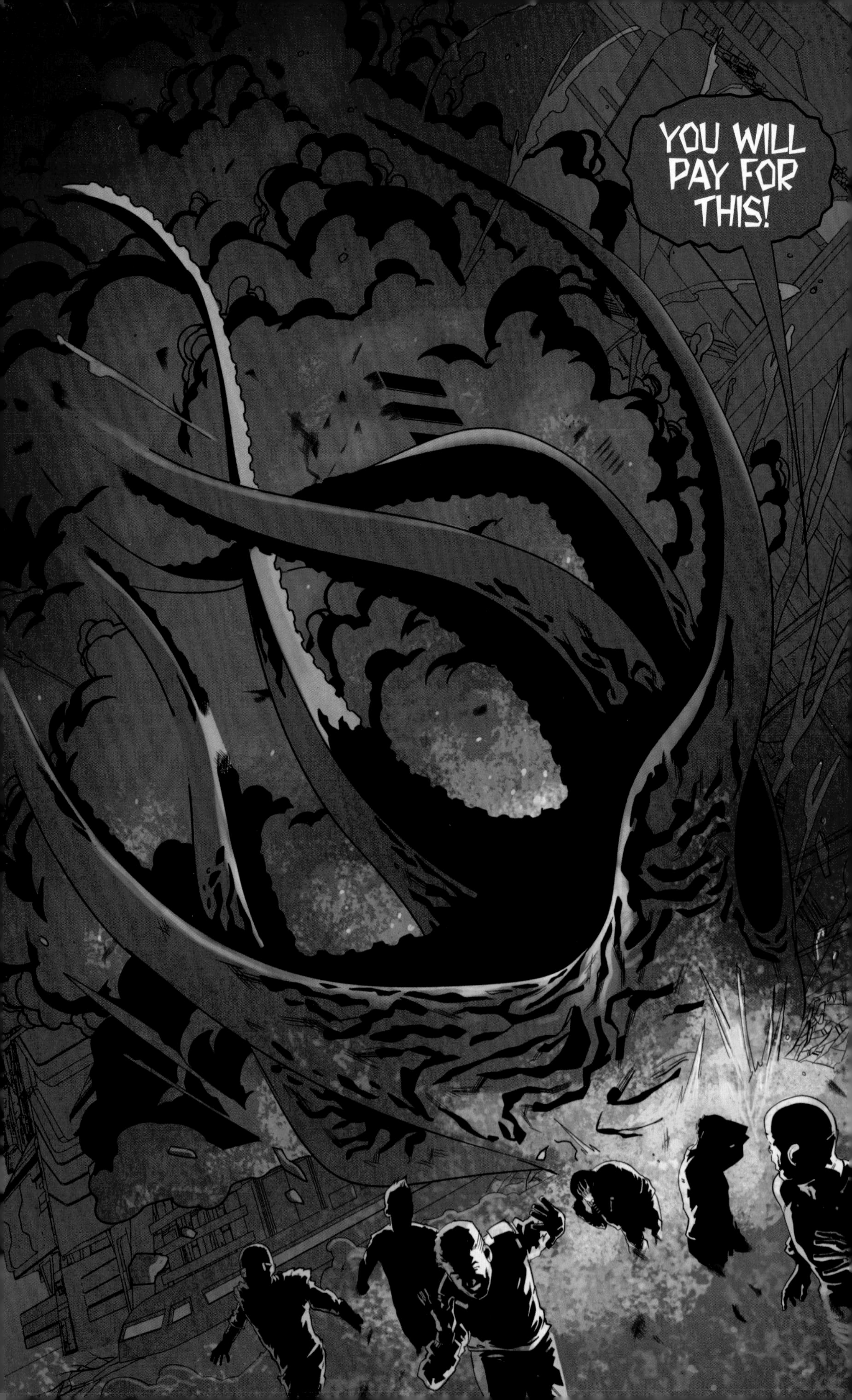
YOU WILL PAY FOR THIS!

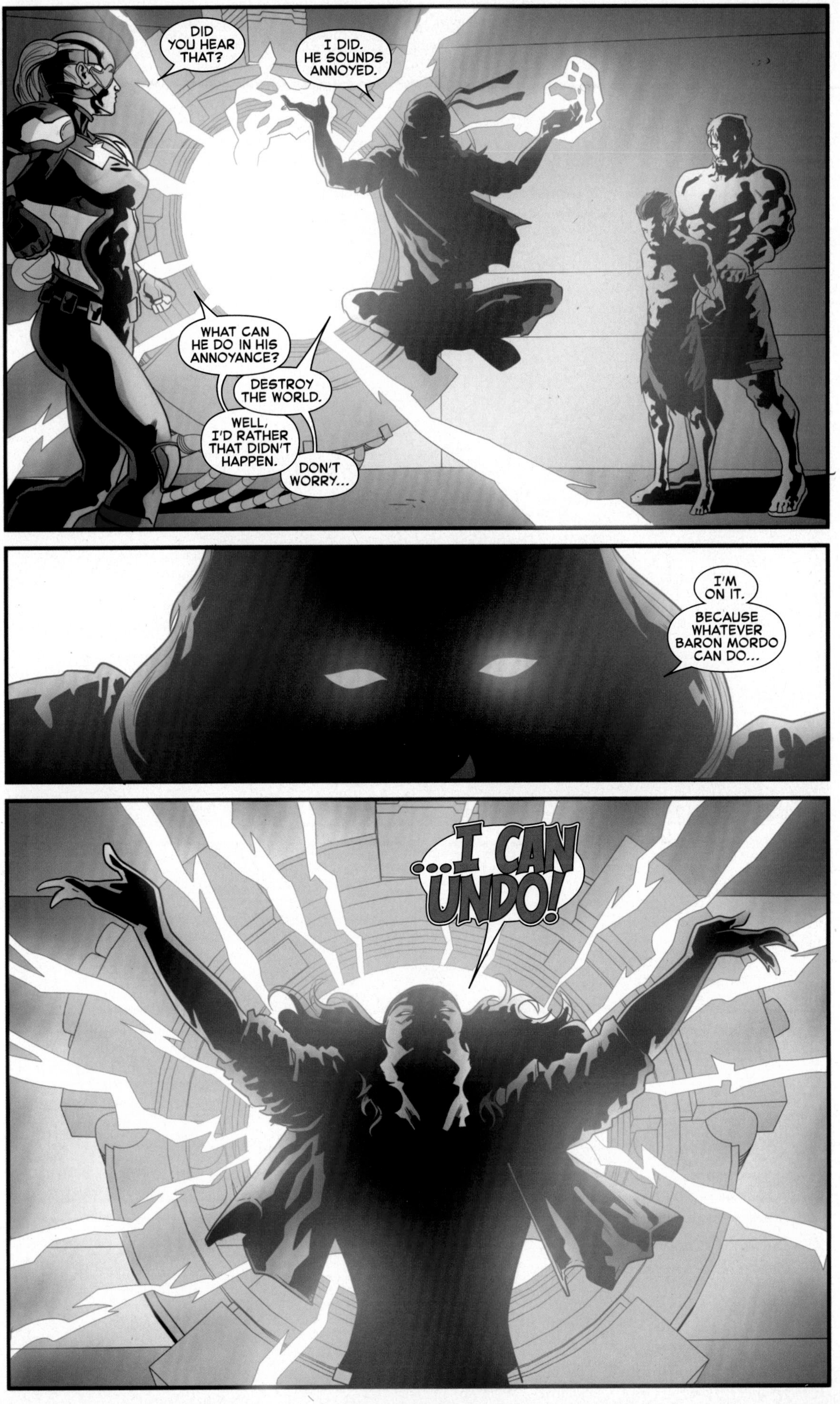
DID YOU HEAR THAT?
I DID. HE SOUNDS ANNOYED.
WHAT CAN HE DO IN HIS ANNOYANCE?
DESTROY THE WORLD.
WELL, I'D RATHER THAT DIDN'T HAPPEN.
DON'T WORRY...
I'M ON IT.
BECAUSE WHATEVER BARON MORDO CAN DO...
...I CAN UNDO!

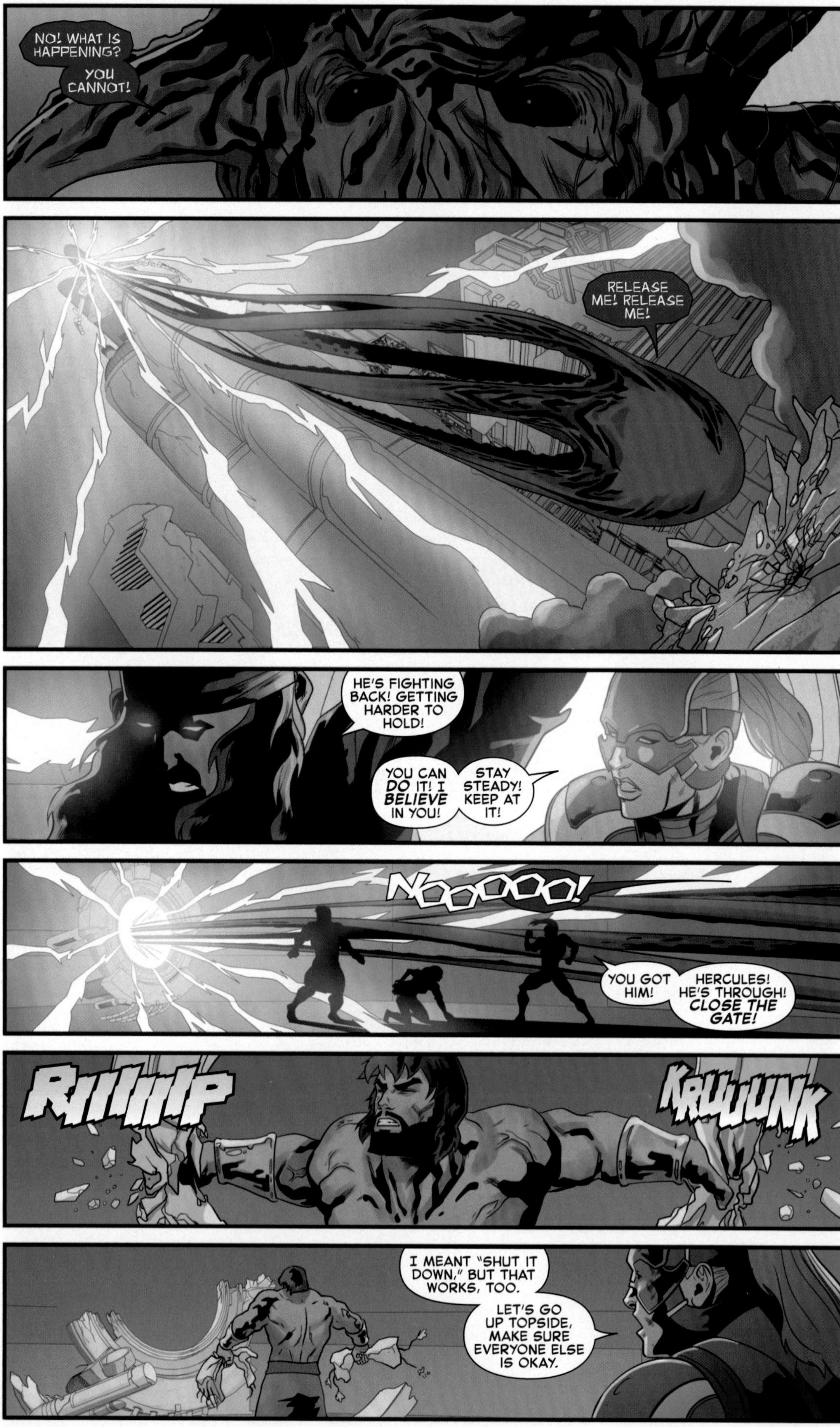
NO! WHAT IS HAPPENING?
YOU CANNOT!
RELEASE ME! RELEASE ME!
HE'S FIGHTING BACK! GETTING HARDER TO HOLD!
YOU CAN *DO* IT! I *BELIEVE* IN YOU!
STAY STEADY! KEEP AT IT!
NOOOOOO!
YOU GOT HIM!
HERCULES! HE'S THROUGH! ***CLOSE THE GATE!***
RIIIIIP
KRUUUNK
I MEANT "SHUT IT DOWN," BUT THAT WORKS, TOO.
LET'S GO UP TOPSIDE, MAKE SURE EVERYONE ELSE IS OKAY.

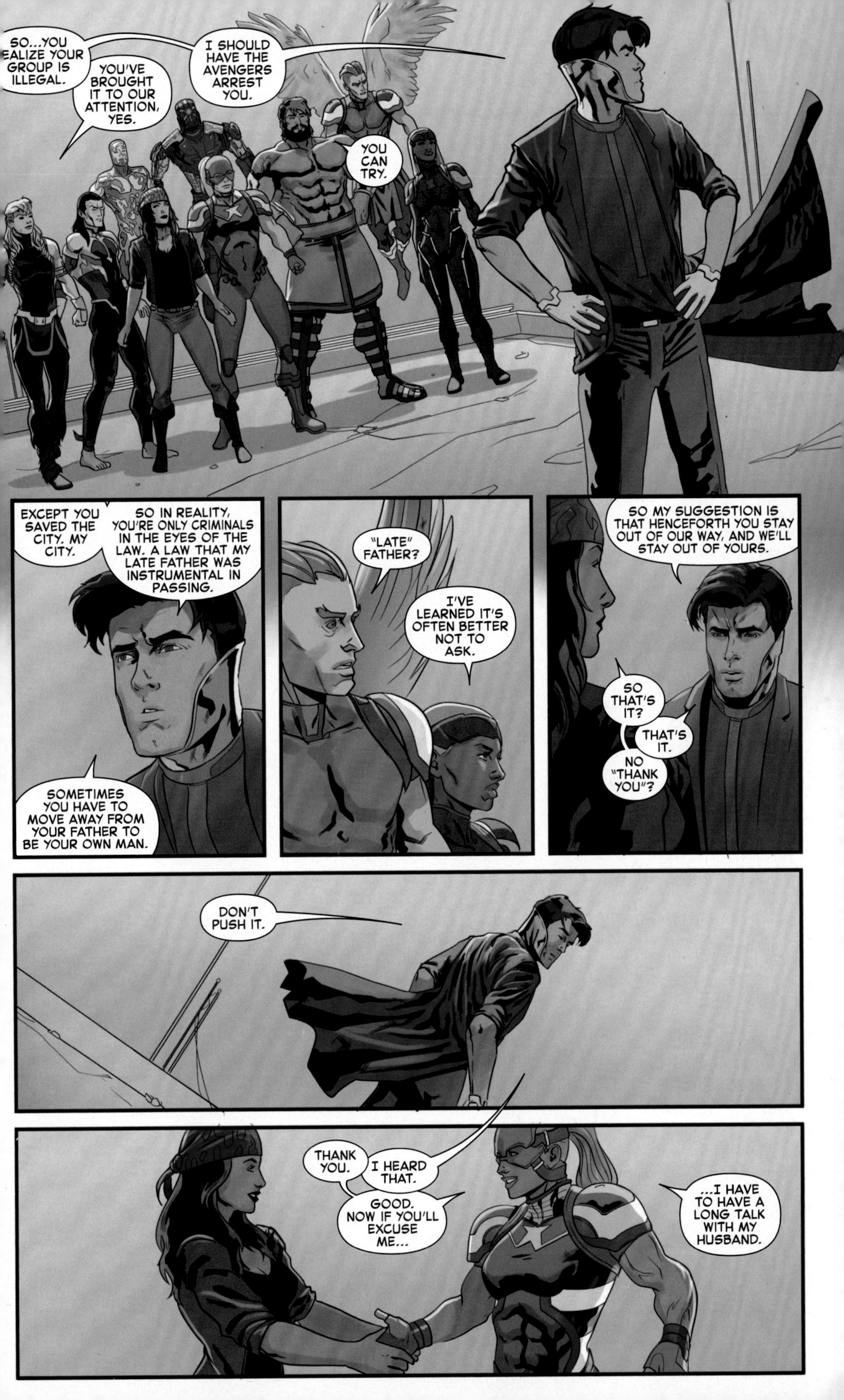
SO...YOU EALIZE YOUR GROUP IS ILLEGAL.
YOU'VE BROUGHT IT TO OUR ATTENTION, YES.
I SHOULD HAVE THE AVENGERS ARREST YOU.
YOU CAN TRY.
EXCEPT YOU SAVED THE CITY. MY CITY.
SO IN REALITY, YOU'RE ONLY CRIMINALS IN THE EYES OF THE LAW. A LAW THAT MY LATE FATHER WAS INSTRUMENTAL IN PASSING.
SOMETIMES YOU HAVE TO MOVE AWAY FROM YOUR FATHER TO BE YOUR OWN MAN.
"LATE" FATHER?
I'VE LEARNED IT'S OFTEN BETTER NOT TO ASK.
SO MY SUGGESTION IS THAT HENCEFORTH YOU STAY OUT OF OUR WAY, AND WE'LL STAY OUT OF YOURS.
SO THAT'S IT?
THAT'S IT.
NO "THANK YOU"?
DON'T PUSH IT.
THANK YOU.
I HEARD THAT.
GOOD. NOW IF YOU'LL EXCUSE ME...
...I HAVE TO HAVE A LONG TALK WITH MY HUSBAND.

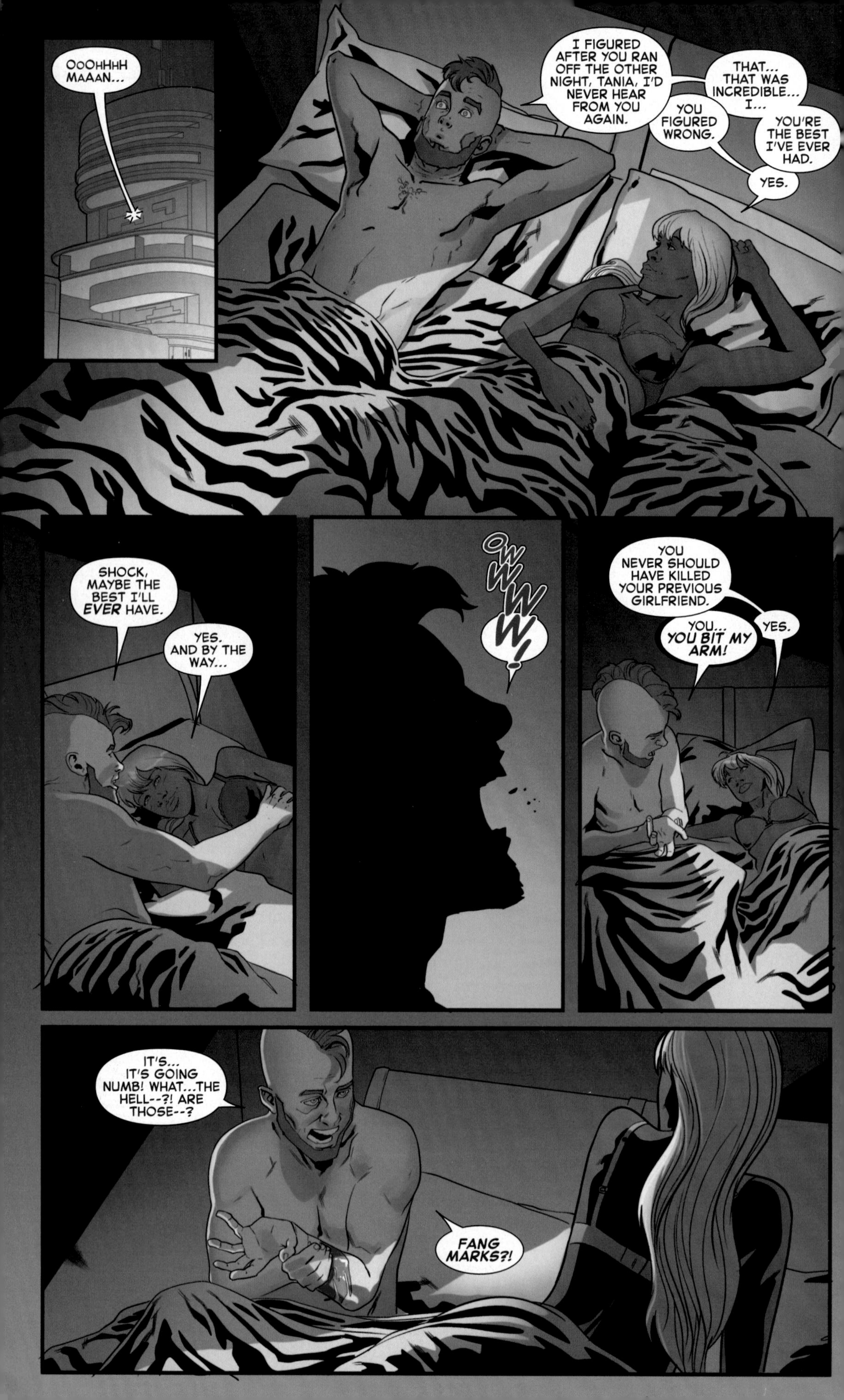
OOOHHHH MAAAN...
I FIGURED AFTER YOU RAN OFF THE OTHER NIGHT, TANIA, I'D NEVER HEAR FROM YOU AGAIN.
YOU FIGURED WRONG.
THAT... THAT WAS INCREDIBLE... I...
YOU'RE THE BEST I'VE EVER HAD.
YES.
SHOCK, MAYBE THE BEST I'LL EVER HAVE.
YES. AND BY THE WAY...
OWWWW!
YOU NEVER SHOULD HAVE KILLED YOUR PREVIOUS GIRLFRIEND.
YOU... YOU BIT MY ARM!
YES.
IT'S... IT'S GOING NUMB! WHAT...THE HELL--?! ARE THOSE--?
FANG MARKS?!

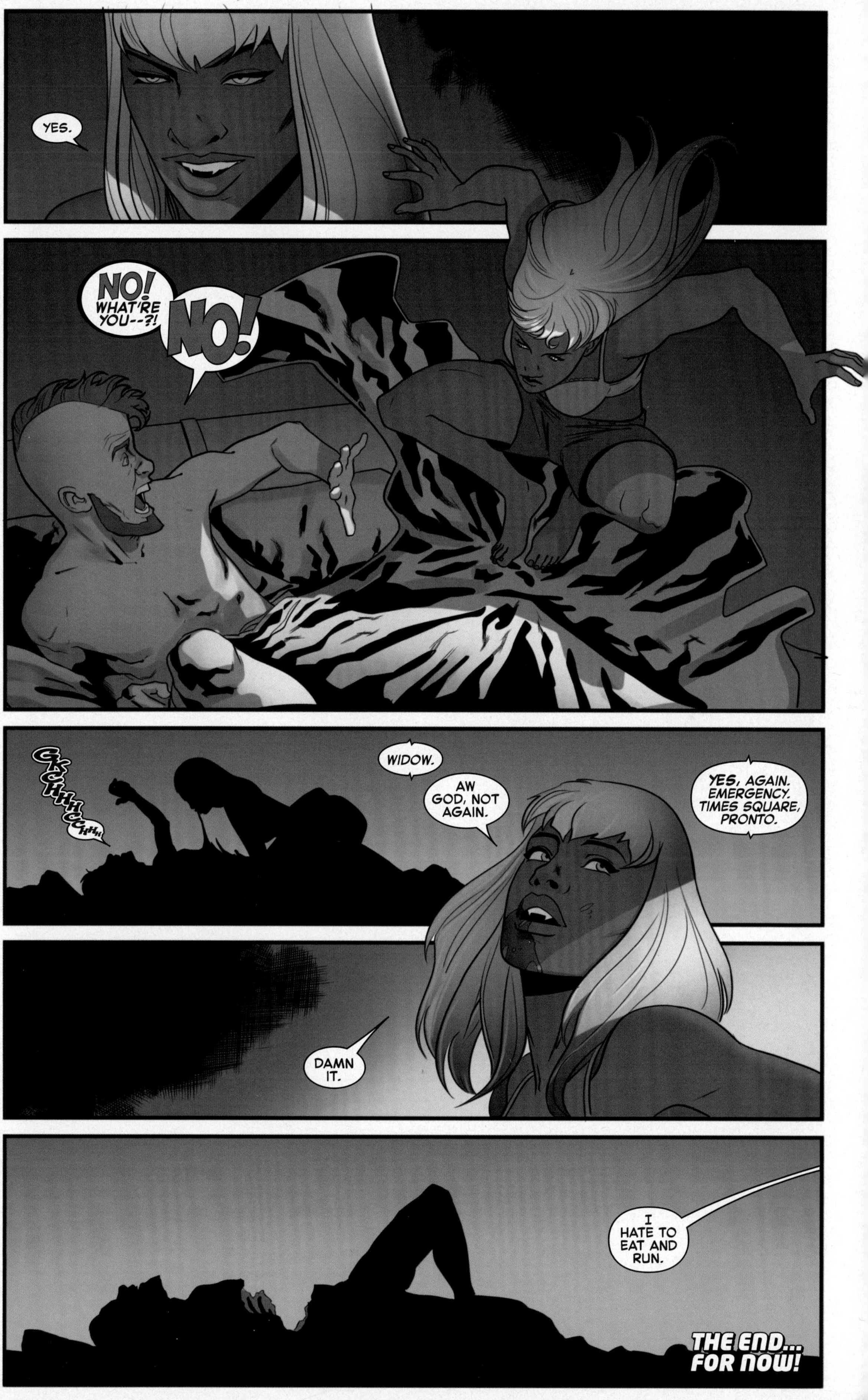
YES.
NO! WHAT'RE YOU--?!
NO!
GKCHHHCCHHH
WIDOW.
AW GOD, NOT AGAIN.
YES, AGAIN. EMERGENCY. TIMES SQUARE, PRONTO.
DAMN IT.
I HATE TO EAT AND RUN.
THE END... FOR NOW!

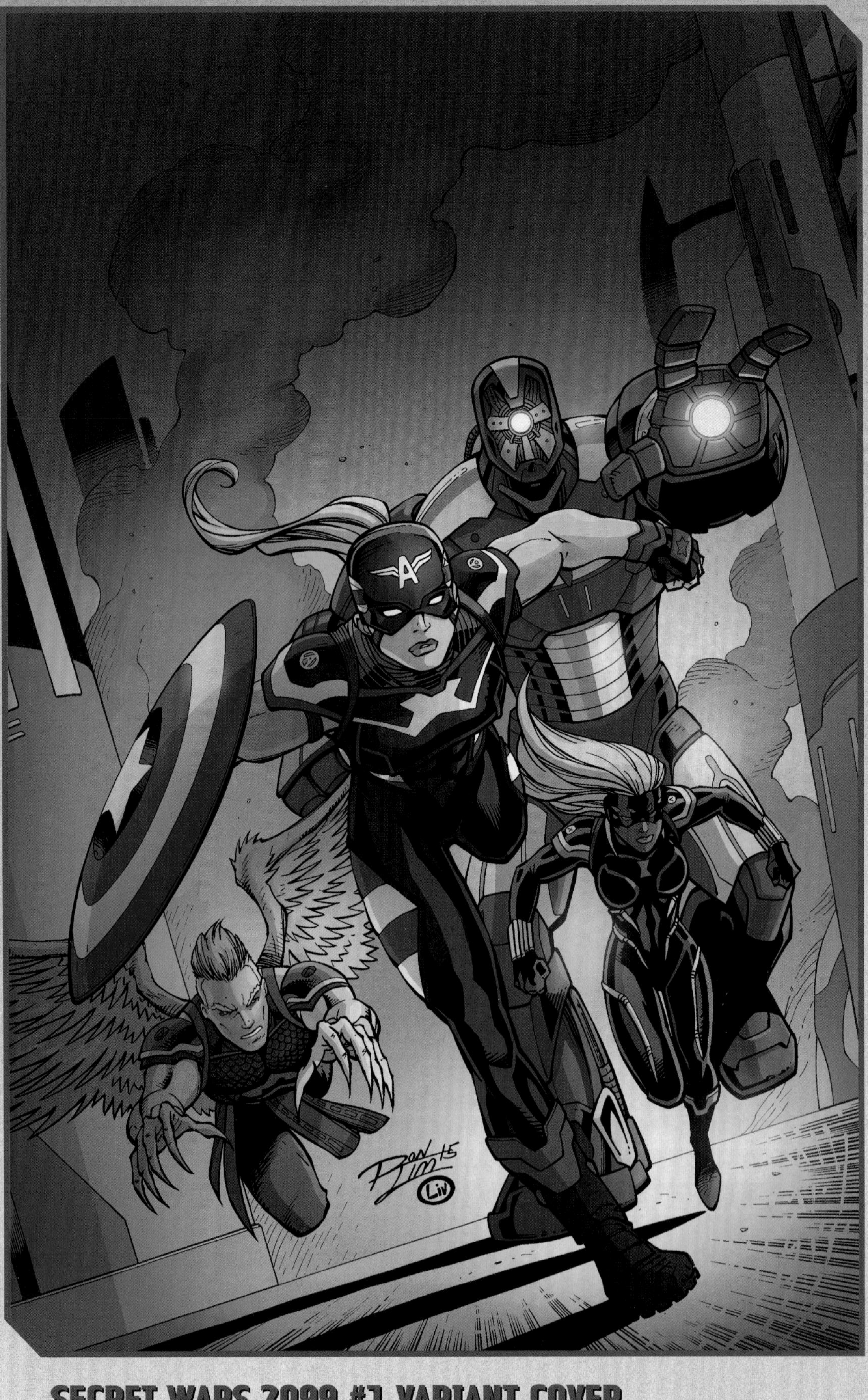

SECRET WARS 2099 #1 VARIANT COVER

BY RON LIM, LIVESAY & JAMES CAMPBELL

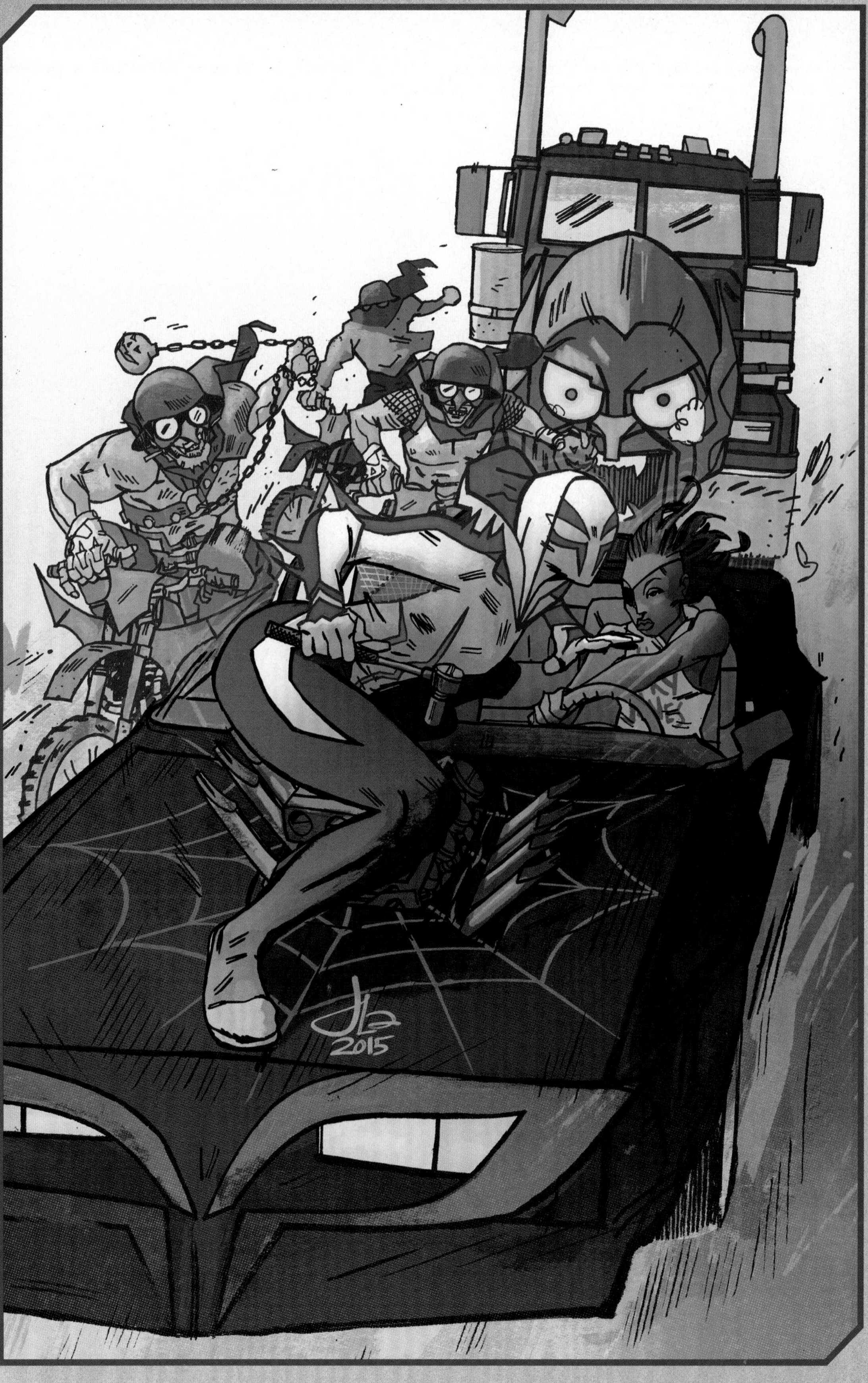

SECRET WARS 2099 #2 SPIDER-GWEN VARIANT COVER

BY JASON LATOUR

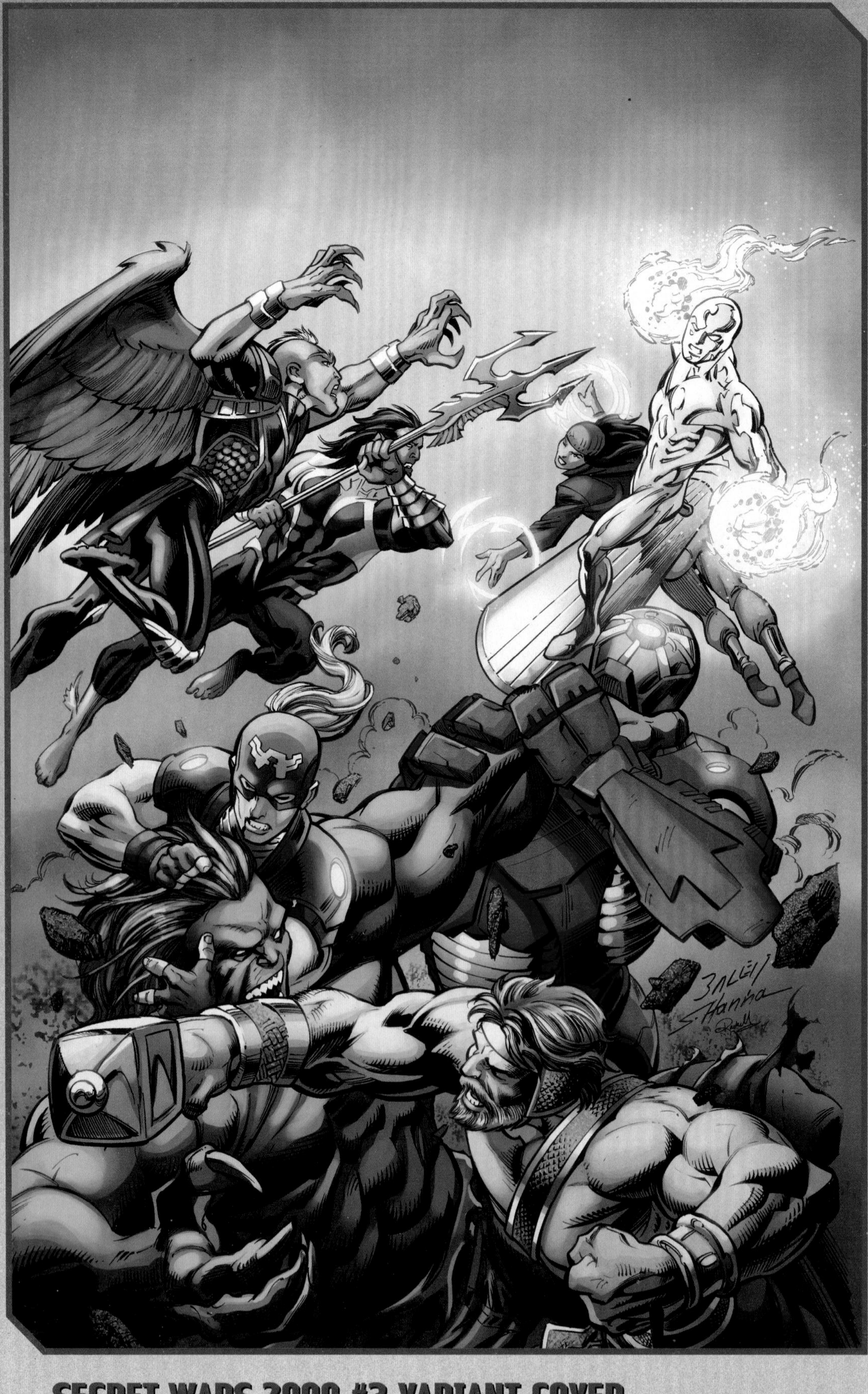

SECRET WARS 2099 #3 VARIANT COVER

BY MARK BAGLEY, SCOTT HANNA & RACHELLE ROSENBERG